SoulTypes

Also by Sandra Krebs Hirsh and Jane A. G. Kise

LifeKeys: Who You Are, Why You're Here, What You Do Best
(Kise, David Stark, and Hirsh, Bethany House)

Looking at Type and Spirituality
(Hirsh and Kise, CAPT)

Work It Out: Clues to Solving People Problems at Work
(Hirsh with Kise, Davies-Black)

Also by Hirsh

Introduction to Type and Teams
(CPP)

Introduction to Type in Organizations
(Hirsh and Jean Kummerow, CPP)

LifeTypes
(Hirsh and Jean Kummerow, Warner Books)

Also by Kise

Find Your Fit: Dare to Act on God's Design for You
(Kise and Kevin Johnson, Bethany House)

The Gift of God's Guidance
(Kise and David Stark, Bethany House, summer 1999)

SoulTypes

Finding the Spiritual Path That Is Right for You

Sandra Krebs Hirsh
Jane A. G. Kise

New York

Library of Congress Cataloging-in-Publication Data
Hirsh, Sandra Krebs.
Soultypes : finding the spiritual path that is right for you / by
Sandra Krebs Hirsh and Jane A.G. Kise. — 1st ed.
        p.   cm.
Includes bibliographical references.
ISBN 0-7868-8289-1
1. Spiritual life.   2. Typology (Psychology)—Religious aspects.
3. Myers-Briggs Type Indicator.   I. Kise, Jane A. G.   II. Title.
BL627.57.H57   1998
200'.1'9—DC21   98-15116
                    CIP
First Edition
10 9 8 7 6 5 4 3 2 1

Book design and text "cloud" photograph by Deborah Kerner

TO ALL SOJOURNERS WHO, ALONG WITH ME,
ARE SEEKING ENRICHED SPIRITUALITY,
DISCOVERING WHO WE ARE,
BUILDING ON THE GIFTS WE'VE BEEN GIVEN,
AND APPRECIATING THE UNIQUENESS OF EACH PERSON'S JOURNEY.

Sandra Krebs Hirsh

TO MY MOM, MURIEL GRIFFIN,
WHOSE LOVE, ENCOURAGEMENT, AND DEEP FAITH
ARE A CONSTANT SOURCE OF INSPIRATION AND MOTIVATION TO ME.

Jane A. G. Kise

Contents

Acknowledgments

We could not have written this book without the assistance of friends, colleagues, and even strangers who were willing to share their personal stories, insights, and spiritual journeys to help us create accurate pictures of spirituality for each type.

Our heartfelt thanks to Nancy Achterhoff, Sarah Albritton, Dana Alexander, Larry Atkinson, Lynne Baab, Lena Bakedahl, Maureen Bailey, Charette Barta, Randi Baxter, Monica Bergman, Paul and Nan Bertleson, Craig Blakeley, Robert Boozer, Polly Bowles, Christine Boyer, Nicky Bredeson, Amy Carrizo-Brennen, Susan Brock, Nancy Brooker, Helen Krebs Bruant, Joan Buchanan, Dee Cauble, Elizabeth Cauble, Laura Crosby, Penny Davis, Jamelyn R. DeLong, Larry Demarest, Jean and Steve Diede, Jari Dostal, Debbie Ducar, Kit Duncan, Terry Duniho, Terri Elton, Binnie Ferrand, Margaret Fields, P. J. Fuller, Barb Gabbert, David D. Getsch, Peter Geyer, Linda Gilligan, Thomas Golatz, Richard D. Grant, Jr., Ken Green, Jean Greenwood, Eva Grolleva, Ellen Griffin, Tom Griffin, Jack and Vicki Griffin, Jane Griffin, Muriel Griffin, Lonnie and Alison Gulden, Kay Hacklander, Madge Hanson, Becky Harris, Kathi Hirsh, Jeanne Hoagland, Diane Huling, Lee Hulsether, Greg Huszczo, Pat Hutson, Myra Hykes, Kevin Johnson, Mary Johnson, Karen Keefer, O. Fredrick Kiel, Christine King, Linda Kirby, Brian Kise, Brenda and Dean Knutson, Paula Kosin, Jindra Krpalkova, Jean Kummerow, Bob Kunzie, Alan Leggat, Rosemary Long, Sharon W. Lovoy, Sally and Rob Lund, John and Meredith Lundgren, Margarita Lycken, Peter Malone, Beverly Mease-Buxton, Jerry MacDaid, Steve Merman, Wayne D. and Jan Mitchell, James Mullins, Steve and Jo Mundy, Andrew Murray, Laurie Nadel, Julie Neraas, Judith E. Nicholas, Ann and Bill Oliver, Tim Olsen, Barbara Olson, Kit Olson, Richard Olson, J. Sam Park, Sue Pepper, Peter Richardson, Helen Marie Plourde, William Rebholtz, Sally Riglar, Judy Ritchie, Ranelle Rulana,

Josef Rzyman, JoAnne Sandler, Fred and Elsie Scaife, William F. Schmidt, Don Smith, Kurt Smith, Sandy Smith, David and Janet Stark, Grace Stewart, Karen Stuart, Randy A. Stricker, Shelley Thompson, Barbara Upton, Sondra Van Sant, Peggy Sue Vojtech, Jay Warren, Hichul Henry Whang, Bob Witherspoon, and Carolyn and Ray Zeisset.

Foreword

My daughter, an active, living-in-the-moment person, consistently turns aside invitations to join me in my various religious or spiritual activities on her visits. A whitewater kayaker, she thanks me very much and says, "My church is the woods and the rivers." With our family's deep heritage in type theory and the gifts of our individual personalities, I can only respect my daughter's approach to spirituality!

Yet, along with Sandra Hirsh and Jane Kise, I have long been puzzled by the fact that several of the sixteen types virtually never appear at the workshops and programs I personally find most rewarding for my spiritual development. *SoulTypes* satisfies my long-standing curiosity as to how other people fulfill their desire for significance and purpose. I read it with growing excitement, a tour de force of effectiveness unscrolling as I turned each page.

The book is ambitious in what it attempts. Using the formulation of Jung's psychological type, as developed by Katharine C. Briggs and Isabel B. Myers in the Myers-Briggs Type Indicator® (MBTI), and through extensive conversations with individuals of each of the sixteen Jungian types, the authors have sketched portraits of the spiritual path most natural to each type. The result is a book that can serve as an invaluable guide to an individual or a group working together on a journey of spiritual growth—a journey sparked by the universal yearning for meaning, balance, and connectedness to one another and to something greater than oneself.

As writers, Hirsh and Kise managed to order what could be overwhelmingly complex material and ideas, leading the reader in gentle, easy-to-understand steps into the richness of complexity without sacrificing meaning for the sake of simplicity. By illuminating each step of spiritual development with the words of people telling their stories, the full richness of the dynamic and developmental aspects of psychological type is imparted.

As researchers, they worked to discover both the differences in spiritual concerns and the practices and patterns that might be common for each type. They shared with me that their role became one of "stewards for these messages" as they tried to let each type speak for itself, defining its unique approach to soulwork.

As authors, they live out in every word their respect for each individual and for each of the many valid paths toward growth and spiritual development. As a result, their book will speak to people of many faiths as well as to nonbelievers and skeptics who are questioning and open to exploration.

The book is carefully crafted for use in daily life and soulwork. The skill with which this is done reflects the years of experience of the authors in workshop leadership and design. Readers will come to understand:

- The many valid forms of spirituality;
- Past frustrations with their spiritual history, opening doors to renewed exploration;
- The spiritual pathway that is most natural to them—that brings the greatest joy, insight, clarity, and practical help; and
- Ways to expand their spiritual practices, thus enriching the journey.

Readers will grasp their uniqueness as well as their commonality with others who possess a similar nature. Ideas from other types will help to bring new creativity and interest to their individual pathways and movement toward balance and wholeness in their personal development.

In an early chapter, the authors confess to sharing a passion for helping others reach their full potential. I was reminded of Isabel Myers and her mother, Katharine Briggs, who found Jungian psychological type so useful in their own lives. Their mission in life became to enable others to have access to this knowledge through the MBTI. Myers and Briggs gave others access to their preference type; Hirsh and Kise in *SoulTypes* have succeeded in providing a step-by-step way of applying that understanding to the never-ending, lifelong process of spiritual growth and fulfilling living.

—KATHARINE D. MYERS

Authors' Note

The authors acknowledge that there are many expressions of spirituality and a variety of religious experiences. While we have tried our best not to minimize any of the differences or slight other perspectives, we are well aware that our writing may be colored by our Judeo-Christian upbringings and traditions. If you have an experience, example, expression, or event that could enlarge our perspective or enrich our understanding, especially from other traditions, we invite you to pass them along to us.

We chose in these pages to differentiate between religion and spirituality and contend that there is a clear distinction. Spirituality does not equal religion, although many people find their spiritual path through a particular tradition. Religions are a way of pursuing spirituality in an organized manner by banding with others who espouse the same dogma or creed.

One of the decisions we made for ease of writing was to refer to the higher power that seems bigger than the sum of humanity as God or Creator. While some may see this as hierarchical or anthropomorphic, using other terms might place this work beyond the limits of acceptance for many people. We encourage you to substitute your preferred phrasing to meet your own needs.

Additionally, we attempted to include the various tangible places where people feel spiritual: church, synagogue, mosque, ashram—they go by many names. We chose to refer to all of them as spiritual communities throughout these pages.

SoulTypes

Introduction

Do you set aside time each day for prayer and reflection? Or does the very thought of it rob you of any spiritual inclination?

Do you enjoy pondering the mysteries of our existence? Or do you dismiss them as irrelevant to the demands of your days?

Are discussions about the meaning of life engaging or a practice you try to avoid?

Does being involved in a spiritual community enrich or entrap you?

Does the topic of spirituality cause you to clam up or clamor for more?

For several years, we have taught classes with a spiritual perspective to help people add meaning to their lives by discovering who they are and what they do best. As we taught about Jungian theory, the 16 psychological types ["type"], and gathered data about the participants, we were struck by the fact that time and again people of certain psychological types were simply *never* present, unlike our experiences in the business world. This book grew out of a desire to better understand the relationship between type and spirituality and why certain types tend to avoid organized forms of spirituality—or even be turned off almost entirely by the subject of spirituality.

As our interest in this topic led to conversations with hundreds of people, our perceptions were confirmed: Each psychological type has a unique slant on spirituality. Some are drawn to traditional forms of spirituality. Others feel detached from the standards of their tradition or the norms of their culture. We hope that these pages might:

- Increase awareness of the many valid forms of spirituality, some of which are distinctly different from the patterns of most organized religions;
- Encourage people who have never felt comfortable with traditional forms of spirituality to take a second look at spirituality; and
- Provide guidance for people who are already on a spiritual path to find new practices that will enhance their soulwork and sustain them through the inevitable difficult times that we refer to as "the storms of life."

As we heard the stories from people of each type, then tried to communicate their points of view, we've done our best to let each type speak for itself, defining its unique approach to soulwork.

However, before delving into the differences among the 16 types, we want to point out a few things that all versions of spirituality have in common:

All types want to have some say in crafting their soulwork, spirituality, or the understanding of their religious tradition. However:

- Sensing types mold their soulwork to authenticate their actions, and by doing so, meet practical needs in their day-to-day lives.
- Intuitive types design their soulwork by synthesizing ideas from several traditions or by accepting some of the dilemmas others might find problematic.
- Thinking types tend to construct their soulwork by doubting at first, then searching for truthful, clear principles; cause/effect relationships; and explanations before espousing a belief system.
- Feeling types personalize their soulwork, wanting to first hear about the practices that have worked for others to find what will help them live out their values.

Each of the types defends its own spiritual way and its integrity:

- Sensing types want to validate their pathways through experience and the simplicity of being.
- Intuitive types want to validate their pathways through the imagination and artistic endeavors.
- Thinking types want to validate their pathways through analysis and philosophical suppositions.
- Feeling types want to validate their pathways through personal meaning and a desire to support others.

The beauty and wonder of the natural world touch all types. However:

- Sensing types tend to benefit from being outside in the world of nature: what they see, hear, smell, touch, and taste supports their soulwork.
- Intuitive types find that being surrounded by nature facilitates the daydreaming that fuels their spiritual ideas.
- Thinking types find soulwork through experimenting with, explaining, classifying, or categorizing things in the natural world.
- Feeling types tend to appreciate the beauty of nature and the way it touches their hearts and souls.

Throughout history and cultures, music has played an important role in spirituality. All types find music conducive to soulwork. However:

- Sensing types find spiritual meaning in the actual words, rhythms, and melodies of music.
- Intuitive types find that music inspires their spiritual creativity.
- Thinking types' spirituality is often enhanced by the majesty and intricacy of the music's structure and sound.
- Feeling types often find that music invokes a change in mood, a remembrance of an emotional state, or recollections of relationships that fuel their spiritual desires for wholeness and healing.

These core similarities provide a common ground for all of the 16 types to journey together spiritually. In unity, the 16 types create a spirituality that honors:

- The gifts of pragmatism (Sensing)
- The gifts of imagination (Intuition)
- The gifts of reason (Thinking)
- The gifts of emotions (Feeling)

In short, a spirituality that leads to wholeness.

However, if all types are to find meaningful soulwork that taps into our spiritual nature, then all of us must become more sensitive to the languages and styles of other types.

Chapter 1

Soulwork
and Spirituality

Religion [spirituality] is a thing not alien to us.
It has to be evolved out of us.
It is always within us: with some, consciously so; with others, quite
    unconsciously. But it is always there.
And whether we wake up this religious instinct in us through outside
    assistance or by inward growth, no matter how it is done, it has
    got to be done, if we want to do anything in the right manner, or
    to achieve anything that is going to exist.

MOHANDAS K. GANDHI[1]

"When I was eight, my dad was killed in a car accident. I responded by
becoming an atheist. However, somewhere along the way that answer
didn't fit me anymore. In the past 10–12 years I've done a lot of personal
growth work through a support group to overcome my dysfunctionalities
around relationships. Now I am going deeper into my spirituality. To me,

soulwork is understanding my personal lessons in the events of my life and how I fit into the Universe."

DONNA, 55, COMPUTER TRAINER

"I know there's more to life than what I can see and touch, but to find my spiritual side I have to look for evidence in the lives of others. For example, I watched the reaction of friends who lost their little boy to leukemia. Earthly reality would have made them collapse under the grief. Instead, the unseen dimension and support of their spirituality allowed them to function, to comfort their friends, and to love and nurture their other children. Their example pressed upon me the urgency of soulwork—I want to have the sort of spiritual base they have before I find myself in need of support."

DAVE, 32, TEACHER

"I have struggled my entire life with being 'different'—too tall, too heavy, too redheaded, etc. Always being the odd one out and acutely aware of it. I had a hard time believing that any God was personally concerned for me. While my mother eventually divorced my alcoholic and abusive father, during my adolescence he constantly belittled me (I was five ten, one hundred thirty-five pounds, and 'so big'!) until he convinced me I would never be loved.

"Years later, as a married woman and a mother, a spiritual community welcomed me with open arms. Only then could I celebrate who and what I was as a person, finally free from the encumbrances of my past. I began to heal and the spirit had free access to my heart and mind for the first time since I was ten."

ADDY, 41, WRITER

"It took me a long time to find my inner spirit or being, what perhaps some people may call soul. This lies within me, but I can only describe it in terms of images of outside experiences.

"For example, one of my symbols involves a very large, beautifully twisted old tree in a magical forest. Between the exposed roots of this tree is *a small tunnel. As you journey down the tunnel toward a large cavern, the walls become studded with amethyst until they are completely encrusted with the gems. Then, in the middle of the cavern is a very large, pure crystal which radiates a golden light that reflects off the walls. Light from one place mixes with others, adding new shades and dimensions—there is no beginning or end to the light. For me, soulwork is imagining myself absorbing the light from this crystal, a source of strength."*

CELIA, 24, POET

These individuals echo the longings of millions of people before them. Throughout history and throughout the world, all cultures have explored spirituality in some form. Humankind seems to look outside the boundaries of common reality and everyday life to deal with what cannot be explained or even changed. Our spirituality can help us interpret our experiences, whether they are providential or tragic, known or hidden, logical or illogical, so we can grow to accept what we cannot understand. Soulwork can also help us with the common perplexities of life:

- We need to learn to live with reality, both the good and the bad.
- We need to come to terms with the brevity of our lives and our purpose for existing.
- We need a set of values that guides our actions and interactions.
- We need to grasp how we individually relate to the actions and experiences of the human race.
- And we need at times to know we are not alone and not without choices.

Spirituality *is* a dimension of life, as real as the physical world, where people who choose to can explore and find untapped resources. For us, delving into our spiritual being provides an increased understanding of who we are. It helps us define a strategy to prepare ourselves for life *and* its fruitfulness while allowing us to approach what heart, mind, hands, and imagination are insufficient to fix.

Life brings discoveries and events that simply cannot be explained by what we think, do, feel, or even imagine. For us, spirituality taps the intangible world, the pursuits and ideas that allow for meaning, purpose, and wholeness in life—the fruit of what we term soulwork. Developing our spiritual nature through soulwork means to respect that sacred part of ourselves and others. It also means that while on the spiritual path, we should be open to the mystical in all of us, reaching toward an understanding of God and working toward conserving all of God's creation.

With the Western emphasis on rational, mechanistic thinking, the value of our inner workings, our souls, is often overlooked. Our spiritual side doesn't scream for our attention in the way that our bodies, our families, our work, or our pocketbooks do. We know when we're hungry for food or water, but the needs of our souls can go undetected. For some, it isn't until they experience things that cannot be explained or solved through their own powers that they begin to seek the spiritual. For others, it may take a major loss—referred to in this book as "the storms of life"—before they encounter the spiritual side of themselves.

Psychological Type and the Soul

Whether soulwork is already part of your life or a new area for exploration, using the concepts of psychological type can help you illuminate the spiritual climates or atmospheres that will help you the most. Melding spirituality and psychological type is natural. *Psyche* (the root of the word "psychology") is defined as "soul." *Soul* is defined as the intangible part of us, or our spirit. Thus, to tap into our spiritual side through the psyche is to combine two schools of thought; both schools are about intangible concepts made tangible by looking at their expression in our everyday behavior.

And the key? For us it is whether soulwork is a part of your everyday life. Have you found a spiritual climate that is comfortable for you? Are you on a spiritual journey? Do your spiritual practices seem congruent with who you really are?

Carl Jung, the modern-day originator of psychological type, observed, "People from all the civilized countries of the earth have consulted me. I have treated many hundreds of patients. Among all my patients in the second half of life—that is to say, over thirty-five— there has not been one whose problem in the last resort was not that of finding a religious [spiritual] outlook on life. It is safe to say that every one of them fell ill because he had lost that which the living religions of every age have given to their followers, and none of them has been really healed who did not regain his religious [spiritual] outlook."[2]

No one is too young or too old to begin soulwork. However, it takes conscious effort, similar to the effort it takes to tend to the needs of our bodies and minds. When we talked with people, they seemed to be at one of three stages on their spiritual journeys.

Stage One—
Choosing to pay attention to the work of the soul

At some point, people decide they are open to the value of soulwork and are ready to respond to the soul's call.

You might begin by exploring why you're here and where you're going—what brought you to this place and what propels you forward. If you haven't taken this step, consider the following questions:

- What gaps exist in your life? Are there yearnings that you can't define or that your current existence doesn't seem to satisfy?
- What benefits do you observe in the lives of people who seem to follow a spiritual path?
- As you look honestly at your past experiences with spirituality and religion, what encouraged or nurtured your soul? What events, practices, or people kept you from the path of soulwork?

What atmospheres or climates helped or hindered you just as you are?

If past experiences are blocking you from soulwork, you are far from alone. For many of the people we interviewed, their spiritual paths, religious traditions, or family upbringings were at direct odds with who they were—their psychological type.

Your personal path to soulwork might begin by reading about your psychological type and discovering how your natural spiritual preferences fit with what was "accepted" in your spiritual tradition. Understanding why some climates or atmospheres led you to react as you did can remove old barriers and create new opportunities for soulwork.

Stage Two—
Crafting soulwork to bring it to the everyday

Thomas Moore, contemporary author of *Care of the Soul,* wrote, "For some, religion is a Sunday affair, and they risk dividing life into the holy Sabbath and the secular week. For others, religion is a week-long observance that is inspired and sustained on the Sabbath."[3] Your type can be your compass, pointing to those practices and environments that particularly suit your individual divine nature and help you find the kinds of soulwork to regularly pursue. These settings and activities offer the energy, support, direction, and even the challenges you need.

"Traditional" soul climates may be contrary to your nature. Most books on spirituality were written by people who thrive on meditation, solitude, study, and discipline. However, what is natural for one type may not be natural to another. There are *many* other avenues to soulwork that are just as valid—and these may be more instinctive for *you*. Finding those avenues that work for you is essential to making spirituality a regular part of your life.

- For some types, being outside in the world of nature or relishing the delights of daily living is the best route to soulwork.
- Some find meaning by exploring paradox and mystery.

- For others, discussing their doubts to find clarity and truth is the best spiritual path.
- Still others carry out their soulwork by interacting with people.

Perhaps this is your opportunity to find what works best for you, for the time to begin soulwork is in the calms of life (possibly right now). People who are able to bring soulwork to their everyday lives are most able to access it when they need it—either to provide direction for the choices they face or to weather the storms of life.

Stage Three—
Soulwork for wholeness, for meaning and purpose

Soulwork takes on an entirely different dimension when we move on from coping with life's storms to becoming all we were meant to be. Perhaps soulwork has been a part of your life for a long time, but has lost a bit of its spark. Or, you want new challenges or insights, or are curious about new experiences. Soulwork at this stage is the avenue to meaning and purpose, fruitfulness, significance—the yearnings are called by many names.

The concepts of psychological type provide direction for this quest: How can we move toward fashioning our own unique identity in a way that respects how we were created, thereby honoring our Creator? As we desire to mature spiritually, our psychological type can guide us in seeking new, enriching practices.

These spiritual stages aren't necessarily sequential. Some people find their spiritual paths at a young age. Some doubt everything, spiritual or not. Others continually struggle with past spiritual experiences that perhaps left almost too much pain to overcome. Still others are catapulted backward by the storms of life, those dark times that we all eventually face—sometimes never to recover.

However, by defining your starting point—the stage where you currently are—you can use this book to craft your spirituality with the soulwork that will mean the most to you and have the greatest possibility of enriching your life.

The Starting Point of Our Own Journeys

Because we as authors are quite familiar with psychological type theory and Jung's concepts of the conscious and the unconscious, we realize that *unconsciously* we may have had a bias as we developed and wrote this book.

Sandra comes from a family that combined, but did not blend, three major religious traditions. Her preferences are for ENFP,* a type that typically is open to possibilities for people and chafes at anything imposed in a heavy-handed way. Sandra tries to use psychological type to help others become more self-aware and in the process find more, not fewer, options for their spiritual life. Sandra believes God works in us and through us in mysterious ways and that one's personal spiritual path is just that—personal as well as individually crafted with God.

Jane, with preferences for INFJ,† finds that she, as well as many others of her type, tends to naturally view life in spiritual terms. For her, it is often easier to look for how God is working all around us than to stay in touch with actual current events. Because so much spiritual literature is written from the IN (Introverted Intuition) standpoint, with its emphasis on silent prayer, study, and meditation, Jane hopes that these pages can help others find the less-known and less-written-about paths for soulwork that are more natural for them.

As NFs (Intuitive Feelers), we share a passion for helping others reach their full potential and trust that these pages might help *you* to:

- Find those spiritual atmospheres or climates that bring you the greatest joy, insight, clarity, or practical help—whatever you personally need from soulwork;
- Understand your past frustrations with spirituality;
- Know how to best provide shelter for yourself and others in the storms of life;
- Discern strategies for personal growth that include spirituality throughout your life.

Extraversion iNtuition Feeling Perception (ENFP). The terminology for psychological type preferences is fully explained in Chapter 2.
†*Introversion iNtuition Feeling Judging.*

I laugh when I hear that the fish in the water is thirsty.
  You don't grasp the fact that what is most alive of all
  is inside your own house;
And so you walk from one holy city
  to the next with a confused look!
Kabir will tell you the truth:
  go wherever you like, to Calcutta or Tibet,
If you can't find where your soul is hidden,
For you the world will never be real!

KABIR, FIFTEENTH-CENTURY HINDU POET[4]

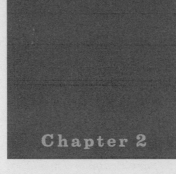

Chapter 2

Understanding Psychological Type—
A Pathway to Finding Your Natural Spiritual Climate

Have you ever met anyone who was *just* like you? Of course not. No two human beings are alike; yet if you carefully study human behavior, certain consistencies and predictable patterns emerge.

Innumerable cultures developed a method for categorizing people to explain behavior, from ancient civilizations on. In modern times, Carl Jung's work on psychological type enhanced the paradigm that human behavior is far from random. Jung's theory became more accessible to the American public through the work of Katharine Briggs and Isabel Briggs Myers, whose efforts to make his theory more practical resulted in the Myers-Briggs Type Indicator® (MBTI®).* The MBTI is one of the most widely used psychological instruments for self-awareness in the world.

Jung's theory of psychological type postulates that we each have natural preferences for:

---

*If you wish to clarify your psychological type, consider contacting your human resources department or local community college to take the MBTI. Or call the publisher, Consulting Psychologists Press, at (800) 624-1765 or the Association for Psychological Type at (816) 444-3500 for more information.

- How we are energized (Extraversion or Introversion)
- How we perceive the world around us (Sensing or Intuition)
- How we make decisions (Thinking or Feeling)
- How we choose to live our outer lives (Judging or Perceiving)

These preferences are innate but can be influenced by our family, education, culture, etc. In much the same way, most of us never give a thought to the hand with which we prefer to write. Take a moment to sign your name with your *non-preferred* hand in the space below:

Think about the experience. Most people describe it as awkward, time-consuming or unnatural, taking more conscious effort. Now write your name with your *preferred* hand.

Was it easier? More natural? Did it take less concentration, as most people find? Your handedness is innate, as is kicking a ball with your preferred leg or focusing a camera image with your preferred eye. However, *with practice*, you can learn to use your non-preferred hand or leg or eye. And so it is with our psychological preferences. We are born into one way of being. That path generally feels more instinctive and typically requires less effort than using the non-preferred ways. However, we can improve our abilities with the other processes.

Type and Spirituality

While there are infinite varieties of people within each of the 16 psychological types, there are also many similarities that provide clues for understanding how each type can best pursue a spiritual path. One of our friends who critiqued part of an early draft of this book commented on his intensive soulwork, "I see from your text that I have once again followed a *type* path: rather disturbing when one thinks one has simply pursued truth apparently with reasonable independence and integrity!" Other people who have participated in workshops on the subject reported:

- *I understand more why my spiritual practices are different from others'—but not wrong!*
- *I learned that my natural form of soulwork is consistent with my type and can be termed prayer.*
- *I want to find out the types of the rest of my family—I have a good feeling that our disputes about spirituality could be aided through the concepts of type.*

If you are not familiar with psychological type, the following pages can give you an approximation of your own, but you may wish to read further. Our suggested reading list at the end of the book provides further clarity and other applications.

Extraversion or Introversion—Our Pathway to Energy

The first of the preference pairings describes how we are energized. Think about all of the different activities and environments you encountered during the past week. Some of them probably left you feeling energetic and refreshed while others were stressful and draining, causing you to seek rest and renewal elsewhere.

In a Nutshell

Extraverts are energized through contact with other people or through engaging in activities.

Introverts are energized through the world of ideas, pulling back from activities to allow time for thought and reflection.

Which way would you have approached the assignment in the following story?

Jane: *"I attended a writers' workshop at a retreat center. One evening our leader dismissed the group to work on the assignment of identifying our strengths as writers and our aspirations for the coming year. As an Introvert, I couldn't wait to get to my room—the evening session had covered so much and I was ready to organize my thoughts on paper. I made a little grid of ideas I wanted to consider. What was most on my heart? The next 90 minutes flew by as my pen filled the paper. For me, this quiet time alone on the retreat was the most meaningful segment of the weekend.*

"The next morning, I heard that several of the participants—including the leader—never quite made it to their rooms to journal. Instead, they chose to use each other as sounding boards, tossing out ideas and dreams to allow those listening to give input on the patterns and strengths they saw. At breakfast, they were still bubbling about the insights they had gained through their discussion."

Jane's preference is for Introversion—she gains energy by retreating, taking time to reflect and process her inner thoughts. Those who stayed together to interact probably preferred Extraversion—they were energized by talking through their thoughts with others. Different methods, same results.

Which method would work best for you—off alone or together in discussion? Now consider the following word pairings as you try to determine your own preference for energy:

Extraversion	Introversion
❏ People and things	❏ Thoughts and ideas
❏ Try, then consider	❏ Consider, then try
❏ Action	❏ Reflection
❏ Breadth; different subjects	❏ Depth on one subject
❏ Outer energy	❏ Inner energy
❏ Interruptions are stimulating	❏ Interruptions are distracting
❏ Focus outside	❏ Focus inside
❏ Say what they are thinking	❏ Keep thoughts to themselves
❏ Discuss to process ideas	❏ Introspect to process ideas
❏ Offer suggestions freely	❏ Hold suggestions until clear

If Extraverted types could design their own atmosphere for soulwork, they would include people, action, and variety; they gain energy from the world around them. Extraverted types learn best by talking through spiritual matters, joining with others for worship, study, or service activities. They see God or the spiritual through their own actions and the words and deeds of others.

If Extraverted types are surrounded by silent environments, attend meetings or services with long pauses for meditation, or are required to sit still or focus on one idea for too long, they *might* conclude that they struggle spiritually.

Solitude, introspection, and privacy for personal reflection are key to spirituality for Introverted types. They gain energy in the world of ideas. Introverted types learn best through study, reading, contemplation, or one-to-one conversations. They may not even pray aloud or discuss their soulwork with close friends.

If Introverted types spend too much time in group discussion, participating in active learning experiences, or are asked to share deep thoughts too freely they *might* mistakenly conclude that they struggle spiritually.

Sensing or Intuition—Our Pathway to Discovery

Information surrounds us every day of our lives: sights, sounds, conversations, readings, events, changes in the weather, and the products of our imaginations. Our *perceiving process* involves sorting through all of this data. We naturally filter the things to which we pay attention. None of us can process it all. There are two ways to perceive, using either Sensing (S) or Intuition (N).*

---

*N *is used for Intuition because* I *was already assigned to Introversion.*

How might you have reacted to this experience?

"I joined a cancer support group that was recommended by a friend. The first meeting was filled with concrete tips on information-gathering, dealing with chemotherapy, and examples of how others had dealt with decisions about cancer care. Then at the end of the session our leader handed each of us a rock. 'Imagine that the weight of this stone is the weight of your personal sorrows and concerns. They weigh on your soul just as this rock weighs down your hand. Let's take a moment to ponder that weight in silence and consider the effect of the burdens we carry. Then as you leave, drop your rock into the basket by the door. Leave your fears about cancer here as well, taking with you only the proactive plan you've developed tonight.'

"Out in the hall, I was amazed to see that some of the participants had tears in their eyes as a result of the closing exercise, saying that they were able to let go of their anxieties as they let go of the rock. This did nothing for me— the rock was a rock, gray, cold, and hard. I felt just as burdened as before. I tried not to make too much of my reaction, but I wondered why I was affected so differently when the others seemed to have shared a meaningful experience."

JON, 54, RETAIL MANAGER

The teller of this story has a preference for Sensing—relying on information that is provided by the five senses. Many of those who found meaning and help in the stone exercise probably had preferences for Intuition—going beyond the facts that provide a starting point for using the imagination and making connections.

Which list of word pairings resonates most with you?

Sensing	Intuition
❏ Five senses	❏ Sixth sense
❏ Common sense	❏ Insight
❏ Accuracy	❏ Creativity
❏ Past experience	❏ Inspiration
❏ Real world	❏ Unseen world
❏ Current reality	❏ Future potential
❏ Immediacy, concreteness	❏ Anticipation
❏ Master, then apply skills	❏ Learn new skills, then innovate
❏ Simplicity, clarity	❏ Complexity
❏ What experience offers people	❏ What possibilities offer people

A NATURAL SPIRITUAL ENVIRONMENT
FOR SENSING TYPES

If Sensing types could design their own spiritual setting, it might be filled with tangible evidence that supports their values and principles, suggestions for activities and tasks, methods for study and prayer, the examples of others who have found soulwork meaningful, and opportunities to serve in practical ways. Soulwork, they might say, should make a difference in the here and now.

Some Sensing types struggle if asked to believe too many assumptions without good facts or evidence. Their preference for concreteness can make them feel somewhat out of place in many spiritual communities, where often the emphasis is on accepting on faith what cannot be proved.

A NATURAL SPIRITUAL ENVIRONMENT
FOR INTUITIVE TYPES

If Intuitive types could design an atmosphere for soulwork, they might fill it with symbols and imagery, the creative, artistic, or poetic— spurs to the imagination that provide inspiration. Learning often comes through synchronistic interactions among ideas, people, and the environment. Change and innovation tend to enrich their spirituality.

Intuitive types might struggle in environments with fixed routines, narrow interpretations, or defined methods for soulwork that leave little room for innovation. If their soulwork becomes too familiar, their minds may wander or their attention be captured elsewhere, leaving them to feel unspiritual.

Thinking or Feeling—Our Pathway to Decisions

We all use our perceiving process, either Sensing or Intuition, to gather information. We also need to sort through that information and act on it. To do so, we operate out of our preference for Thinking or Feeling. Both approaches are *rational*, decision-making processes; however, only one can be termed *logical* while the other might be described as *values-centered*. Think how often these styles play out in our day-to-day conversations: "I *think* we should do this." "Well, I don't *feel* that way at all!"

In a Nutshell

Thinking types base their decisions on impartial criteria—cause-effect reasoning, constant principles or truths, and logical analysis.

Feeling types consider the impact of their decisions on people— their needs and those of others, the values to be served, and circumstantial or community variables.

◈

Our decision-making style has a profound impact on how we evaluate experiences, define our beliefs, and view the actions of others. Consider how you might react in this situation:

Sandra: *"In a seminar on the soul at work, our instructor asked us to ponder what our life work might be. As music played softly in the background, several members of the class jotted down their thoughts while I simply closed my eyes.*

The discussion that followed impressed me with the heartfelt reflections about purpose and fulfillment. One person mentioned a value his life work needed to fulfill. Another mentioned striving toward a change she hoped to bring about in employee-employer relationships. As the stories and affirmations about our life work continued, the man next to me interjected, "I'm beginning to wonder about the kind of planet I landed on tonight. As I pondered my life work, I concluded that I don't need to analyze all of this other stuff. I like my work and I'm good at it. My corporation serves a useful purpose, we've created products that fill a need—why look beyond the work I am doing right now?"

Many of the class participants were looking to define their life work in terms of the impact they could have on other people or on society, perhaps out of their preference for Feeling. The last speaker had examined his work through a logical framework of usefulness and productivity, a more Thinking process.

Which of the words in the pairings below seem to fit your decision-making style?

Thinking	Feeling
❑ Easily sort ideas about data and things	❑ Easily sort ideas about people
❑ Acknowledge differences	❑ Acknowledge common ground
❑ Critique	❑ Appreciate
❑ Logical, analytical	❑ Harmonious, personal
❑ Reasons	❑ Values
❑ Head knowledge	❑ Heart knowledge
❑ Fair but firm	❑ Empathize, make exceptions
❑ Analyze	❑ Sympathize
❑ Content of message	❑ Impact of message
❑ Convince through impartiality	❑ Convince through personal meaning

If Thinking Types could design their atmosphere for soulwork, they would start with the intellect, searching for universal principles and sacred truths. Their skepticism often precedes conviction. Learning occurs through debate and dialogue, logical explanations of issues, categorizing practices and beliefs, and working to establish standards and structures. They may discount or distrust the emotional aspects of spirituality.

If Thinking types find themselves in atmospheres that emphasize soulwork through personal encounters or relationships with their Creator, they may consider themselves inadequate without these spiritual experiences. They may also struggle unless others let them probe and question—a type of soulwork that feels threatening to some.

If Feeling types could design their own atmosphere for soulwork, they would start with the heart, searching for personal meaning and values. Relationships with others are often key to their spirituality. Learning occurs through direct acts of service as well as trying to explain the motivations, inspirations, and experiences of others. They also want compassionate environments that put people and their needs first.

If Feeling types find themselves in atmospheres that enforce rules without love, require logical, objective rationale for what they believe, or take an impersonal approach to soulwork, they may struggle spiritually.

Judging or Perceiving—Our Pathway to Soulwork

People tend to approach life in one of two ways: Judging types like to plan their work and work their plan, soulwork included. Perceiving types prefer to go with the flow, remaining open to soulwork as opportunities arise.

Can you place yourself in this story?

"When my spouse suggested a daily family time to connect with each other, it seemed like a wonderful idea—a planned activity, a chance for everyone to report on their day, a question to ponder—perhaps ten or fifteen minutes after dinner. At first, I shared the enthusiasm for these times, but after awhile I began to feel locked in and duty-bound. Instead of enriched, I felt smothered, dreading the daily dinner 'ritual.'

"My spouse, who really enjoyed this time, was upset when I said I preferred not to continue. For a long time, I felt guilty about backing out and canceling the routine. I wondered how one of us could find these moments so meaningful and the other find the structure and predictability so deadening."

CYNTHIA, 42, CAREER COUNSELOR

Our storyteller prefers the Perceiving process, approaching life as it comes and finding richness and joy in spontaneity. Her spouse took a more Judging approach, enjoying the planning of their family time. Consider your own preference in the following word pairings.

Judging	Perceiving
❏ Planned events	❏ Serendipitous events
❏ Work before play	❏ Work and play coexist
❏ Stress reduced by planning ahead	❏ Stress reduced by identifying contingencies
❏ Enjoy making the decision	❏ Enjoy gathering information

❑ Goal-oriented	❑ Discovery-oriented
❑ Tasks in order	❑ Several tasks at random
❑ Settled and decided	❑ Open to late-breaking information
❑ Choose one option, then explore	❑ Explore many options, then choose
❑ Select the best experience	❑ Experience as much as possible
❑ Settled, orderly	❑ In the moment

A NATURAL ENVIRONMENT FOR JUDGING SOULWORK

If Judging types could design their atmosphere for soulwork, the key elements might be discipline, organization, and schedule. They might develop regular routines for their devotional practices, using benchmarks for recording progress and accomplishments. Learning often occurs through structured exercises or regular classes.

If Judging types are in environments where things don't start and end on time, there is no discernment, others aren't prepared, or stated goals aren't accomplished, their frustrations may cause them to lose their desire for soulwork.

A NATURAL ENVIRONMENT FOR PERCEIVING SOULWORK

If Perceiving types could design their atmosphere for soulwork, it would be flexible, full of options, stocked with resources, and able to adapt time frames to the needs of people or circumstances. Learning comes as much from departures as from staying on task, being open to more facts and possibilities, and experiencing as many avenues for soulwork as possible when opportunities arise.

If Perceiving types are corralled in environments that are too structured, they may either feel inadequate or concerned that they lack the discipline others say they need to grow spiritually. They often find that systematic spiritual disciplines (which permeate literature on prayer and other writings on enriching one's soulwork) threaten to dampen their chances of finding the sacred as they go about experiencing life.

These eight preferences combine to describe 16 different psychological types. Because you might find it interesting and because our writing comes from who we are—our personality—Sandra's preferences are for Extraversion, Intuition, Feeling, and Perceiving, more easily written as the type ENFP. Jane's preferences are for Introversion, Intuition, Feeling, and Judging, more easily written as the type INFJ. For brevity, the preferences are known by the first letter in the word (remember that the *N* stands for I*n*tuition—the *I* was used for "*I*ntroversion"). As you read through the previous description of each of the eight preferences, which seemed most like you? You can record your four-letter type in the spaces below:

E or I   S or N   T or F   J or P

_____   _____   _____   _____

A Few Observations About Type

While we want to emphasize that type is only one tool for soul-work, it provides key insights for many people as they work to enrich their spiritual journey. However:

- Psychological type is *not prescriptive*. It is a tool for describing recognizable distinctions between people.
- Psychological type is *not a pigeonhole*—human behavior is much too complex to be described through a single framework. In addition, there is infinite diversity among human beings and within each of the 16 psychological types. People with the same type will share some common characteristics, but each will have many unique characteristics of his or her own.
- Psychological type is *not deterministic*. While Jung believed that you are born a certain type (think of the differences in siblings you know!), you are also born with a free will that gives you latitude for your behavior. You also have your own particular life circumstances that shape the expression of your type.
- Psychological type offers little information about your particular skills, competencies, abilities, or knowledge base.
- Psychological type is *not an excuse* for certain behaviors or for avoiding certain tasks.

- Psychological type is *not about putting barriers* in the way of your personal or spiritual growth.

For this book, *type is a tool*, not the answer, for understanding yourself and learning how to make your spiritual life more meaningful. As you look to use this book to strengthen your soulwork, keep the following in mind.

- *Type is a way to understand yourself in general, not in specifics.* Read the specific chapter for advice about the most natural paths to soulwork for people of your type, but then read the other chapters to understand similarities, differences, and new paths for enrichment.
- *Type is a logical framework for explaining some of the consistencies of human behavior.* As such, for spirituality it can:
    Improve communication
    Emphasize the value of diversity
    Identify potential conflicts
    Offer an appropriate language to deal with emotional or stressful issues.
- *Finally, type is a dynamic theory, not a method for placing people in unchanging boxes.* As the next chapter describes in detail, type can be used to explore strategies for growth and development over the span of life as well as help anticipate responses to the inevitable storms of life.

Chapter 3

Psychological Type
and Personal Development

W hat is your favorite climate? Some people like four distinct seasons, others want the tropics all year, or the thin air and clear
sunshine of high altitudes, or the moist breeze of the seashore.

But even if one of these is your favorite, you probably occasionally
want to explore a different one—and may even need to do so. You can't
snow ski in Florida and you can't appreciate the aurora borealis in the
middle of a city. Type is like that. You've identified your favorite atmosphere for soulwork, but enrichment and fulfillment are to be found by
visiting the natural climates of other types. The theory of *type dynamics*
acts as a guide for where to explore and what to expect.

Type is more than just your four letters—it is also a theory about
growing toward wholeness and adding meaning to your life. Herein
lies its value in pursuing soulwork. To understand the implications of
type theory, consider for now just the two middle letters of your
type—S, N, T, or F. These four preferences describe how we *function*.
The order in which you learn to use these preferences will also say
something about your spirituality.

The following chart shows the typical order of preferences for each of the sixteen types. Find your type on the chart so that you can refer to it throughout the next sections.

ISTJ	ISFJ	INFJ	INTJ
1. Sensing	1. Sensing	1. Intuition	1. Intuition
2. Thinking	2. Feeling	2. Feeling	2. Thinking
3. Feeling	3. Thinking	3. Thinking	3. Feeling
4. Intuition	4. Intuition	4. Sensing	4. Sensing
ISTP	**ISFP**	**INFP**	**INTP**
1. Thinking	1. Feeling	1. Feeling	1. Thinking
2. Sensing	2. Sensing	2. Intuition	2. Intuition
3. Intuition	3. Intuition	3. Sensing	3. Sensing
4. Feeling	4. Thinking	4. Thinking	4. Feeling
ESTP	**ESFP**	**ENFP**	**ENTP**
1. Sensing	1. Sensing	1. Intuition	1. Intuition
2. Thinking	2. Feeling	2. Feeling	2. Thinking
3. Feeling	3. Thinking	3. Thinking	3. Feeling
4. Intuition	4. Intuition	4. Sensing	4. Sensing
ESTJ	**ESFJ**	**ENFJ**	**ENTJ**
1. Thinking	1. Feeling	1. Feeling	1. Thinking
2. Sensing	2. Sensing	2. Intuition	2. Intuition
3. Intuition	3. Intuition	3. Sensing	3. Sensing
4. Feeling	4. Thinking	4. Thinking	4. Feeling

The Role of the Dominant Function

Each of us has a dominant function, the function listed first in the above chart. Consider it as the central or core aspect of psychological being, the natural climate for each type. People use their dominant preference first in most situations and it develops earliest in life. This is the dominant force of your personality; generally the other preferences act to support it.

Consider your childhood:

- Many dominant *Sensing types* were described as sensible or matter-of-fact youngsters.
- Many dominant *Intuitive types* were described as imaginative or creative children.
- Many dominant *Thinking types* were described as inquisitive kids, full of questions, frequently asking, "Why?"
- Many dominant *Feeling types* were known as empathetic children, considerate of the feelings of others and concerned that everyone be included.

For most people, approaching spirituality through their dominant function allows them to find a natural pathway.

The Role of Extraversion and Introversion

Your preference for Extraversion or Introversion tells the *orientation* of your dominant function. Extraverts show their dominant function to the outer world. Introverts use their dominant function in the inner world—the life of the mind. Jane as an INFJ, for example, processes her ideas internally, generating possibilities and connections on her own. *Introverted* Intuition is her dominant function. In contrast, Sandra as an ENFP processes aloud with others, getting her ideas from the world at large, what she sees and what others say. *Extraverted* Intuition is her dominant function.

The Role of the Auxiliary Function

Complementing each type's natural element, the dominant function, are the gifts of the *auxiliary* function, the second one for your type in the above list. Without a well-developed auxiliary function, people lack balance. Together, the dominant and auxiliary make up the two middle letters of your type code.

If your dominant function is one of the perceiving functions: Sensing or Intuition	Then your auxiliary function is one of the judging functions: Thinking or Feeling This function enables you to act on all of the information your dominant function gathers
If your dominant function is one of the judging functions: Thinking or Feeling	Then your auxiliary function is one of the perceiving functions: Sensing or Intuition This function gives you information for the decision-making process of your dominant function

The auxiliary function is the next to develop in life. By young adulthood, most people are able to use this function efficiently, allowing them to both gather information and make decisions.

The *orientation* of the auxiliary function is opposite that of the dominant function. For example, since Jane's dominant function, Intuition, is *introverted*, then her auxiliary function, Feeling, is *extraverted*. In order to understand her feelings and the effects of a situation on people, Jane often finds it helpful to talk things through with others or engage in activities to gain new perspectives. As we worked on this book, Jane spent considerable time interviewing people to understand their soulwork and determine what might be included in these pages.

Sandra's dominant function, Intuition, is *extraverted*, so her auxiliary function, Feeling, is *introverted*. Sandra often needs time by herself to consider exactly how she feels about a situation. In writing this book, Sandra reflected alone on what might be most helpful for others and how to make our treatment of the subject as inclusive as possible.

The Third Function

So far we've explained the middle letters of your type. However, the letters that *aren't* there influence you as well.

Type theory suggests that during the first half of life, we operate mostly through our dominant and auxiliary functions. This makes sense if you consider that the first half of life is about separating from our families of origin, establishing our careers, building our primary relationships, and perhaps becoming parents. Success in these endeavors often comes through operating out of our most natural functions.

However, as we move toward the second half of life, the focus changes. Perhaps there is a vague yearning for more.

"Is this all there is to life?"

"I can't understand . . . "

"I've been successful, but what have I really achieved?"

Carl Jung held that our first two functions are not enough to bring fulfillment in life—we must learn to access our non-preferred processes. He stated it thusly: "We cannot live in the afternoon of life according to the program of life's morning. For what in the morning was true, will at evening have become a lie."[1]

For many people, the other two functions now come into play. Generally, we begin to access our third function next—for both Jane and Sandra, Thinking is an avenue to adding richness. Sandra describes it this way: "Between Intuition and Feeling, my first two functions, I am acutely aware of the potential in other people and how I might help them. I was quick to say 'yes' to any request where I believed others could grow or develop through my actions. But as my consulting grew, requests overwhelmed me. Now, Thinking helps me choose more wisely. Whereas my Feeling function tends to guide my decisions in terms of the needs of others, Thinking allows me to set more impartial criteria. As I evaluate opportunities, I consider the physical, financial, and emotional costs as well."

Not as much is known about the third function. Carl Jung wrote that for most of us, this process is sometimes conscious, sometimes unconscious: this third function may act to support our dominant and auxiliary functions (the ones we consciously use), but may more *typically* link with our fourth function (the least conscious of the functions). Whichever way it acts, the third function is more difficult for us to access and for most people is not as well-developed as the dominant and auxiliary functions.

Whereas we describe the first, second, and fourth functions in terms of extraversion and introversion, we cannot say the same about the third function. Some writers say that the third function can be either extraverted or introverted at different times. However, we *do* know that:

- **Sensing, the gift of seeing** *what is,* **is the third function for ENTJs, ENFJs, INFPs and INTPs.** These types tend to be more adept at perceiving through their auxiliary Intuition function. However, taking a commonsense approach to life, being aware of facts and specifics, is occasionally required. For these four types, developing their third function of Sensing can help them back up their Intuitive insights with the necessary details.
- **Intuition, the gift of seeing** *what could be,* **is the third function for ESTJs, ESFJs, ISTPs, and ISFPs.** These types tend to be more adept at perceiving through their auxiliary Sensing function. At times, however, adding insight and inspiration can be useful. For these four types, developing their third function of Intuition can help them enlarge their view of reality, value the big picture, and be open to new ways of doing things.
- **Thinking, the gift of** *logic and clarity,* **is the third function for ESFPs, ENFPs, ISFJs, and INFJs.** These types tend to be more adept at making decisions through their auxiliary Feeling function. However, by developing their third function, Thinking, they may find it easier to debate and logically support their viewpoints, adding objectivity to their decision-making process.
- **Feeling, the gift of** *understanding and appreciating* **the values and viewpoints of others, is the third function for ESTPs, ENTPs, ISTJs, and INTJs.** These types tend to be more adept at making decisions through their auxiliary Thinking function. At times, however, focusing on subjective values or analyzing the impact of different alternatives on people can be useful. For these four types, developing their third function, Feeling, can soften their more tough-minded decision-making style.

How people use their third function in soulwork varies greatly. Each type chapter provides information on how the third function can be accessed. You can also look at the summary pages for Sensing, Intuitive, Thinking, and Feeling spirituality, whichever is the third function for your type, for more ideas.

The Fourth or Inferior Function

Lastly, there is the fourth function, often known as the *inferior function*, which typically develops at midlife and beyond. For most people, their inferior function is the opposite of their dominant and by far the most difficult to learn to use effectively. It is hard to discern the facts and the possibilities (S and N) at the same time. It is hard to be objective and subjective (T and F) at the same time. This means that the inferior function can be the source of many problems for each of us.

- **Dominant Sensing types (ISTJ, ISFJ, ESTP, ESFP)**, so versed in identifying *what is*, may have difficulty accessing what *could be*— the realm of their inferior Intuitive function.
- **Dominant Intuitive types (INFJ, INTJ, ENFP, ENTP)**, so adept in using their imagination and developing new insights, may struggle in dealing with day-to-day details or realism—the realm of their inferior Sensing function.
- **Dominant Thinking types (ISTP, INTP, ESTJ, ENTJ)**, with their ease at being objective and analytical, may struggle with interpersonal matters where subjectivity and harmony are valued—the realm of their inferior Feeling function.
- **Dominant Feeling types (ISFP, INFP, ESFJ, ENFJ)**, acutely aware of the impact of events and ideas on themselves and others, may find it difficult to deal objectively with tough issues—the realm of their inferior Thinking function.

However, while often being a source of trouble, the inferior function also adds a richness and many rewards to the second half of life. New vistas are available for those who tap this fourth function.

"As a dominant extraverted Feeling type, I had one use for my sailboat—parties! For me, the more people, the better. I'd have twenty on the boat with me and twenty more on shore waiting for the next round. I skippered, kept the buffet table full and the soda flowing, in short being the life of the party.

"Last year, though, something changed for me. The boat became a means of getting away from people in order to think. The lapping of the water and the feel of the breeze were all but unnoticeable when I was surrounded by dozens of people. Sometimes I pull in the sails and drift in silence as my mind ponders a decision. My inferior introverted Thinking now can provide the peace and wisdom I used to look for from others."

KEITH, 68, RETIRED
RELIGIOUS PROFESSIONAL

While the dominant function is often the initial spark as people pursue spirituality, some of the deepest growth is fed through this inferior function. Perhaps this is because few things that are extremely important to us come easily. In addition, as long as we are using our dominant function, most of us are in control of ourselves and the processes we are pursuing. When we enter the domain of the inferior function, few of us can effectively control the process. We need to be more deliberate, more disciplined to use this fourth function. For many of us, this is where God can get our attention—we stop trying to control and are more open to the Creator.

"For a long time, I was envious of how some people could close their eyes, relax, and suddenly have profound experiences—they seemed to find answers to questions with which they had been struggling. I wanted to have the experience, too, but as a Sensing type, try as I might, nothing much ever happened.

"I took several spiritual growth classes and tried to ground my images in a place I knew well and visited frequently. The first time I tried I managed to visualize my favorite meadow, but nothing else happened. Later on in a similar exercise I felt more of a presence of peace as I imagined this special place, but that was it.

"Then a few years later, I took another class in guided imagery. This

time I could sense that I was enthusiastic about going to my familiar meadow. I imagined the walk there in great detail. And all of a sudden, other things started to happen. The leader suggested we imagine a symbol that would feed our souls, and an animal came, to my total surprise! As the course proceeded, the leader suggested we go to the top of a mountain to ask questions of our Creator. I went there and I got answers! In time, I came to trust these answers more than some of the more realistic ones based on facts I gathered."

RORY, 56, TEACHER

As you continue on in these pages, remember that while some spiritual pursuits may be labeled as more Sensing, Intuitive, Thinking, or Feeling, *all of us* can benefit from operating outside of our normal ways. However, it helps to know that this is what we are doing.

"For years I thought that I was 'bad' at prayer. My mind always wandered and I felt guilty about it, even though prayer time often fed, illuminated, delighted and comforted me. Now I understand that my Intuition was at work, connecting one thought with another and providing new insights. Instead of condemning myself, I bought a notebook to list the things I want to be consistent about in prayer. Now I can choose to flit or focus!"

ESTHER, 48, PHOTOGRAPHER

To make your own choices of whether to "flit or focus," we suggest that to use this book you do the following:

- Start with the chapter on your own psychological type.
- Read the summary pages for your dominant function.
- Try what fits, take what you want, leave the rest.
- Keep in mind that because one of your first two functions is extraverted and one is introverted, you need both outer and inner approaches to soulwork. *This does not mean that you must join an organized spiritual community or discipline yourself for extended periods of solitude.* It simply means that Extraverts will flourish by finding *some* time for reflection and Introverts will flourish by finding at least a few like-minded souls as companions on their spiritual journey.

- Decide what your third function can bring to your soulwork.
- Look at the chapter for your opposite type to gain a real sense of the differences between your dominant and inferior functions. While the chapter on your type has examples of how some people use their inferior function, you may want to observe the spirituality of people whose preferences are opposite from yours—or talk with them—to gain vivid images of the gifts of their natural soulwork.

In families or relationships:

- Become aware of the different psychological types of your family members and their natural avenues for soulwork.
- Look through the chapters to find common ground for spirituality.
- Decide where you can support each other—which practices and opportunities does each person need the chance to pursue.
- Encourage each other for richness and spiritual development.

And finally, for those of you who are spiritual directors or leaders, we ask you to reconsider any "shoulds" and "oughts" through the lens of type. What would honor *all* types, or at least respectfully acknowledge type differences?

The year's at the spring

And day's at the morn;

Morning's at seven;

The hillside's dew-pearled;

The lark's on the wing

The snail's on the thorn:

God's in his heaven—

All's right with the world.

R OBERT
B ROWNING[1]

Sensing
Spirituality

Sensing Types Find Satisfying Soulwork Through:

- Living the spiritual life with an emphasis on what's happening in the here and now
- Enjoying the gifts of being alive, the delights of this world
- Appreciating the beauty of nature and creation, the joys of "what is"
- Seeing tangible applications for the day-to-day real world and practical works and needs
- Learning in an orderly, step-by-step fashion about facts, history, or methods of spirituality
- Observing concrete examples of what's worked for others
- Commemorating spiritual traditions and events

Preferred Extraverted Sensing Soulwork (ESTP and ESFP)

- Prayer/meditation in the moment, as an event, blessing, or need occurs
- Soulwork through activities, nature, being with others
- Spontaneous spiritual life, happiness in the midst of the celebration of life
- Service through action to solve immediate problems concerning people, organizations, natural world

Preferred Introverted Sensing Soulwork (ISTJ and ISFJ)

- Prayer/meditation through consistent, private conversation with God
- Soulwork through an appreciation of the continuity of traditions and creeds
- Sequential, structured spiritual life, typically with set times or routines
- Service, often behind the scenes, organizing to meet current needs

Suggestions for Sensing Soulwork

1. Sometimes our most effective praises are for the little things in life. Verbally, or by writing a litany of praise in your own style, give thanks for the simple things as did the poet below:

God who created me
Nimble and light of limb

In three elements free,
  To run, to ride, to swim;
Not when the sense is dim,
  But now from the heart of joy,
I would remember God
  Take the thanks of a boy.

H. C. BEECHING[2]

You might also look to the poetry of Emily Dickinson, e. e. cummings, or the Hebrew Psalms for examples of thanksgiving over the wonders of *this* life.

2. Think of a person you love and admire or activity you enjoy. Contemplate *or* journal:

Person	**Activity**
How does that person enhance my spirituality?	How does this activity make me feel spiritual?
What special gifts does that person share with others?	What gifts come to me through this activity?
What meaningful times have we shared together?	What special memories resulted from this activity?
How has this person enriched my life?	How has this activity enriched my life?
Pause to be thankful for this person.	Pause to be thankful for this activity.

You might also use these questions as you think about a person you struggle to like or an activity that you dislike but in which you must occasionally participate.

3. Go to a favorite spot, either outdoors or indoors, where you feel in touch with your soul. Look and listen for specific signs of God's love, beauty, wisdom, and goodness. How has God been revealed in the events of your life? In your history? You may wish to write down your praises to God.

4. **For the discipline of study:** Notice the wonders of the natural world. Spend most of your time simply appreciating the delightful feel of water, the wonder of migrating birds, the miracle that flowers actually bloom, the sounds of rustling leaves when the city is still enough to hear. Then consider what new spiritual information these observations could have for you. What might they mean for you? How might you apply lessons from nature to your life?

5. **For the discipline of meditation or prayer:** Think of a habit you'd like to change, an attitude you'd like to improve, or someone you'd like to help or who needs prayer. Come up with a *very* short phrase that captures your request or petition. Examples might be:

Teach me patience	Help me appreciate what I have
Guide my actions in service	Bring strength/peace/love to [name]

Then, let the activities of the day bring your prayer to mind—when the phone rings, as you perform your daily tasks, while dropping off to sleep. You might keep the same prayer for a few days or a few months. If you begin to forget to bring the prayer to mind, consider whether it is time to change it.

6. **For the discipline of simplicity:** Examine your life to determine what things bring joy. What things take away joy? Many Sensing types discover that the complexities of modern life separate them from the things that bring them closest to their souls. What simple pleasures are you missing or no longer able to do? How can you bring those pleasures back into your life?

7. **For the discipline of celebration:** Take time to mark the milestones of your life with a special festivity—add candles to the dinner table, call a good friend for a walk, take a special photograph to commemorate an event, give a small dinner party, treat yourself to an afternoon at a place that is sacred to you, etc. Besides birthdays or anniversaries, you could celebrate a job well done, the reaching of a specific goal for soulwork, or the gift of a beautiful day.

8. What could you add to soulwork that would engage your senses? If you write, try brightly colored pens or one that is superbly smooth. Buy a special notebook for journaling. Purchase a distinctive candle. Find a favorite kind of coffee or tea and save it for your reflective moments. Get that bicycle, set of skis, or pair of walking shoes you've always wanted if it will draw you more often to the work of your soul.

9. Consider framing a poem, favorite saying, or passage from your sacred readings. Keep it on your desk or by your bedside as a reminder for your soulwork.

10. Turn your refrigerator, bulletin board, or scrapbook into a place to record your blessings. Add pictures of friends and families, tickets from events, particularly meaningful greeting cards, or copies of expressive poems or sayings. As occasional soulwork, gaze at or page through these reminders and offer thanks.

11. Prepare a special place for your soulwork—perhaps your favorite easy chair, a corner of a room, a beautiful walking route, or a bench by a local pond. Make sure that you can be there frequently. If it is a spot in your home, what might you do to make it more welcoming? Add a flower vase? Stock it with special mementos? Have music nearby? Clarify with others that this space and time is for you and your soulwork. Ask their support in not disturbing you.

12. Record several of the favorite and familiar songs that speak to your soul onto one tape so that you can have uninterrupted music for soulwork.

13. Find a friend (or two or three) who enjoys your favorite activity. Brainstorm together on how you might do it more regularly together. As you golf, walk, fish, work on crafts, cook, stargaze, garden, etc., be aware of your sense of gratitude at what God provides.

14. Sensing soulwork includes tangible acts of help or service to others or projects. At the end of the day, pause to reflect on or write

down all of the tasks you've completed or the help you've been able to give to other people. Pat yourself on the back and be thankful that you *see* what needs to be done.

15. Think of someone whose spirituality you'd like to emulate. How is your spirituality like/not like theirs? What kinds of soulwork do they practice? Which ones appeal to you? How can you add these practices to your own life?

16. Consider forming a *small* group. Decide together your plans for study, activities, or service opportunities to jointly tackle. Set up expectations and determine a schedule so that the group can remain together for a few months.

17. Reinvestigate your spiritual history, roots, or rituals. Look at the creeds, prayers, or other components of the spiritual tradition you embrace. Which ones might you add to your current soulwork? Which ones could be refreshed? Which ones could be replaced to make time for something more meaningful to you?

18. Keep a written record of your concerns for yourself and others— the requests you offer in prayer or the situations about which you pray or meditate. Look back periodically to see which have changed for the better and rejoice. Which ones are still issues? What might be their spiritual lessons for you?

> Embrace your:
>
> > **Common sense**
> > **Experience**
> > **Realism**
> > **Present focus**
> > **Proven talents and skills**

Chapter 4
ESTP

Extraversion, Sensing, Thinking, Perceiving

Finding spirituality
in the outer world
of events
and adventure

General Description: ESTPs tend to be action-oriented, outgoing, pragmatic, and resourceful. They like to be where the excitement is and where they can use their quick thinking at just the right time to solve problems. They are to-the-point, lively, and efficient. Enjoying life each day, they help others participate fully in the here and now.

> ### THE GREATEST GIFT FOR ESTPs:
> ### EXTRAVERTED SENSING WITH THINKING
> *Making the most of the present moment; seizing opportunities for renewal for themselves and others, yet seeing reality and dealing with it objectively, and capably.*
>
> ### THE ESTP ROLE IN COMMUNITY:
> *Meeting practical needs in the most proficient way; adding an energetic spark to any endeavor they find worthwhile; reminding others of the joys in this life.*

Extraverted Sensing is the **dominant function** for ESTPs, the function that develops earliest in life, is most comfortable to use, and is easiest to access. Using the dominant function is the natural avenue for each type to pursue soulwork—this is where the soul resides. In other words, for soulwork to be meaningful, the ESTP's extraverted Sensing must be satisfied.

◆

ESTP Spirituality: Atmospheres for Soulwork

ESTP spirituality is often about appreciating and engaging fully in the life given to us. "Our Creator made an interesting world with endless possibilities for adventure and excitement, so let's enjoy it," might be their statement of faith. They tend to be keenly aware of and delight fully in the sights, sounds, smells, tastes, touches and wonders of nature, whether in the majesty or the details of their environment. For many, this gratitude for the attractions and challenges available daily to each of us is the essence of their soulwork.

ESTPs like to blend the spiritual, intellectual, social, recreational, and vocational aspects of life. Many combine their soulwork with their daily activities, such as exercising, cleaning, lawn chores, or commuting to work. Rather than compartmentalize their soulwork, they turn their thoughts over to the experiences they are having in the moment, celebrating them as they happen. ESTPs can sometimes feel a sense of spiritual inadequacy because they engage more sporadically in some of the spiritual disciplines that other types view as essential. Yet ESTPs may view those practices, especially solitary ones, as the equivalent of "la la land"—a waste of time that could be used for the more active experiences that feed the ESTP's soul.

"Either one's belief system is of practical value or it is pretty useless," ESTPs might say. They tend to look for soulwork that will first help them cope in the here and now and secondarily help them grow as they mature. While ESTPs don't need the emotional reinforcement of a group, they often flourish spiritually in environments where they are free to be themselves and are inspired when intangible concepts such as mercy or generosity are made real through the actions of others. Less formal settings suit them best, especially when people dress casually and at least *appear* to enjoy the process.

In fact, ESTPs may rather relish the role of a rebel in those places they view as too staid—either by ignoring the formal codes, asking the tough questions, or avoiding anything that smacks of emotion, pretense or bureaucracy.

"The group's conversation was so tiresome that I couldn't help but interject my reaction to a rather racy movie I'd seen the night before. The focus of my comment was the predictable and vapid story line that served only as a vehicle for luridness, but the others didn't get beyond the fact that I'd actually dared to see such trash. I rather enjoyed their shock and, not surprisingly, the group never invited me back!"

MAYA, 58, DIETITIAN,
MARRIED TO CLERGYPERSON

Often ESTPs are convinced of the importance of soulwork through an event or the experience of someone close to them. For some ESTPs, these events can pull soulwork to the top of their priority list until they eventually work out their own spirituality.

"One of my friends, an all-state athlete, broke his neck in a freak accident. He eventually recovered full use of his limbs, but he said, 'Lying there, facing the prospect of never walking again, I poured out my fears and doubts to our rabbi. He told me stories of how Job and others had been angry as well. I started to see that life could be okay even if I were a quadriplegic. Working out the real reasons for existing is the only way to get through the tough times.'

"This friend had faced what I fear the most—being unable to pursue my active lifestyle. He urged me to work out my own spirituality well before I might have a desperate need to do so and I took his advice. For me, this great world is evidence enough that there is a Being. I now know that God is there for the tough times; otherwise it's my job to cope with the little stuff."

BERN, 22, TEACHER

"When I lost my job, a friend dragged me to a support group. I was surprised at the number of mainstream business-executive types there who considered their spirituality essential to their work. Their sincerity and integrity impressed me then, but I was blown away by the amount of personal help they gave me as I searched for a new position. They didn't just sit around talking about how I might get help, they provided assistance themselves out of their convictions."

LERON, 34, MANAGER

Spiritual Paths Using Extraverted Sensing

Whether soulwork is new to them or they desire to enrich their spiritual practices, ESTPs generally prefer soulwork that applies directly to life. Some of these activities and methods include:

• Considering the wonders of God's creation while out enjoying them, integrating spirituality and real-life activities that bring renewal. They may especially enjoy finding others with similar avocational interests (biking, fishing, sports teams, etc.) and joining them on these types of outings. Often ESTPs then form strong common bonds that make it possible to discuss spiritual matters.

"I didn't join my spiritual community just to play softball, but when I heard there was a team, I knew I'd find some friends and people who look at life the way I do."

REUBEN, 29, PILOT

• Experiential soulwork—visiting a wide variety of spiritual communities, engaging in rather than reading about other practices. Even when ESTPs have already chosen a particular formal religion or developed their own spiritual pathway, many pick up additional helpful suggestions for soulwork from such experiences.

• Learning opportunities that emphasize the importance of soulwork in the context of everyday concerns. ESTPs might enhance their spirituality through classes on parenting, workplace ethics, or inspirational talks from people for whom soulwork has made a difference.

- Working with other people in outcome-oriented teams, where they can *tangibly* see that they are needed and that their efforts make a difference. ESTPs enjoy single-focus projects where they can solve problems. They often know just what to do to efficiently finish a task, taking action with gusto.
- Linking up with others in informal settings for active, joyous celebration of the good things in life we all have. ESTPs often bring their gifts of spontaneity and fun to those with whom they join in soulwork.

Clouds That Hinder Soulwork

When the gifts of the dominant function of Sensing are violated, or if ESTPs are not affirmed in the soulwork that is most effective for them, their desire to nourish their spiritual side may be dampened. Major factors that can get in the way of ESTP spirituality include:

- Being drawn to the myriad and immediate things life offers in the press of daily living. ESTPs often find that they have little time for spiritual matters. In any context, ESTPs look for hands-on learning experiences that they can apply directly. In many venues for spiritual understanding, these active experiences are tough to find.
- Getting stuck by longing for a tangible occurrence that is a direct proof of faith. When spiritual practices or experiences do not provide dramatic or recognizable evidence of spirituality, ESTPs may feel the effort was useless or that *they* somehow missed the boat. This feeling of "lacking a miracle" may be especially true if others claim to have profound spiritual experiences.
- Becoming discouraged as they search for those who share their spiritual preferences—like-minded souls. ESTPs want to join with people who appreciate the lighter side of the spiritual journey. This can be difficult since many ESTPs opt out of spiritual communities or seldom openly discuss their soulwork.
- Avoiding structure and schedule. ESTPs may have difficulty with soulwork because what is spiritual to them may not be con-

sidered so by others. One of the greatest gifts people can give to an ESTP is the chance to explore and develop their own soul-work.

"My mom always said, 'You don't have to be a Catholic like me, but someday you'll be glad you know God.' Watching her worship and pray with sincerity all through my childhood convinced me that a belief in God was important. Once out of her house, though, I started visiting other denominations and reading about other religions. I found more meaning in campus ministry events than in formal church services. I need to keep adding new flavor to my spirituality or the zest for it in my life fades away."

BRAM, 22, STUDENT

The Second Gift for ESTPs: Introverted Thinking

ESTPs have introverted Thinking as their **auxiliary function.** The gifts of introverted Thinking include using objective criteria to solve problems, clarify principles, and search for truth.

While ESTPs often begin their spiritual journey through the stimulation of the outer world with all its happenings, their auxiliary function of introverted Thinking makes it necessary for them to pull back for introspection, to choose among the options they see, define for themselves what is true and relevant, and bring their intellect to bear on their spiritual experiences.

To critically examine which avenues are best for their soulwork, ESTPs may need to seek solitude for reflection in order to engage their introverted Thinking function. Because ESTPs place a high value on having their spirituality bear fruit in everyday life, this solitary time can help them evaluate whether they need to reorder their priorities and how well they are living by their principles. ESTPs may find it helpful to complete exercises to clarify what matters most to them. Others might list exactly what they want to achieve and then flow-chart the activities that will help them reach their goals. Doing cost/benefit analyses, writing out the pros and cons of a choice, or using logic to examine the possible benefits or consequences of any decision can help ESTPs confront their principles to determine what is true. Some ESTPs seek out structured learning experiences, such as seminars or retreats, for this purpose.

Rather than *total* solitude for reflection, ESTPs might develop some discipline for their soulwork by taking part in regular classes or small groups. Their auxiliary Thinking function allows them to process topics or course work in private, but the stimulus of group interaction often encourages them to continue their focus. Some ESTPs schedule time for meditation, organized study, or writing.

Thus, the auxiliary function provides balance: While extraverted Sensing helps ESTPs appreciate the gifts of life, introverted Thinking points them toward appropriate choices. This brings the context of their soulwork from the world at large to their own private realm to establish a framework for making decisions.

The Third Gift for ESTPs: Feeling

Not as much is documented or agreed upon about how the third, or tertiary, function expresses itself in any of the 16 types.* The **third function** for ESTPs is Feeling. The domain of the Feeling function includes weighing values; discerning what is important for themselves, others, and community; and determining the impact of decisions on people.

For all of the 16 types, the third function tends to evolve later in life, typically after the first two functions are clearly developed. The age at which ESTPs pay attention to their Feeling function may depend on the amount of experience they have using their Feeling function to make decisions and influence others. Without this orientation, given the emphasis in most educational tracks on logical decision-making, ESTPs may find that it takes considerable concentration and energy to use their Feeling function. However, as they seek to enrich their spirituality, ESTPs may consciously use their third function, Feeling, to:

---

*Whether the third function is extraverted or introverted is not well documented in theory or practice. We therefore suggest that people observe how they use it in both the outer (extraverted) and inner (introverted) worlds at different times to see which is most helpful.

- Tailor their soulwork to improve their relationships with people and with their Creator; and
- Further refine their priorities, clarify their values, and then ensure the way they are living their lives is congruent with their values.

ESTPs in the Storms of Life

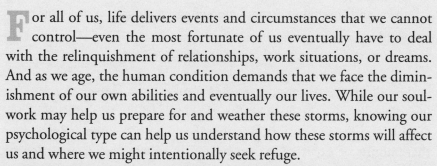

The Least Accessible Gift for ESTPs:
Introverted Intuition

For all of the 16 types, the fourth function is called the **inferior function** because it is the most difficult to use consciously and effectively. The inferior function can be a source of irritation and oversights that can threaten career, competency, relationships, or even meaning and purpose—but at its best it can be a source of rest or richness in the storms of life, in moving toward deeper spirituality, or in exploring issues as we age. For ESTPs, the inferior function is introverted Intuition.

For all of us, life delivers events and circumstances that we cannot control—even the most fortunate of us eventually have to deal with the relinquishment of relationships, work situations, or dreams. And as we age, the human condition demands that we face the diminishment of our own abilities and eventually our lives. While our soulwork may help us prepare for and weather these storms, knowing our psychological type can help us understand how these storms will affect us and where we might intentionally seek refuge.

The dominant extraverted Sensing function of ESTPs provides some natural coping skills. ESTPs are masters at dealing with reality, acting quickly when a crisis arises. They expect life to have a certain amount of ups and downs and tend to see their task as working to solve the immediate problems.

The auxiliary function of introverted Thinking also provides some help. ESTPs are able to remain objective about many situations. By moving away from outer distractions, ESTPs can find the space to resurrect their inner guidelines, logical principles, and systems of procedures and rules before making decisions. Sometimes Thinking also helps ESTPs to put aside the feelings of self-doubt, future catastrophes, or doom that their inferior Intuition function can manifest.

"I calmed down as I laid out some specific parameters for deciding how we might take care of my elderly mother. She disliked being alone. She needed to keep her cat. She had to be closer to my home. Narrowing the field like this gave me renewed energy to analyze the pros and cons of the remaining choices and brought about a useful solution to the dilemma my mother and I faced."

GILLIAN, 34, CRAFTSWOMAN

When the Storms Overwhelm

However, the bigger storms of life often swell beyond our natural capacity to cope. While life's tragedies strain all of us, no matter how intense our soulwork and regardless of our psychological type, the stormy times for ESTPs can be intensified if the circumstances include any of the following factors:

- When they can't control the time frames for making decisions about their future. ESTPs typically detest having their options cut off. They want clear direction and enough information so they don't make wrong choices. If too many future possibilities are presented, they may feel overwhelmed and throw them all out.
- When the present is no longer enjoyable and they fear that things may not get better. The marring of their own health or physical abilities is especially troubling to ESTPs.
- When the crisis or storm prevents them from pursuing the activities that bring them renewal. Lack of time or opportunities for renewal can magnify their stress.
- When the predicament imposes unnecessary structure on their lives. Being realists, ESTPs appreciate that some structure is

useful, but too much gets in the way of producing quick, direct results.

In the most despairing moments, all types can be caught by overuse of their strengths, relying too much on their dominant function. The worst time for ESTPs is when they bring their energy to bear on the immediate needs of the storm, then have reason to doubt whether their actions are working toward the right outcome. They may have overused their dominant Sensing function and underestimated the seriousness of a situation—or assumed that the shortest distance between two points is *always* a straight line. When these dark times come, ESTPs may continue their unexamined flurry of activity to counteract their feelings of dread for the future. In the worst storms, a totally different approach to soulwork may be their only refuge.

"I'd kept my nose to the grindstone at work despite the massive layoffs and general atmosphere of doom and gloom. With ten years invested in a job that had basically been satisfying, I was in no hurry to find anything new. Then one day I realized that I was like the little Dutch boy whose one finger in the dike held back the floodwaters—but no one was going to come to my aid. Only when the evidence became overwhelming did it occur to me that I needed to turn my energy toward finding a new job."

WALI, 44, SALES

"In college, on my own initiative, I read a great deal of pop psychology and theology to make sense of who I was and how I could be a healthier person emotionally and spiritually. In retrospect, I believe that I was depressed then, but didn't realize it. The more I searched, the harder I applied my efforts to finding a spiritual framework that would solve my problems. However, it wasn't until I stumbled into a new job that affirmed my strengths that I began to feel better. I now spend my days in new activities that allow me to be successful and to be myself."

ADRIA, 40,
HUMAN RESOURCES PROFESSIONAL

| Clues that ESTPs are being overwhelmed: | • Uncharacteristic gloom, tiredness, hypersensitivity |
| | • Avoidance of their normal activities or a tendency toward a withdrawn state |

| How to help ESTPs: | • Aid them in reevaluating their catastrophic thinking and true feelings about the situation |

| For self-help: | • Imagine the worst outcomes and come up with contingency plans |
| | • Make time for the activities that bring true renewal, no matter how *urgent* other matters seem to be |

The Gifts of the Inferior Function—Rest and Richness

Even though using one's inferior function can be stressful, an irony of psychological type is that *a path to serenity and rest is to intentionally use the inferior function.* For the ESTP, the inferior function of Intuition is opposite the dominant function of Sensing. Therefore, its *conscious use* requires shutting down what is most natural and easy— the Sensing function—which may have gotten out of control while trying to cope with the storm.

For ESTPs, pursuing practices that engage their inferior function, introverted Intuition, forces them to concentrate, focus, and slow down the whirlwind of activities. Through introverted Intuition, ESTPs can get in touch with their own dreams and the possibilities for the future. Ways to intentionally engage the introverted Intuition function include:

• Developing contingency plans. Consider the impact of a decision six or twelve months from now, or even two to five years into the future. If the worst really does happen, what are the options? Mapping out available help or possible different courses can lessen despair over losses. A controlled exploration of what the current circumstances might mean for the future can be helpful.

- Watching television programs or reading books that involve theories or hypothesizing about what could be. The topics might include scientific developments or even science fiction if an imaginary journey is substituted for the ESTP's normal pragmatic approach.
- Engaging in activities that require thinking through possible outcomes. One ESTP played tabletop world conquest games where he had to consider several different strategies. Others envisioned remodeling projects, daydreamed about finding a financial windfall, or imagined a successful personal, family, or business venture.

In soulwork for each type, richness, depth, and development come through the inferior function. As useful as it is to understand the inferior function in the storms of life, it provides more benefits as we seek to grow.

In the first half of life, we define ourselves, both in work and relationships, through our dominant and auxiliary functions. In the second half of life, the gifts of our inferior function can aid us as we seek to become all that we can be. When we don't take advantage of this natural development of our psychological type, we can become stuck.

Midlife also gives clarity to the brevity of our lives. This compels many of us almost unconsciously to seek richness from unfamiliar experiences as well as to complete the psychological tasks we may have bypassed at an earlier age. As we journey toward wholeness and completion, we can open ourselves to new avenues that are outside of our routines by relinquishing the control our dominant function exerts. Adding spiritual practices that incorporate the attributes of our inferior function can give our soulwork new dimension and zest.

The first two functions, Sensing and Thinking, give ESTPs an enjoyment of the present that fuels their soulwork and a set of principles that helps them apply their beliefs pragmatically. To continue to grow, ESTPs need the spiritual richness of introverted Intuition. Though making space for reflection tends to be difficult in the midst of their activities, ESTPs need to explore their insights, hunches, and dreams through their introverted Intuition.

This involves:

- Developing a consistent, deliberate, and intentional relationship with God;
- Dialoguing internally about the future possibilities that are imaginative and broad in scope;
- Concentrating on what is unseen, inexplicable, and mystical about spirituality; and
- Looking at life's events with a sense of the reality of the impossible that involves purposes bigger than we can comprehend.

ESTPs become reacquainted with the spiritual as they find meaning in things they previously overlooked. While they may continue many of their favorite methods of soulwork, renewal may come from the spiritual pathways that are naturally the domain of INFJs and INTJs:

- *At least once a year, I disengage from the real world and participate in a structured spiritual retreat. I take time to nurture my relationship with what is unseen in this world and contemplate the direction I'm headed. If I don't actually get away, my spiritual life has a low priority. My pragmatic side gives little time to it.*
- *I've always struggled with the concept of any type of afterlife, perhaps because I love this world so much that I can't imagine how anything could be better. Recently, though, I've studied in depth many sacred texts that portray Heaven, Sheol, or whatever else you might want to call it. I read and then consider what my next existence might be like.*
- *I've started paying close attention to my dreams. When I was younger, I assumed they had no connection with real life. Now I find I can interpret them with ease and can rely on the information. I've also learned to write down my hunches. I don't always look for the proof—now there are actually things I "just know."*
- *I no longer need to categorize my spirituality. I can live with an undefined Creator. Somehow I find new comfort in this acceptance of "awesomeness" instead of viewing it as disconcerting mystery. If I quiet my soul, I sometimes feel as if I am looking at what I might describe as "Glory" through a doorway.*

- *I used to spend time taking inventory of my physical, financial, and personal resources. Now I actually take time to think about my non-material assets. My more spiritual focus has given me a much-needed wider perspective.*

I am thankful for

My love of this life
My realistic grasp of situations
My resourcefulness and quick responsiveness
The way I can catch the joys of the moment

In the storms of life, I can find shelter by

Making time to pause and reflect
Envisioning the future with positive expectations
Assessing my true priorities

To honor myself and my pathway to God, I can

Search for ways to integrate soulwork and the activities
I enjoy
Seek the company of others who find spirituality in the
midst of life
Retreat, if only rarely, to give my spiritual side the
attention it needs

Chapter 5
ESFP

Extraversion, Sensing, Feeling, Perceiving

Finding spirituality
in the outer world
of events and
practical activities

General Description: ESFPs tend to be fun-loving, friendly, outgoing, and exuberant. They are relationship-oriented and in touch with people's needs for encouragement, comfort, and inclusion. They are sympathetic and generous with their time and support. ESFPs engage others in living life to its fullest. Practical and realistic, they are often where the action is.

THE GREATEST GIFT FOR ESFPs:
EXTRAVERTED SENSING WITH FEELING
Lighting up any setting with their easygoing nature, enthusiasm, and love of life; accepting people and situations as they are in a straightforward yet sensitive way.

THE ESFP ROLE IN COMMUNITY:
Serving as a resource of time and talents; reminding others how to appreciate God through the five senses; adding warmth and informality to spiritual endeavors through their desire to put others at ease.

Extraverted Sensing is the **dominant function** for ESFPs, the function that develops earliest in life, is most comfortable to use, and is easiest to access. Using the dominant function is the natural avenue for each type to pursue soulwork—this is where the soul resides. In other words, for soulwork to be meaningful, the ESFP's dominant function, extraverted Sensing, must be satisfied.

ESFP Spirituality: Atmospheres for Soulwork

ESFPs might describe their spirituality as an essential appreciation of the gifts we all have and the richness of our experiences. For many ESFPs, spirituality is about connecting—to self, others, nature, and life. This focus on being thankful for our blessings adds a new dimension to their own and others' thoughts and actions. ESFPs like to combine soulwork with their other activities. Some discovered early on that they feel closest to God while physically out in nature, preferably with people whose company they enjoy—often their best spiritual venue.

While ESFPs certainly acknowledge the complex and philosophical aspects of soulwork, they tend to value a simple and direct spirituality. ESFPs focus more on activities and "in-the-moment" encounters. They notice the details that other types miss—a kind word or an attentive presence. Spiritual practices that honor the very small and "seemingly" insignificant things are meaningful to ESFPs. They might find it easy to identify with Ramakrishna, who stated, "There is no need for much reading of the Scriptures. You would be inclined to argue and debate. What you gain by repeating the Name of God with love ten times is the very essence of the Scriptures."[1] While ESFPs are as capable of seriousness as any other type, when choosing books or studies about spirituality, they prefer stories of others' actual experiences rather than doctrines or polemics.

Many ESFPs know that for them soulwork consists of service and action. Others can count on ESFPs to add celebration to any endeavor they undertake. They have a knack for welcoming strangers, planning festivities, being positive, fostering loyalty, and jumping in with both feet where they see a need. They often are aware of just what other people need in a crisis and readily provide tangible help, such as running errands, providing transportation, or offering other personalized assistance.

"Several friends and I joined together to conduct recreational activities for teens. While we have a secular organization, we all are very aware of how God is at work in our lives and the lives of the teens. The spiritual questions these kids asked encouraged me to seek a more spiritual path for myself. So you might say I found myself and my spiritual roots in being of help to young people as they mature."

PERRY, 32, FACTORY SUPERVISOR

The most satisfying moments for ESFPs often come through experiences in the outer world when they see concrete evidence of the spiritual.

"The first time in my life I really felt spiritual was at a youth camp. Most of our days were spent swimming, hiking, and challenging other cabins to 'capture the flag' and 'counselor hunts.' Each evening, though, we gathered around the campfire to sing and listen to a talk about God. Out there under the stars, with the chirps of crickets and the occasional cry of a loon, it seemed as if I could almost reach out and touch our Creator. As an adult, if my soul needs renewal, I try to go to 'camp' again! I organize outings for my close friends—hiking, antiquing—once we even went to a dude ranch. Somewhere along the way we usually recreate the 'campfire' experience as well as connect with each other and nature."

BRYCE, 43, SCHOOL-BOARD OFFICIAL

"My desire for soulwork was fueled when my sister became involved in what we now know was a cult. In my search to understand how she could accept the leader's distortions and rules, I figured out my own beliefs of right and wrong. When she emerged from the cult's influence and we reviewed her experiences there, I saw that my less complex view of issues was just right for me. I learned very quickly that I was not comfortable in

the role of judge—there are too many contradictory facts concerning many issues."

KAYLA, 36, TEACHER

Spiritual Paths Using Extraverted Sensing

Whether soulwork is new to ESFPs or they desire to enrich their spiritual practices, pathways that enlarge and extend their experiences are most rewarding. Some of these activities include:

- Being a part of vibrant, joyful expressions of spirituality. ESFPs prefer atmospheres where the senses can be engaged directly: music that is uplifting and activities that are relevant to their own experience. Otherwise, if things become staid and boring, with too much that seems esoteric to the realities of life, they may leave to find a better fit for themselves.
- Retreating from normal routine for playful activities such as camping, skiing, or sight-seeing. These are made even more "spirit-filled" when done with close friends with whom meaningful discussion is possible.
  "My elderly mother, sister, and I spend the High Holy Days together. We visit arboretums, botanical gardens, or the small town were my grandparents grew up. These excursions allow us to share our family stories while experiencing our connections with our roots, the soil, and to earth and life itself."

JASON, 46, RESTAURANT MANAGER

- Visiting the sick and elderly, aiding people in emergencies, and appreciating how God can be reflected in these charitable acts.
- Hearing about others' experiences as well as finding personal examples of how God works through reading novels or biographies, and watching television or movies.
- Spending time with close friends to share spiritual journeys to see and understand how God is at work.
  "Spirituality for me comes alive through relationships. I don't want to study, participate, or worship in large groups anonymously. I want to

be with people who know about me and understand the joys and needs that I and those close to me have."

JAY, 52, CONSULTANT

Clouds That Hinder Soulwork

When the gifts of the dominant function of extraverted Sensing are violated, or if ESFPs are not affirmed in their strengths, they may struggle to regain their realistic view and specific sense of awe about life being a divine gift. Major factors that can get in the way of ESFP spirituality include:

- When their spiritual communities or influential people around them require that spirituality be formal or "by the book."
  "I seldom take the time to just be still. Praying aloud rather than silently helps my thoughts take on clarity, but I probably don't do it enough. I feel guilty about my efforts because I think I should be doing more. Lately, though, I've come to realize that I feel most spiritual during my exercise time—I know I'm doing something good for myself while at the same time I can also talk to God in prayer."

SUZANNE, 59, PUBLIC-HEALTH NURSE

- Focusing more on outer than inner reality because of their attention to immediate circumstances. The needs of friends, the weather, or choices of activity may have more pull than any organized spiritual pursuits. Because ESFPs concentrate on action in the here and now, they may miss the underlying need for soulwork to ready themselves for the future.
- Becoming busy, too involved and overloaded in helping others. ESFPs can overlook their own spiritual needs to the point that their helping becomes an excuse or justification for putting off their soulwork.
- Engaging in any activity, hobby, or spiritual path too intensely can eventually rob it of the spontaneity that brings joy.
  "I was a ranked tennis player as a young adult, then quit cold turkey when I realized that the concentrated, disciplined, and scheduled

effort needed to move to the next level would eliminate any other pursuits from my life. I think this happens in my spiritual walk as well. When it gets too routine and heavy it becomes only another obstacle for me to overcome. I like to keep soulwork more fluid and easygoing."

STEPHEN 31, MARKETING MANAGER

The Second Gift for ESFPs: Introverted Feeling

ESFPs have introverted Feeling as their **auxiliary function.** The gifts of introverted Feeling help them to sort through their activities to choose the most important ones, those that clearly match their deeply held and internalized values.

While ESFP soulwork begins in activities and comes directly from their experiences, many ESFPs benefit from a turning away from external demands in order to allow time for inner processing, the domain of their auxiliary function, introverted Feeling. These "down-times" for reflection are often experienced as a natural pattern. One ESFP noticed that even as a child she enjoyed being at home by herself. Although she loved people, she begged her parents to occasionally leave her behind when they went to visit friends and family for this reason.

Seeking solitude and quiet time, often on long walks, helps ESFPs identify what is truly meaningful to them and understand how they feel about various people or events in their lives. Other ESFPs find that they prefer the company of one close, trusted person with whom to talk through their heartfelt concerns.

"My friend joined me for walks frequently during the month following my mother's protracted illness and eventual death. I realized that I felt guilty about my sense of relief at not having to nurse her anymore. My friend helped me see that after my day in/day out care of her, my relief from the heavy physical and emotional burden was practical, not selfish."

JANE, 29, RECREATION LEADER

Thus, the auxiliary function provides balance: While extraverted Sensing allows for appreciation of life as it unfolds, introverted Feeling allows ESFPs to order their lives so they can live more congruently with their values, bringing a focus and direction to bear on their soul-work.

The Third Gift for ESFPs: Thinking

Not as much is documented or agreed upon about how the third, or tertiary, function expresses itself in any of the sixteen types.* The **third function** for ESFPs is Thinking. The domain of the Thinking function includes logical argument, cause-effect reasoning, objectivity, and a search for clarity.

For all of the 16 types, the third function tends to evolve later in life, generally after the first two functions are clearly developed. However, many ESFPs are assisted early on if they choose one of the many educational tracks that emphasize logical reasoning and decision-making, the domain of Thinking, their third function. Thus, many ESFPs benefit from being able to reach logical conclusions about matters that are important to them when they *consciously* try to do so. As they seek to enrich their spirituality, many ESFPs use their third function, Thinking, to:

- Evaluate the spiritual traditions or faith systems to which they were exposed by taking an objective look at their own beliefs and seeking consistencies, logical proofs, or evidence of truths; and
- Participate in rigorous and objective studies to establish what is just and fair, right or wrong, and true or false as they work to establish their own spiritual criteria and standards.

Whether the third function is extraverted or introverted is not well documented in theory or practice. We therefore suggest that people observe how they use it in both the outer (extraverted) and inner (introverted) worlds at different times to see which is most helpful.

The Least Accessible Gift for ESFPs:
Introverted Intuition

For all of the 16 types, the fourth function is called the *inferior function* because it is the most difficult to use consciously and effectively. The inferior function can be a source of irritation and oversights that can threaten careers, relationships, competency, or even meaning and purpose—but at its best it can be a source of rest or richness in the storms of life, in moving toward deeper spirituality, or in exploring issues as we age. For ESFPs, the inferior function is introverted Intuition.

For all of us, life delivers events and circumstances that we cannot control—even the most fortunate of us eventually have to deal with the relinquishment of relationships, work situations, or dreams. And as we age, the human condition demands that we face the diminishment of our own abilities and eventually our lives. While our soul-work may help us prepare for and weather these storms, knowing our psychological type can help us understand how these storms will affect us and where we might intentionally seek refuge.

The dominant extraverted Sensing function of ESFPs provides some natural coping skills. ESFPs tend to look on the sunny side of life, so it takes them longer to give in to doom and gloom. Often, ESFPs see the immediate tasks in front of them, and their experiences provide a framework of common sense for them to do what is needed.

The auxiliary function of introverted Feeling also provides some help. ESFPs often find that quiet time alone in nature or sharing one-on-one gives them a chance to reflect in the midst of their very busy lives.

Quiet, natural settings can also allow the ESFP to tap into the processes of introverted Feeling.

"When life is rosy, I seldom just sit by the lake—I swim, boat, ski, fish, or sail. However, when the future seems dark and heavy, I take a blanket down by the shore and gaze at the waves lapping the beach, the families of

ducks paddling by, the clouds reflected on the water. I observe the cycles of the seasons and gain hope that the seasons of my life will pass on to warmth and spring again."

F I O N A , 3 0 , S E C R E T A R Y

When the Storms Overwhelm

However, the storms of life often swell beyond our natural capacity to cope. While life's tragedies strain all of us, no matter how intense our soulwork and regardless of our psychological type, the stormy times for ESFPs can be intensified if the circumstances include any of the following factors:

- When their circumstances force too much speculation, creative problem-solving, or long-range planning. Because introverted Intuition is their inferior function, ESFPs frequently envision negative outcomes for the future. This only adds to their burdens.
"I was asked to prepare a new training program at work and found myself in a dither because there were so few guidelines and so much riding on a successful outcome. I couldn't imagine how many hours it would take to cover the content, much less how much time to give to each topic because all of it was new to me. Once I decided on the format and taught the class several times, I felt more comfortable because of my experience—I knew what to expect and the class took shape with real people in real time—I was no longer speculating and the class was a success."

A U B R E Y , 2 9 , C O R P O R A T E T R A I N E R

- When the situation causes them to acknowledge the march of time and the finality of separation. ESFPs become vulnerable to stress when the present moment loses its delight or relationships are permanently severed.
"When one of my students dropped out of school, I became discouraged. I had given so much individual attention to this child, apparently to no avail. Then a colleague pointed out that the story wasn't over—perhaps I had truly planted seeds that had not yet borne fruit.

Now I am trying to place my faith in unseen results, not only what I can verify."

KEVIN, 28, HIGH-SCHOOL TEACHER

- When the present is no longer enjoyable and they are uncertain of whether the future will be better. ESFPs can be particularly depressed by the marring of their own physical health or capabilities.
- When they are forced to add too much structure to their lives.

"First and foremost, I wanted to help my sister. Driving her to physical therapy seemed a natural avenue. However, I grew crabbier and crabbier each day as my alarm sounded and I struggled out of bed to make the trip. After some thought, I finally realized that it wasn't the early hour as much as the loss of options for my morning. Now instead of reading the paper, going for a walk, or any of the other things I used to do before work, I had to face a demanding, daily routine. *This realization helped me cope—I didn't resent helping my sister; I just needed to find a new place in my day for some unstructured time."*

MATT, 52, RETAIL MANAGER

In the most despairing moments, all types can be caught by overuse of their strengths, relying too much on their dominant function. The worst time for ESFPs is when the immediate needs of a crisis give them little chance to assess their own feelings and needs. They may become so overwhelmed with helping others that they neglect themselves. They have overused their dominant Sensing by trying to address all the things their practical nature says should be done. When these dark times come, ESFPs may continue their flurry of activities rather than face the forebodings they feel. In the worst storms, a totally different approach to soulwork may be the only refuge.

"When my husband's best friend was diagnosed with terminal cancer, we did everything we could for his family. We looked after the children so that he and his wife could have some time alone. I organized meal delivery and made all the arrangements for special equipment so that he could be nursed at home. I helped plan a prayer service and checked that it met his spiritual

preferences. I made sure that my husband encouraged our other mutual friends to support him. When our friend finally died, I realized that I'd taken no opportunity to come to grips with what this dear friend's life meant to me. I couldn't even attend the funeral. I needed to withdraw from all of my activities for several days as I grieved."

NANCY, 48, HOMEMAKER

"People used to tell me how brave I was in caring for our special-needs child, but actually that was the easy part for me. I had the medical knowledge, the skills, and of course the love for my son. Frankly, I didn't take the time to consider whether I should feel burdened or if life was fair. I seldom allowed myself to dwell on his future until after his recent death. Then I realized how taxing his future would have been for me and our entire family—never-ending responsibilities and a lifetime of being his advocate. Now it seems so very overwhelming, but it wasn't that way when he was alive."

DARLENE, 40, DAY-CARE PROVIDER

Clues that ESFPs are being overwhelmed:	• A negative perspective on thoughts about the future • Priorities that seem out of balance, particularly when making major decisions
How to help ESFPs:	• Listen in a supportive, accepting, and nonjudgmental way as they talk over their problems
For self-help:	• Reduce external activities to allow time to process feelings • Consciously work to project the future from the facts at hand, focusing on being realistic instead of pessimistic, as a way to return to normal optimism

The Gifts of the Inferior Function—Rest and Richness

Even though using one's inferior function is stressful, an irony of psychological type is that *a path to serenity and rest is to intentionally use the inferior function.* For the ESFP, the inferior function of Intuition is opposite the dominant function of Sensing. Therefore, its *conscious use* requires shutting down what is most natural and easy— the Sensing function, which may have gotten out of control while trying to cope with the storm.

For ESFPs, engaging their inferior function, introverted Intuition, forces them to slow down the whirlwind of activities in order to be open to new perspectives. Through introverted Intuition, ESFPs can get in touch with their own dreams for the future. Ways to intentionally engage the introverted Intuition function include:

- Becoming deeply involved with a creative interest that might open up the imagination to new avenues for soulwork. Consider themes of wholeness or spirituality while painting, writing, listening to or performing music.
- Designing or planning a complex future event like retirement or financing children's education.
- Spending time in solitude, reading for enjoyment, or reflecting and journaling on the events and concerns of life. Look beyond the facts for different interpretations and implications for the future.

In soulwork for each type, richness, depth, and development come through the inferior function. As useful as it is to understand the inferior function in the storms of life, it provides more benefits as we seek to grow.

In the first half of life we define ourselves, both in work and relationships, through our dominant and auxiliary functions. In the second half of life, the gifts of our inferior function can aid us as we seek to become all that we can be. When we don't take advantage of this natural development of our psychological type, we can become stuck.

Midlife also gives clarity to the brevity of our lives. This compels

many of us almost unconsciously to seek richness from unfamiliar experiences as well as to complete the psychological tasks we may have bypassed at an earlier age. As we journey toward wholeness and completion, we can open ourselves to new avenues that are outside of our routines by relinquishing the control our dominant function exerts. Adding spiritual practices that incorporate the attributes of our inferior function can give our soulwork new dimension and zest.

The first two functions, Sensing and Feeling, give ESFPs an appreciation of life and an understanding of what is important to themselves and others. However, to continue to grow, ESFPs need the spiritual richness that introverted Intuition provides. They need to pay attention to their insights and things not yet seen or experienced.

INTROVERTED INTUITIVE SOULWORK

This involves:

- Developing a consistent, deliberate, and intentional relationship with God;
- Discussing internally future possibilities that are imaginative and broad in scope;
- Concentrating on what is unseen, inexplicable, and mystical about spirituality; and
- Looking at life's events with a sense of the reality of the impossible that involves purposes bigger than we can comprehend.

ESFPs become reacquainted with the spiritual as they find meaning in things they previously overlooked. While they may continue many of their favorite methods of soulwork, renewal may come from the spiritual pathways that are naturally the domain of INTJs and INFJs:

- *Recently I participated in a silent retreat. It was so unexpectedly beneficial that I plan to do it again. Day to day, I seldom have time to myself. I was amazed at the insights into my values and dreams that this quiet time gave me.*
- *A friend who is quite intuitive taught me how to tap into what you*

might call my sixth sense. He uses a framework that highlights the differences between our view and God's view of the world. I better understand that there are:

A spiritual reality and a physical reality;
An eternal perspective and a present perspective;
The impact of our deeds as well as the deeds themselves;
Spiritual laws as well as physical laws;
God-centered thinking and human-centered thinking; and
A preoccupation with the unseen as well as a preoccupation with
     what is seen.

We use this framework together to brainstorm the different perspectives a situation might present. It helps me look beyond what the facts and my own experience give me to understand the events of my life.

- As I watched a friend go through the agony of dealing with a parent with Alzheimer's, I was acutely aware that my friend's patience, caring, and love could not be adequately explained by the tangible aspects of this world. It wasn't her training or schooling or past experiences that supported her throughout the difficulties, but her spirituality and reliance on God that gave her endurance. This was the best reason I've ever had for pursuing soulwork.

- I used to be concerned with God only to help me deal with the here and now. Those songs and teachings about eternal life held little appeal for me. Now, though, with the death of a close friend and my own recent illness, I find myself wondering about a future life and dreaming about what it may bring.

- I've learned to effectively use my imagination to more fully understand what the present means to me. For example, when I was laid off recently, at first I focused only on my financial situation and my family's needs. Later, though, I listed out all of the things that had been wrong with my job: a cold and dominating boss, a lack of teamwork, etc. When I considered realistically what my future might have been there, I decided that the future held much more potential somewhere else.

I am thankful for

> My enjoyment of each new day and the fresh wonders
> it brings
> The varied ways I offer practical help to others
> The enthusiasm I add to each endeavor and to those
> around me
> My openness to exploring, experimenting, and
> experiencing spirituality in different ways

In the storms of life, I can find shelter by

> Seeking support from those who know me well
> Reserving some time so that I'll have renewed energy for
> myself as well as for others
> Focusing on the unseen, those inexplicable aspects of
> our lives

To honor myself and my pathway to God, I can

> See God in the here and now by experiencing the Creator
> in all of creation
> Connect with others to join in celebrating our spiritual
> journeys
> Become comfortable with listening to my dreams and
> hopes for the future

Chapter 6
ISTJ

Introversion, Sensing, Thinking, Judging

*Finding spirituality
in the inner world of
experiences and
organizing principles*

General Description: ISTJs tend to be systematic, painstaking, thorough, and hardworking. They honor their commitments, keep track of specifics, follow standard operating procedures (when they make sense), and get their work done on time. Careful with details, clear about facts, they are dependable, straightforward, and stable.

THE GREATEST GIFT FOR ISTJs:
INTROVERTED SENSING WITH THINKING
*Seeing what is, using their internal awareness of what has worked
in the past, conscientiously and dutifully bringing order and
logic to all they do.*

THE ISTJ ROLE IN COMMUNITY:
*Upholding and conserving the splendor of tradition; building clear
structures; modeling responsibility and follow-through; using past
experience to provide stability to the present.*

Introverted Sensing is the **dominant function** for ISTJs, the function that develops earliest in life, is most comfortable to use, and is easiest to access. Using the dominant function is the natural avenue for each type to pursue soulwork—this is where the soul resides. In other words, for soulwork to be meaningful, the ISTJ's dominant function, introverted Sensing, must be satisfied.

◆

ISTJ Spirituality: Atmospheres for Soulwork

ISTJs, who arrive at their spiritual precepts through experience, logic, and purposes behind their beliefs, tend to hold deep spiritual convictions. They often look to the results of spirituality in the lives of others and the events in the history of their traditions, using the practices and disciplines as guidance for their own lives. Their soulwork is evident in their dedication to any endeavor they undertake.

For ISTJs, what they see and experience helps them evaluate and understand their private spirituality. Spiritual understandings often come from real situations involving real people. Lessons from the lives of people they admire and direct experiences with the observable wonders of life—such as the birth of a child—are often what draw ISTJs to a spiritual journey. One ISTJ stated, "Spirituality is a process of growing both in understanding and in dependence. Little by little, I've found enough concrete proof that I can trust God with the details of my life."

Many ISTJs appreciate the richness of traditions surrounding creeds, religious rituals, and holy days. However, they often prefer to define or find a rational basis for spiritual practices before giving them a try. Their acceptance of the many aspects of the faith in which they were raised comes from an acknowledgment of the considerable merit of ceremonies or spiritual principles that have stood the test of time. In any spiritual pursuit, many ISTJs want to clearly grasp the purpose and benefits.

"Even the words 'Systematic Theology' appeal to me. I know the subject will be presented objectively, the concepts will build on each other logically,

and the topic of theology holds my interest. For me, doctrinal statements are worthy of study and the creeds that connect me with generations of long ago are essential. Either these basic elements are solid and can hold water, or I'll pursue my spiritual life elsewhere."

TED, 48, EMPLOYEE-TRAINING MANAGER

ISTJs often look to their soulwork for a framework for decisions in their day-to-day lives. ISTJs want to determine how the teachings of their spiritual tradition apply to specific situations, how to behave responsibly toward others, and how to be good stewards of what is entrusted to them. Once they clarify their own spiritual outlook and select their regular practices, they then tend to "go by the book" to discern what is right and what is wrong.

"I've always been grateful to my parents for the early religious exposure they gave me. For me, the services and ceremonies were never rote, but simply seemed the right thing to do. I knew that my mother, grandfather, great-grandfather, and maybe even generations further back had done the same things, held to the same beliefs, and had given God a major place in their lives.

"To me, providing spiritual training is just part of parenting. People who don't expose their children to any faith are robbing them. Whether they accept everything or not, a faith tradition gives them a history lesson, good standards for moral instruction, and a framework for values. Additionally, I make sure my kids know exactly why we chose our spiritual community."

EDEN, 39, HOMEMAKER

"For a long time, my soulwork was fairly straightforward. I like to know where I stand, what to do, and what is expected of me—and that was the basis of my spirituality. Then I had an experience which was truly a departure from my spiritual norms that enriched my soulwork tremendously.

"Somehow I was convinced to go with our teenage son on a service project to build homes for single-parent families. My heart, usually so under wraps, was touched as I watched our team work cooperatively. The last

evening, everyone brought a token of themselves to seal in one of the walls of the new house. As I watched my son tuck in his prayer for the new residents, I clearly recognized that God is a source of love, not just a source of order."

DUANE, 42, SUPERVISOR

Spiritual Paths Using Introverted Sensing

Whether soulwork is new to ISTJs or they desire to enrich their spiritual practices, pathways that build on experience and provide tangible results are most rewarding. Some of these methods include:

- Engaging in structured approaches to worship, prayer, or study. ISTJs often join study groups, take classes, or use books that provide precise programs to follow.
- Serving as a resource to others seeking just and fair ways to handle matters of faith. ISTJs often are able to recall facts and details that assist them in making decisions. Coupled with their ability to remain impartial and their tendency to build their own principled foundation, they can often discern inequities and provide useful solutions.
- Completing hands-on projects or crafts that meet practical needs and allow for self-expression. With their ability to attend to detail, ISTJs can express their spirituality through meticulous activities such as quilting, woodworking, or handling all the specifics of a project.
  "In my job as director of community services for the elderly, I ensure that the meals delivered each day meet the individual health requirements of each recipient. I feel that on a daily basis I provide the hand of God tangibly to those in need—a common theme in all faith traditions."

  HEATHER, 57, SOCIAL-SERVICES DIRECTOR

- Reading or seeing tangible examples of God in action. ISTJs may learn more about compassion from watching someone meet with people experiencing loss than through classroom work on counseling.

- Taking time alone for reflection about the realities of life.

"My friends often ask me to pray for them. They comment that I remember the concerns each person raises and add an appreciation for the constant role our Creator plays. Really, it's the sort of detail-oriented solo work I enjoy the most. Others might provide advice or a casserole, but I usually pray with or for someone in crisis."

AMANDA, 31, MEDICAL TECHNICIAN

Clouds That Hinder Soulwork

When the gifts of the dominant function of introverted Sensing are violated, or if ISTJs are not affirmed in their strengths, their desire to find and apply the types of soulwork that meet their needs may be weakened. Major factors that can get in the way of ISTJ spirituality include:

- Finding that behavior does not always match "spiritual" people's speech. Even though it's only common sense to expect that some people are not all they say they are, ISTJs still can be turned off by the hypocrisy of people or institutions.

"While I have fond childhood memories of choir, youth groups, roast beef dinners, and camps, I have not been successful in providing that same experience for my children. I think this is primarily because as an adult I see 'faithful' people gossiping about each other and generally acting on their spiritual values only when they're in a spiritual setting."

ANDREA, 48, COMPUTER PROGRAMMER

- Having too many responsibilities to add the "burden" of spirituality. Many ISTJs are already involved in "giving," serving others through roles at work, in the community, or for their family. Even if ISTJs pursue a spiritual path that doesn't require involvement in an organized community, they can feel guilty that they don't make room for one in their busy lives.

"My relationship with God continues to evolve—I guess I'm sort of a difficult case! I consciously have to set aside all of my duties and give myself the luxury of being still long enough to hear my soul."

SAMUEL, 45, ACCOUNTANT

- Being in environments that place little emphasis on soulwork. Especially affected are ISTJs whose families of origin ridiculed or abandoned spiritual practices. Without any direct experiences to influence their opinion of soulwork, ISTJs may not be open to new ideas related to the spiritual realm.
- Setting standards for their spirituality that are too high. ISTJs can be all too aware of their own needs for improvement. Coupled with their focus on doing good deeds and solving practical problems, ISTJs may find their efforts at soulwork come up short of their expectations.

"As willing as I am to help, I need to know from others that my efforts are useful. Otherwise, I sense I'm not doing what I thought I could and then find myself demoralized."

BEVERLY, 42, SMALL BUSINESS OWNER

The Second Gift for ISTJs: Extraverted Thinking

ISTJs have extraverted Thinking as their **auxiliary function.** The gifts of extraverted Thinking include using logic and objectivity to assess situations, determine goals, and set courses of action.

While ISTJs tend to begin their spiritual journey with an inner focus on actual life experiences, their auxiliary function of extraverted Thinking often fosters a need for some sort of community setting, whether a small group or a large organization. ISTJs understand that their own experiences need to be analyzed through their logical principles for them to be most effective. In addition, the experiences of others can broaden their point of reference as they work to establish those standards. Meeting with people to discuss and debate what is truthful about issues of faith provides a sound basis to guide their actions.

"As an introverted male, sharing my problems with anyone, let alone another man, is extremely difficult. Recently though, I joined a men's fellowship group. Through our questioning and critiquing of each other's core principles, I've been able to build a framework for my spirituality. In addi-

tion, we've developed a level of trust with each other that allows us to talk about the difficulties in our personal lives."

ANDERS, 37, ADMINISTRATOR

Other ISTJs use extraverted Thinking to evaluate the merit of different interpretations, beliefs, or spiritual practices and to work out their own personal standards.

"I used to struggle with questions like, 'If God is sovereign and already knows what I want, why should I bother praying?' Through studying with others, I now understand that prayer affects how I might handle a situation or approach a change. Through it I can be a part of the answer—prayer has become a more rational process for me."

Thus, the auxiliary function provides balance: While introverted Sensing concentrates on what can be verified and focuses on concrete reality, extraverted Thinking assists ISTJs in determining what best might be done in a given situation. This brings their soulwork from their private realm into useful activities with others and the world at large.

The Third Gift for ISTJs: Feeling

Not as much is documented or agreed upon about how the third, or tertiary, function expresses itself in any of the 16 types.* The **third function** for ISTJs is Feeling. The domain of the Feeling function includes weighing values; discerning what is important for self, others, and community; and determining the impact of decisions on people.

◈

Whether the third function is extraverted or introverted is not well documented in theory or practice. We therefore suggest that people observe how they use it in both the outer (extraverted) and inner (introverted) worlds at different times to see which is most helpful.

For all of the 16 types, the third function tends to evolve later in life, typically after the first two functions are clearly developed. The age at which ISTJs pay attention to their third function may depend on the amount of experience they have using their Feeling function to make decisions and influence others. Without this orientation, given the emphasis in most educational tracks on logical decision-making, ISTJs may find that it takes considerable concentration and energy to use their Feeling function. However, as they seek to enrich their spirituality, ISTJs may consciously use their third function, Feeling, to:

- Tailor their soulwork to improve their relationships with people and with their Creator; and
- Further refine their priorities, clarify their values, and then ensure that the way they are living their lives is congruent with their values.

ISTJs in the Storms of Life

The Least Accessible Gift for ISTJs:
Extraverted Intuition

For all of the sixteen types, the fourth function is called the **inferior function** because it is the most difficult to use consciously and effectively. The inferior function can be a source of irritation and oversights that can threaten careers, competency, relationships, or even meaning and purpose—but at its best it can be a source of rest or richness in the storms of life, in moving toward deeper spirituality, or in exploring issues as we age. For ISTJs, the inferior function is extraverted Intuition.

For all of us, life delivers events and circumstances that we cannot control—even the most fortunate of us eventually have to deal with the relinquishment of relationships, work situations, or dreams. And as we age, the human condition demands that we face the diminishment of our own abilities and eventually our lives. While our soul-

work may help us prepare for and weather these storms, knowing our psychological type can help us understand how these storms will affect us and where we might intentionally seek refuge.

The dominant introverted Sensing function of ISTJs provides some natural coping skills. For ISTJs, the first reaction to the storms of life might be to recall what has worked well in the past, using that to bring the situation under control. They may then busy themselves with the tasks directly in front of them, list what needs to be done, obtain the required resources, and get down to the job at hand.

The auxiliary function of extraverted Thinking also provides some help. ISTJs can remain objective and dispassionate as they seek solutions. Often, ISTJs analyze the situation with others—who did what, where the problem arose, how people failed to do their parts, and why a different approach might be better. This analysis is especially helpful when they have had considerable experience with a given project or situation.

Other ISTJs find that extraverted Thinking helps them regain control.

"I learned how to flow-chart in my early computer classes. Now I use the technique to be sure I'm sticking to a plan that can actually work, not letting any of the steps get ahead of others. I develop as complete a plan as possible for a small area of my life and work to bring that under control. Once that's accomplished, I feel more ready to tackle the bigger hurdles, one by one."

GRETCHEN, 61, BANK TELLER

When the Storms Overwhelm

However, the storms of life often swell beyond our natural capacity to cope. While life's tragedies strain all of us, no matter how intense our soulwork and regardless of our psychological type, the stormy times for ISTJs can be intensified if the circumstances include any of the following factors:

- When the situation forces them to depart too far from their normal routine or familiar tasks—what the ISTJ knows will work.

- When people offer nonspecific advice or help. ISTJs keep their commitments. When they offer to help, they'll follow through, so they are disappointed when others do not.

"As we awaited the arrival of our new baby whom we knew had major health problems, I grew frustrated with all of the platitudes even our closest friends offered. Don't say, 'I'd love to lend a hand'—say you'll mow the lawn, drive my kids to soccer practice, or stay at home with our other children. And don't say everything will soon be normal again, because it may not be. We will have to redefine what is normal after this blows over."

BARRETT, 29, ATTORNEY

- When they are asked to create something entirely new in response to changing circumstances.
- When they look toward the future and all options and possibilities seem to be bleak.

"Dental school had been my goal for nearly six years; yet there I was, just five months into the program, when I realized that I had no aptitude for the sculpture work that makes up the majority of a dentist's day. The thought of completing the program, knowing I'd struggle with the skills, was paralyzing. I felt that I had no choice but to drop out of school and try some different work before investing any further in education. Fortunately, a friend helped me rethink the facts—I was very close to a degree in chemistry and with little effort I could at least graduate and get a job."

TARA, 36, CHEMICAL ENGINEER

In the most despairing moments, all types can be caught by overuse of their strengths, relying too much on their dominant function. The worst time for ISTJs is when they continue on the same track, trying to be reliable and efficient, as if sheer effort will prevail. When the outcome is not assured, they may start to question themselves and even whether their sense of duty was misplaced. When these dark times come, ISTJs can further isolate themselves by working harder, but probably *not* smarter, until fatigue or illness sets in. In the worst storms, a totally different approach to soulwork may be the only refuge.

"We experienced a significant family crisis several years ago. The distress was so severe that I lost twenty-five pounds, became an insomniac, and grew despondent. During that time I did not miss one day of work. Only a small handful of close, personal friends knew of my difficulties. All of my pain was dealt with privately. On the surface, things often appeared status quo to others. I finally took some time off and sought professional counseling, even though it was very hard for me to do both."

ROSALIE, 51, BOOKKEEPER

"I read all of the books about parenting, quit my job to be home with my children, put in the quality time, fed them nutritious meals, read endless stories—I followed all the rules, yet my youngest child threw tantrums at the slightest provocation. I was afraid to try preschool—what if they thought I was a terrible mother? The more I watched my children, the more I was sure I hadn't done enough or they wouldn't have these problems.

"I realize now that I didn't spend enough time with other mothers. *The wider my circle of friends and the more open I became, the more I realized that all families have their problems—good parents or not."*

HANNAH, 46, INTERIOR DECORATOR

Clues that ISTJs are being overwhelmed:	• Trouble handling details and specifics, usually their strength • Overly impulsive actions or worrying obsessively about the future
How to help ISTJs:	• Help them relax, perhaps by assisting them with their many duties
For self-help:	• Reconsider the overall, big picture of the crisis in the scheme of life • Seek help from others, *take time off,* and reevaluate priorities

The Gifts of the Inferior Function—Rest and Richness

Even though using one's inferior function is stressful, an irony of psychological type is that *a path to serenity and rest is to intentionally use the inferior function.* For the ISTJ, the inferior function of Intuition is opposite the dominant function of Sensing. Therefore, its *conscious use* requires shutting down what is most natural and easy—the Sensing function, which may have gotten out of control while trying to cope with the storm.

For ISTJs, pursuing activities that use their inferior function, extraverted Intuition, forces them to set aside the verifiable facts and known outcomes and turn to enjoyable outer activities and actions to lend new perspectives. Ways to intentionally engage their extraverted Intuition function include:

- Imagining the worst possible outcome, then planning the best approach. Often in this process a better awareness of what is involved surfaces. Then ISTJs can use a step-by-step approach to work toward resolution.
- Concentrating on the big picture—determine what will *really* matter a year or five years from now. What is the overall goal, not the specific details? What could possibly change and what effects will that have?
- Joining with others to create something from scratch that's engaging and entertaining. For example, ISTJs might join a theater group, take a cruise, or go to another locale to gain a fresh perspective.

In soulwork for each type, richness, depth, and development come through the inferior function. As useful as it is to understand the inferior function for the storms of life, it provides more benefits as we seek to grow.

In the first half of life we define ourselves, both in work and relationships, through our dominant and auxiliary functions. In the second half of life, the gifts of our inferior function can aid us as we seek to become all that we can be. When we don't take advantage of this natural development of our psychological type, we can become stuck.

Midlife also gives clarity to the brevity of our lives. This compels

many of us almost unconsciously to seek richness from unfamiliar experiences as well as to complete the psychological tasks we may have bypassed at an earlier age. As we journey toward wholeness and completion, we can open ourselves to new avenues that are outside of our routines by relinquishing the control our dominant function exerts. Adding spiritual practices that incorporate the attributes of our inferior function can give our soulwork new dimension and zest.

The first two functions, Sensing and Thinking, give ISTJs an awareness of their own and others' past experiences and a set of principles to guide their lives. However, to continue to grow, ISTJs need the spiritual richness of extraverted Intuition. They need to pay attention to their insights, be open to new possibilities in the world of action, and at times adopt a positive future outlook.

EXTRAVERTED INTUITIVE SOULWORK

This involves:

- Experiencing the sacred in future possibilities and exploring idealism in self, others, and new opportunities;
- Being attracted to new avenues and untried practices for spiritual expression;
- Exploring with others the mysteries of spirituality, accepting things that have neither concrete proof nor practical applications; and
- Using imagination to discern new insights, to muse about the big meanings behind simple stories and commonplace events.

ISTJs become reacquainted with the spiritual as they find meaning in things they previously overlooked. While they may continue many of their favorite methods of soulwork, renewal may come from the spiritual pathways that are naturally the domain of ENFPs and ENTPs:

- *Whereas "big picture" lessons used to drive me up a wall, I now find that I seek out teachers who let go of the details in favor of conveying information about the trends and ramifications.*
- *All my life I've viewed everything as a project to organize. More recently, I've tried to relinquish my "project-manager" control of my spiritual life. I've let friends choose my spiritual books and activities.*

I'm exploring new music as a way to open my mind to other ways of thinking of God. I even tried a retreat center that had an entirely different approach to spirituality.

- *Traveling, especially immersing myself in different cultures or visiting the geographical wonders of our country, big or small, helps widen my spiritual perspectives.*
- *As I look toward retirement, I feel a need to drastically change my habits. I plan to move from the city to a small, rural community to experience life anew. My activities, spiritual practices, and friendships will all have a fresh start, too.*
- *A few years ago I realized that my spiritual routine had gone dry. I found that I needed an element of the unpredictable. I visited different spiritual communities—a little hand clapping, different songs, more emotion. Mine was a sort of bread-and-butter spirituality, good, stable, and wholesome, but a bit stale. Now I've discovered that every now and then a bit of 'new wine' gives me a fresh outlook.*

I am thankful for

My gifts of sensibility and logic
My awareness of the merit of learning from and building on
    past experiences
My ability to follow through on commitments
The ease with which I handle details and facts

In the storms of life, I can find shelter by

Looking for guidance from what has worked before and how
    things are resolved through faith
Turning over some of my responsibilities to others
Asking for help to assess the big picture—the larger meaning

To honor myself and my pathway to God, I can

Seek the practices that fit into my routine
Understand and apply unchanging truths in this changing world
Explore other traditions or spiritual disciplines to open the
    boundaries of my soul without violating what I know to
    be true

Chapter 7

ISFJ

Introversion, Sensing, Feeling, Judging

*Finding spirituality
in the inner world of
experience and
unifying values*

General Description: ISFJs tend to be dependable, considerate, and conscientious. They value harmonious settings with well-defined roles and responsibilities, and practical ways to be useful. Each person's welfare is important to them. They dutifully conserve resources while organizing things to meet the needs of people they serve.

THE GREATEST GIFT FOR ISFJs:
INTROVERTED SENSING WITH FEELING
*Having a sensitive, helpful, orderly, and matter-of-fact approach to
reality; understanding what circumstances realistically mean for
themselves and others.*

THE ISFJ ROLE IN COMMUNITY:
*Offering tangible and dignified service that meets the needs of specific
individuals while honoring order and tradition; enrolling others to
contribute cooperatively to the spiritual community.*

Introverted Sensing is the **dominant function** for ISFJs, the function that develops earliest in life, is most comfortable to use, and is easiest to access. Using the dominant function is the natural avenue for each type to pursue soulwork—this is where the soul resides. In other words, for soulwork to be meaningful, the ISFJ's dominant function, introverted Sensing, must be satisfied.

ISFJ Spirituality: Atmospheres for Soulwork

ISFJs are realistic and clearly see what is, especially when it involves people. They are aware of good and evil, the practical and impractical, the useful and useless activities all around them. These opposing ways of the world lead them to search for concrete answers to major issues of spirituality. They want to develop a spiritual awareness that allows them to deal with the unvarnished actualities of life. Often their search results in a deep knowing that "something" besides themselves is at work—in daily events that have no tangible explanation, unexpected or unearned kindness or generosity, or the brightening of people's moods.

ISFJs are also concerned about modeling and seriously carrying out their faith's directives in the real world. Generally, ISFJs see their role as implementers of the plans of others. While they are capable leaders, they often prefer to remain supportive in the background. Doing good, helping others, and nurturing their families and those in their care come naturally to ISFJs. This task of giving support to others *and* receiving that support when they themselves are needy is one of the most important aspects of their soulwork.

"My spirituality means that I do those things that serve the common good. I keep my soul open to God's presence through prayer, meditation, walking in natural settings, participating in my spiritual community, and doing things which directly help others."

JON, 23, CHILD-CARE PROVIDER

ISFJs flourish spiritually in settings where there are strong values for loyalty, responsibility, and steadfastness in faith. With their desire for clear structure and order, ISFJs who are raised in spiritual traditions are often able to accept and internalize much of what they are taught. While they may instinctively relate to a Creator or God, a loving force who is greater than they are, their faith is far from an unexamined one.

Soulwork that makes their faith more tangible and oriented to what needs doing at the present time is most appealing to ISFJs. For ISFJs, spirituality is most meaningful when it helps them as individuals appreciate life and the joys it brings, understand what they have to offer others, and trust beyond what they can directly experience.

"Our family life centered around the traditions, celebrations, stipulations, and activities of Judaism. I never questioned my faith, it was so much a part of what we did as a family. In those early years of my life the Law provided a structure and a haven for me. It wasn't until college, where I took formal classes about my faith, that I found I had questions. Mostly these were about legalistic positions or the role of evil—when bad things happen to good people. Eventually I came to realize that I could reconcile my beliefs with my questions. I remind myself that I'm not God and I don't have to understand the whole picture to be faithful."

MARGO, 52, LIBRARIAN

"My spirituality became concrete as I studied the Amish. They are a people who seem to 'walk the talk' more than any other group of Christians. I studied them to gain ideas about how they integrate religion, family life, and work with their basic beliefs. They have one of the most successful systems in the world—little alcoholism, addiction, abuse, crime—and about seventy-five percent of the children choose to remain in the community. Strange, since they are generally thought of as 'backward,' not modern at all. The main insights I gained from them were their focus on group values and their view of labor as a blessing, not 'Adam's curse.' As I work with other people, I constantly urge them to think in terms of what would be best for everyone, not their own needs."

FORD, 58, EXECUTIVE COACH

Spiritual Paths Using Introverted Sensing

Whether soulwork is new to ISFJs or they desire to enrich their spiritual practices, pathways that deepen their understanding of what they have experienced are most rewarding. Some of these methods include:

- Looking for evidence of God in the details of life.
  "After my husband died, I was struck by the many small ways in which I'd been prepared for my new life as a widow. He'd been unable to go with me to our spiritual community for some time, so I was used to being alone there. Our home repairs were all completed, so there were no worries about maintenance. With his dietary problems, I'd grown accustomed to cooking for one. As major as the loss was, I had these small reminders that God had been with me all along."

  MARJORIE, 75, RETIRED TEACHER

- Participating in retreats for renewal, especially in quiet, peaceful, or beautiful settings that allow for relaxation and introspection.
- Taking part in small, structured groups or committees for study, prayer, or meaningful discussion of spiritual matters. ISFJs often cultivate supportive and close relationships within organized, ongoing learning and support groups.
- Studying or reflecting about spiritual matters and how the information applies to the teachings of their spiritual tradition as well as in their own lives. ISFJs might also discern what practices, methods, or parallels in their sacred texts can be useful for daily life in the modern-day context.
- Actively serving others in a one-on-one fashion or by supporting those efforts in which they believe.
  "I think people like me are wired to carry the 'burden' of feeling and identify with the suffering of others and of the world. By nature, I feel compelled to do something about it. We seem to notice more readily and easily what human needs are being presented and have an internal drive to do something to meet those needs and alleviate the pain."

  BARBARA, 60, NURSE

Clouds That Hinder Soulwork

When the gifts of the dominant function of introverted Sensing are violated, or if ISFJs are not affirmed in their strengths, they may lose their desire to explore soulwork in order to understand and apply what has worked well for others or in their own past. Major factors that can get in the way of ISFJ spirituality include:

- Experiencing circumstances that are lacking in love, courtesy, or harmony. Many ISFJs find it difficult to entertain thoughts of a compassionate Creator when their life circumstances are devoid of the premises of doing good and following the rules.
  "My mother's belief was full of judgments and 'thou shalt nots' and I could not accept this. I had to find my own belief system. Because I did not feel *loved as a child, I did not think of God as a loving, caring being. Only when I had the experience of being fully accepted by others close to me was I able to grasp that God was loving."*
  MARISSA, 45, TEAM-BUILDING CONSULTANT

- Knowing that a spiritual atmosphere does not honor everyone's contributions, including their own. Because they often do their best work and make the biggest contributions "behind the scenes," ISFJs can feel forgotten. Their input may not be directly acknowledged even though it is vital to people or the task. In spiritual circles, this can make them feel that either they or their ideas aren't important.
- Finding that others or organizations lack integrity. If someone, especially in a leadership position, does not model what they preach, or a trusted structure or tradition stumbles, ISFJs may find the discrepancy between word and actions discouraging.
- Doing everything as best they can, then finding the outcome looks like they did nothing at all or did something badly. This may cause ISFJs to withdraw from soulwork for a while unless they can assuage their feelings of guilt or failure.
  "I don't see God as someone to bargain with or as pulling the strings and controlling people, but sometimes I wish that faith were more logical. As a mother, I did the best I could and yet my oldest com-

mitted suicide. I prayed so intensely for my son's depression to lift and it did for awhile, but then it came back with the deadliest result. My soul seems unable to move beyond this tragedy, yet I long for it to do so."

PAMELA, 56, EXECUTIVE SECRETARY

The Second Gift for ISFJs: Extraverted Feeling

ISFJs have extraverted Feeling as their **auxiliary function.** The gifts of extraverted Feeling include being aware of the reactions, needs, and values of others, discerning what is of most importance; and reaching out to people.

While ISFJs tend to begin their spiritual journey with an inner focus on actual life experiences, their auxiliary function of extraverted Feeling often fosters a need for some sort of spiritual community, whether a small group or a large organization. With their ability to see practical needs, ISFJs bring their devotion and loyalty to deserving spiritual organizations. Acting quietly but determinedly for the greater good, ISFJs serve as islands of calm to those about them.

ISFJs also enjoy meeting with people who share similar beliefs for learning and fellowship experiences. They look for role models and examples that they can emulate on their spiritual journeys. ISFJs often come to new understandings when they talk through their own feelings and impressions.

"Meeting regularly with others helps me reinforce my already-strong spirituality. I enjoy the encouragement and spirit of support and nourishment that comes from others who also value the same spiritual traditions and want to keep the historical aspects of our faith alive. My skills and talents are needed as well—as long as I can organize our meetings, I'll feel a vital part of the group."

ANNE, 71, RETIRED RECORDS TECHNICIAN

ISFJs might also focus their appreciative Feeling function on themselves.

"I always saw myself as coming up short. Then one day I thought to myself that I'm a child of God with gifts that were given uniquely to me. Now I truly value and honor what is solely mine to share. I thank God for my strengths in a humble yet honest way."

BOB, 33, PEDIATRICIAN

Thus, the auxiliary function provides balance: While introverted Sensing concentrates on what can be verified and focuses on concrete reality, extraverted Feeling points ISFJs toward appropriate and considered action, bringing their soulwork from their private inner realm into their relationships with others and the world at large.

The Third Gift for ISFJs: Thinking

Not as much is documented or agreed upon about how the third, or tertiary, function expresses itself in any of the 16 types.* The **third function** for ISFJs is Thinking. The domain of the Thinking function includes logical argument, cause-effect reasoning, objectivity, and a search for clarity.

For all of the 16 types, the third function tends to evolve later in life, typically after the first two functions are clearly developed. However, many ISFJs are assisted early on if they choose one of the many educational tracks that emphasize logical thinking and decision-making, the domain of Thinking, their third function. Thus, many ISFJs benefit from being able to reach logical conclusions about matters that are important for them when they *consciously* try to do so. As they seek to enrich their spirituality, many ISFJs use their third function, Thinking, to:

- Evaluate the spiritual traditions or faith systems to which they are exposed by taking an objective look at their own beliefs, seeking consistencies, logical proofs, or evidence of truths; and

---

Whether the third function is extraverted or introverted is not well documented in theory or practice. We therefore suggest that people observe how they use it in both the outer (extraverted) and inner (introverted) worlds at different times to see which is most helpful.

- Participate in rigorous and objective study to establish what is just and fair, right or wrong, and true or false as they work to establish their own spiritual criteria and standards.

ISFJs in the Storms of Life

The Least Accessible Gift for ISFJs:
Extraverted Intuition

For all of the 16 types, the fourth function is called the **inferior function** because it is the most difficult to use consciously and effectively. The inferior function can be a source of irritation and oversights that can threaten careers, relationships, competency, or even meaning and purpose—but at its best it can be a source of rest or richness in the storms of life, in moving toward deeper spirituality, or in exploring issues as we age. For ISFJs, the inferior function is extraverted Intuition.

For all of us, life delivers events and circumstances that we cannot control—even the most fortunate of us eventually have to deal with the relinquishment of relationships, work situations, or dreams. And as we age, the human condition demands that we face the diminishment of our own abilities and eventually our lives. While our soul-work may help us prepare for and weather these storms, knowing our psychological type can help us understand how these storms will affect us and where we might intentionally seek refuge.

The dominant introverted Sensing function of ISFJs provides some natural coping skills. ISFJs typically rely on their common sense to size up what needs to be done by whom and when to help bring the situation under control. In addition, many ISFJs find the practical precepts inherent in their spirituality a source of strength, using them as examples or guidance for what steps to take.

The auxiliary function of extraverted Feeling also provides some help. ISFJs may find the support they need by talking through or acting on their feelings or concerns with a close friend who is a good listener. The friend's encouragement may help reduce any anxiety ISFJs may have about the future.

"When my wife was very ill, some of our close friends were so helpful. The men took me out for lunch while the women stayed at our home. I knew that my wife's needs were being met and I had a chance to be with friends who listened, laughed, and shared their own fears about losing a spouse. By interacting with them, I gained new perspectives on my situation."

ROY, 66, RETIRED
RELIGIOUS PROFESSIONAL

Other ISFJs use their Feeling function to evaluate which of their activities merit their time and attention. Because they see what needs doing and do it often before others even become aware, it can be helpful for ISFJs to realize that someone else could benefit from doing a given task. Knowing this may keep ISFJs from feeling like they have to do it all. While ISFJs can find it therapeutic to help others with their problems as an antidote to their own concerns, they also need to be sure they care for themselves, too.

When the Storms Overwhelm

However, the storms of life often swell beyond our natural capacity to cope. While life's tragedies strain all of us, no matter how intense our soulwork and regardless of our psychological type, the stormy times for ISFJs can be intensified if the circumstances include any of the following factors:

- When people close to them deny verifiable facts and "givens" in a situation, impractical ideas are acted upon in inappropriate ways, or common sense is overruled.
- When there is no clear sense of direction. ISFJs work to smooth transitions and are vexed when they are unable to arrange things that way.
- When future outcomes are unclear or the situation is taken out of their hands. ISFJs can easily dwell on the worst that might happen.

  "I am well aware that intuition is not my strong suit—I can easily put two and two together and come up with seventeen! I recently placed a small plaque by my bedside with words from Browning—

'God's in his Heaven, All's right with the world.' To me the poem is a beautiful reminder of that overarching truth. I gave the same plaque to my daughter, who is away at college. Both of us use it as a reminder to pray."

ALAN, 63, ENGINEER

- When they go too far in deferring their own needs to meet those of others.

  "For my husband's job, we moved our family ten times in twenty years, first across the United States and then to Europe. I always wanted to put down roots—especially to be near my mother and the town where I was raised—but the chance came too late. For consolation at the time, I read and studied the life of Sarah, Abraham's wife. You know, Sarah had her problems and things did not work out her way, yet she was a survivor. I know I'm a survivor, too."

  ELISABETH, 67, HOMEMAKER

In the most despairing moments, all types can be caught by overuse of their strengths, relying too much on their dominant function. The worst time for ISFJs is when they are in the midst of change and there is no clear and understandable way to proceed—no concrete direction. They are so caught up by the needs of the present that they find it difficult to see beyond it. When ISFJs focus on what needs to be done, getting through day by day, their attention may be drawn away from the overall awareness of how problematic the situation really is. In the worst storms, a totally different approach to soulwork may be the only refuge.

"During the divorce process, I kept my attention on all the details and on my children. Only after the divorce was final could I really see how awful our marriage had been. I have to get through a loss experience before I can evaluate it in a larger perspective. Then I can be more realistic."

GREG, 46, CUSTOMER-SERVICE MANAGER

"I was totally wiped out by the death of my sister. We'd always been close, best friends, and I could not imagine my future without her. I became housebound and depressed when a friend came to visit. We talked about

all the theories and philosophies of death and the afterlife. I related how much I was struggling with these issues. My friend, who had also experienced a tragic death in her family, said she preferred a more straightforward and even simple approach to the topic. 'When my daughter died I concentrated on my belief that there is a heaven, where we will someday meet again. I also think of her as being very happy there.' The sincerity of my friend's belief helped me immensely and brought me back to equilibrium."

LEE, 29, SOCIAL WORKER

Clues that ISFJs are being overwhelmed:	• Excessive pessimism and forebodings about the future • So set on the "givens" of a situation that they can't think through alternatives
How to help ISFJs:	• Listen to their concerns, help them evaluate their feelings, and assume some of their burdensome tasks
For self-help:	• Consider what others can do for you • Reconsider the overall bigger meanings of the crisis in the scheme of life—look for a possible silver lining

The Gifts of the Inferior Function—Rest and Richness

Even though using one's inferior function is stressful, an irony of psychological type is that *a path to serenity and rest is to intentionally use the inferior function.* For the ISFJ, the inferior function of Intuition is opposite the dominant function of Sensing. Therefore, its *conscious use* requires shutting down what is most natural and easy— the Sensing function, which may have gotten out of control while trying to cope with the storm.

For ISFJs, pursuing activities that use their inferior function, extraverted Intuition, forces them to set aside their day-to-day concerns and turn to enjoyable outside activities and actions to gain new perspectives. Ways to intentionally engage the extraverted Intuition function include:

- Taking a negative situation and thinking of at least three positives that could come from it. Or, consider the most terrible thing that could happen and figure out how to deal with the worst-case scenario in order to break the logjam of gloomy thinking.
- Asking questions about the who-what-when-where-why-how of the current and future state of affairs, then discussing with friends to determine what it all means in the larger context.
- Engaging in a creative activity, such as art, writing, or woodworking, where there is no pressure for a given outcome, and giving over to the process of seeing who or what else emerges.

In soulwork for each type, richness, depth, and development come through the inferior function. As useful as it is to understand the inferior function for the storms of life, it provides more benefits as we seek to grow.

In the first half of life we define ourselves, both in work and relationships, through our dominant and auxiliary functions. In the second half of life, the gifts of our inferior function can aid us as we seek to become all that we can be. When we don't take advantage of this natural development of our psychological type, we can become stuck.

Midlife also gives clarity to the brevity of our lives. This compels many of us almost unconsciously to seek richness from unfamiliar experiences as well as to complete the psychological tasks we may have bypassed at an earlier age. As we journey toward wholeness and completion, we can open ourselves to new avenues that are outside of our routines by relinquishing the control our dominant function exerts. Adding spiritual practices that incorporate the attributes of our inferior function can give our soulwork new dimension and zest.

The first two functions, Sensing and Feeling, give ISFJs a practical, realistic sensibility along with the ability to understand the needs and feelings of others. However, to continue to grow, ISFJs need the spiritual richness of extraverted Intuition. They need to pay attention to their insights, be open to new possibilities in the world of action, and adopt, at times, a positive future outlook.

This involves:

- Experiencing the sacred in future possibilities and exploring idealism in self, others and different opportunities;
- Being attracted to new avenues and untried practices for spiritual expression;
- Exploring with others the mysteries of spirituality and accepting things that have neither concrete proof nor practical applications; and
- Using imagination to discern new insights, to muse about the big meanings behind simple stories and commonplace events.

ISFJs become reacquainted with the spiritual as they find meaning and pleasure in things they previously overlooked. While they may continue many of their favorite methods of soulwork, renewal may come from the spiritual pathways that are naturally the domain of ENTPs and ENFPs:

- *Now that I have the time, I decided to take a creative writing class. It's a very spontaneous process. We take a topic such as "God's love" and just write our thoughts about it. I'm often amazed at the insights I come up with when I practice making associations and connections.*
- *When I'm walking my dog in the evening, I begin to wonder about the magnitude of God's creation. I let the images float by and use them as a way to reminisce about the beauty of the world. My inner sense for having to have my every act be useful has been turned down some. My "flights of fancy" offer me new vistas!*
- *My granddaughter is so full of curiosity—she stimulates my thinking with her myriad of questions. She doesn't want simple answers, she wants me to create imaginative stories for her. I oblige and find that I enjoy using my imagination—I feel pretty good about it, too.*

- *I've learned not to make lists because they reinforce and restrict me to linear thinking. Instead, I put my name in the middle of a page and draw arrows out to different possibilities, like spokes on a wheel. Recently I used this method to consider what I could do with my new leisure time—I drew lines between activities that I could undertake at the same time and came up with all kinds of new ideas.*
- *Before, I enjoyed classes that used day-to-day examples and emphasized practical applications. Recently, I have a new appreciation for more global themes and subject matter. Because I have my own small corner of life pretty well organized, I am curious to explore what new knowledge I can gain for other arenas.*

I am thankful for

My practical outlook, which sees things as they truly are
My sense of duty, service, and responsibility
The fulfillment I feel when I've helped another
The beauty of nature and the company of friends

In the storms of life, I can find shelter by

Finding a listening friend who can act as a compass as I try out new directions
Broadening my perspective by reading sacred texts and the testimonies of others who faced similar circumstances
Appreciating and honoring my own needs, talents, and gifts

To honor myself and my pathway to God, I can

Seek quiet times for reflection and relaxation
Use my imagination to open my spiritual practices to the richness in life that exists beyond the tangible and concrete
Invest time with God, knowing God is in control and therefore I don't have to be

*The imagination is the secret
and marrow of civilization.
It is the very eye of faith.
The soul without imagination
is what an observatory would
be without a telescope.*

HENRY WARD
BEECHER[1]

Intuitive
Spirituality

Intuitive Types find satisfying soulwork through:

- Living the spiritual life with optimism and hope
- Enjoying insights, imagination, creativity, novelty, for things seen and unseen
- Appreciating and contemplating the inexplicable and the mystical aspects of life
- Seeing applications for future possibilities, meaning, growth, and change
- Learning through synchronistic interaction between ideas, occurrences, people, and scholarship
- Observing meanings and connections behind the events, stories, or practices of spirituality
- Designing new avenues, traditions, or rituals for soulwork

Preferred Extraverted Intuitive Soulwork (ENFP and ENTP)	Preferred Introverted Intuitive Soulwork (INFJ and INTJ)
• Prayer/meditation in community	• Prayer/meditation in solitude
• Soulwork through interaction with others and the environment to enhance the future	• Soulwork through musing with God about what could be different or might be in store
• Spontaneous spiritual life, as perceptions or needs arise	• Structured and special times set apart expressly for spiritual matters
• Service through action to make things better for people, organizations, or the natural world	• Service through conceiving paradigms, envisioning and organizing the structures for change

Suggestions for Intuitive Soulwork

1. Imagine that you could invite any three spiritual giants to serve on a panel for discussion. Who would you invite? What would you want to ask them? What could you explore together? What might you hope to discover? How could they be a stimulus for your soulwork?

2. Thoreau said "The youth gets together his [*sic*] materials to build a bridge to the moon, or, perchance, a palace or temple on the earth,

and, at length, the middle-aged man [*sic*] concludes to build a woodshed with them."[2] Are there areas of your life where you have built woodsheds instead of palaces? What could you change to recover your dream?

3. Choose a favorite story that has meaning for you spiritually. It could be from the writings of your spiritual heritage, an oft-told tale about an ancestor, a person you admire, or a fictional character. Imagine yourself as a character in the story *or* reconsider the plot, lesson to be learned, or causes of what occurred. What new insights do you receive? What new messages are there for you in the story?

4. **For the discipline of study:** Go steep and deep with a short passage from your sacred texts, favorite poems, or teachings from someone you admire. Understand the facts it presents, but then look for other meanings and interpretations. Stick with the same reading until you garner new insights. When you have gained new awareness, consider the truth of your ideas and the impact they might have on you or others.

5. **For the discipline of meditation or prayer:** Find ways to use your imagination to support your meditation/prayer life:

   • Picture a future event and the outcomes you hope will occur.
   • Bring to mind a person and the change or blessings you'd like to see for that person.
   • Imagine the results of changes you hope to see in yourself.
   • Place yourself in the presence of God or your Creator. What messages might you receive? Are there lessons God is trying to help you learn?
   • Create in your mind an image of joy, calm, repentance—whatever your greatest need at the moment—and envision what life would/could be like.

6. **For the discipline of simplicity:** The minds of many Intuitive types are easily distracted from soulwork. What are your major distractions? Involvement in too many good causes? Interests in too many

subjects? Reading too many "informative" magazines? Too much time surfing the Internet? If less is more, then imagine what your work, family, emotional well-being, and leisure time might gain from ridding yourself of some of these distractions and adding time for soulwork.

7. **For the discipline of celebration:** Rejoice in your creativity. Devote time to your novel ideas, your music, your art, your writing, your designing—whatever the gifts God gave to you. Allow yourself opportunities, alone or with others, to browse at a bookstore, visit an art museum, attend a concert, etc., thankful for the insights you receive. Use your creativity to celebrate and offer thanksgiving— make cards instead of buying them, designate certain foods or table settings as festival items, invite friends for an evening of games, indulge in a walk in the middle of a day, even turn the music up a bit louder. Take notice of little events worth celebrating, other than holidays and anniversaries. Commemorate the first new flower in the garden, reading a book that fed your soul, receiving a wonderful letter, and other things that brought joy to your day.

8. Think of or journal about three people in your life who encouraged you. What did they see as your future? What did they think you did well? How could their dreams/insights about you help you now? Imagine yourself as a young person. From your adult perspective, what do you view as your own potential? What can you do to bring that potential forward into the future?

9. If time and money were no object (and after the trip around the world!), what would you attempt to do or be? Envision yourself carrying out your dream. What would it be like? How would it fulfill you? How can you incorporate steps toward that fulfillment into your life right now?

10. In what type of environment do you really dream best? At the seashore? By a favorite window? In a bookstore? On a walk in nature? Driving or biking through a pleasant scene? When were you last there?

Go to one of these spots today, even if only in your mind, and be conscious of what happens. What insights did you receive for your work? Your relationships? Your soulwork? How can you make more time for this essential soulwork? If you can't go to your sacred spot regularly, recreate it in your mind. Picture the journey there, the sights, sounds, and smells, and what you would do along the way and once you arrive. Allow yourself time to be in these environments so that you can access your spiritual potential.

11. Envision yourself 10 or 20 years from now. Will you be pleased with what you are doing or who you have become? If so, what do you need to do *now* to make your future a reality? If not, how can you work to modify your life now? How do you think your future self would regard your current activities?

12. Allow yourself at least 30 minutes alone with music that calls to your soul—consider making a tape of favorite songs just for your listening pleasure. Sit back with your journal, art, clay, tablet, computer (or walk with a set of headphones) and let the music inspire you.

13. With whom do you share your dreams and disappointments? Is there someone who will be trustworthy yet will challenge you if needed? Risk sharing your ideas for growth and change. As you converse, how do you feel? Excited? Confident? How can this person serve as a springboard to help you to make your dreams become reality?

14. Remember that as an Intuitive type, daydreams can be rich areas for insights. Even as you daydream, pretend that your are discussing your ideas with God. Don't immediately censor "wild thoughts." What might God be trying to suggest? Are you open to discoveries in this manner? What are your longings? How could these longings be the voice of your soul?

15. When did you last play the piano, guitar, flute, sing, dance, sculpt, etc.? For many introverted Intuitives, these activities can be a major source of peace and renewal. When did you last go to a

public space, perhaps with a friend, and observe the action? For many extraverted Intuitives, these observations can be a major source of inspiration and renewal. Use these activities and others like them as ways to inspire your soulwork.

16. Who are your favorite spiritual heroes? What about them inspires you? Read enough about them so that you can imagine the realities of their day-to-day living and perhaps find new meaning in their writings or deeds. In what context did their insights come? How is your life similar to theirs? What can you do to emulate them?

17. If your soulwork becomes too incidental or accidental, try using meditative resources to bring specific actions for soulwork to fruition.

    Introverted Intuitive types: Keep lists of petitions and praise in a notebook. Decide on a format for prayer, include set supplications or readings, and other reminders to keep your soulwork focused.

    Extraverted Intuitive types: Use an object or picture for meditation to anchor your thoughts. Perhaps placing an icon or sacred object on your dresser, in your billfold, by your desk, etc., could serve to remind you to meditate or pray.

18. Change the patterns of your soulwork frequently. Read different inspirational texts, take a different route on your walk, set aside a spiritual practice or discipline before it becomes too boring.

Embrace your:

> Creativity
> Insights
> Optimism
> Future outlook
> Autonomy and independence

Chapter 8

ENTP

Extraversion, Intuition, Thinking, Perceiving

*Finding spirituality
in the outer world
of challenges
and possibilities*

General Description: ENTPs tend to be independent innovators and change-masters. They enjoy originality of expression, questioning ideas and norms, and developing models. ENTPs follow their hunches and investigate new, intriguing possibilities for systems and organizations. The call of adventure, allowing for freedom of action, entices ENTPs.

THE GREATEST GIFT FOR ENTPs:
EXTRAVERTED INTUITION WITH THINKING
*Conceptualizing what needs to be by integrating divergent ideas;
bringing insight to complex and challenging situations
in order to overcome obstacles.*

THE ENTP ROLE IN COMMUNITY:
*Planning and leading new projects with enthusiasm and energy;
assuming the risks for visionary endeavors;
and advocating strategies for the future.*

Extraverted Intuition is the **dominant function** for ENTPs, the function that develops earliest in life, is most comfortable to use, and is easiest to access. Using the dominant function is the natural avenue for each type to pursue soulwork—this is where the soul resides. In other words, for soulwork to be meaningful, the ENTP's extraverted Intuition must be satisfied.

◈

ENTP Spirituality: Atmospheres for Soulwork

ENTP spirituality is as varied as ENTPs are. When challenged to find answers, many ENTPs discover avenues for soulwork that allow for ever-deepening understanding. Others enjoy a continuing exploration of different spiritual traditions, practices, or philosophies. What seems consistent, though, is a remarkable curiosity fueled by their dominant function, extraverted Intuition.

ENTPs need to understand and reconcile their own perceptions about spirituality with what they've learned, read, or imagined. Many ENTPs claim that figuring things out is their favorite pursuit and the impetus behind their spiritual quest. Some maintain that they are perpetual seekers who hesitate to choose a single spiritual path because there are simply too many possibilities—too many ways of knowing.

ENTPs often feel compelled to define spiritual concepts, ideas, and terms for themselves as they search for meaningful soulwork. They have a natural distrust of rigid structure or hierarchies, and of accepting a set of beliefs or rules without examination. However, to best serve their dominant extraverted Intuition they often seek out spiritual communities for the fellowship they offer. These group experiences are often important to them as another means to intellectual inquiry. In formal settings or with a close-knit group, ENTPs relish the chance to question, debate, and explore spiritual topics. Engaging with thought-provoking people offers ENTPs a "home base" from which to doubt, experiment, and take risks.

Because ENTPs are used to relying on their own initiatives and power, some may see little reason to pursue soulwork. For these

ENTPs, it is only after some adversity or hard-to-master challenge in their lives that they explore a more spiritual, rather than their customary intellectual or logical, point of view. These trying situations become the spurs to look more deeply at who or what could provide strength outside themselves. In many cases, adversity leads ENTPs to acknowledge God, a Higher Power, or a sense of a universal Soul. Often, their most spiritual moments result from difficult situations, whether exciting or tragic, where they are called to put their ingenuity to work.

"I was only seven years old when in the space of a few months three children in our neighborhood died. The uncertainty of life was underscored in a way that was far beyond my maturity to grasp, but I understood that in some ways and aspects of life, things were beyond my control. No matter how competent I was in matters of the mind (I was already the best reader in class), body (a natural athlete), and heart (I had many friends), I knew that life was still like water—you couldn't hold onto it in your hands. I knew I had to find something deeper, what I now refer to as my soul, to guide me through life."

CRAIG, 48, STRATEGIC-PLANNING CONSULTANT

"My upbringing didn't include any spiritual tradition, so I had no spiritual tradition to overcome. However, I'm a curious type and like to figure things out. As a young adult, when my life was not working the way I wanted it to, I searched to discover what was missing.

"I learned that soulwork in my life was nonexistent—and that I enjoyed being with others I viewed as spiritual. When I see the positive results of people of faith in action, I'm able to turn off my analysis and engage my intuition, which brings me closer to the true meaning of soulwork. However, I'm still searching—any God worthy of the name needs to stand up to a bit of scrutiny. While there may be few recognizable changes in my outer self, at midlife I have a clearer recognition of who I am and why I am here. There are enough ideas out there that my frame of reference can shift from research to belief."

PAULA, 48, HUMAN-RESOURCES MANAGER

Spiritual Paths Using Extraverted Intuition

Whether soulwork is new to ENTPs or they desire to enrich their spiritual practices, pathways that allow for discovery and insight are most rewarding. Some of the methods or techniques that ENTPs use include:

- Traveling, attending local classes, or participating in retreats with others to experience different cultural and spiritual traditions. While ENTPs find the religious or cultural differences in beliefs to be intriguing, they also look for the common patterns and threads among those they explore.
- Participating in humanitarian projects where they feel they can have an impact. ENTPs find themselves orchestrating refugee relief, managing trips for 300 teens, running building-fund campaigns, and in general being in leadership positions where they can change the status quo and direct efforts in new and uncharted waters.

    "While chaperoning a youth ski trip, I became so frustrated with the lack of planning and coordination that I took on the responsibility of running the trips for the next couple of years. I could see what needed to be planned and knew how to trust my intuition when it came to handling unexpected events—like being stranded in the middle of Nebraska for twenty-four hours by a blizzard!"

    DREW, 55, CONSULTANT

- Joining with others to celebrate the possibilities and energy that come with exploring spirituality in community. Many ENTPs gain enthusiasm and feel a sense of being connected with a bigger purpose from formal gatherings.
- Serving on long-range task forces or committees that anticipate and strategize to meet the spiritual needs of others.

    "I generally end up in leadership positions. At times I have felt like the true pioneer, musket balls in my rear from getting too far ahead of the troops—perceived as the enemy rather than the visionary."

    HANS, 61, SMALL-BUSINESS OWNER

- Learning, reading broadly, or researching to define spiritual principles and truths for themselves. ENTPs typically enjoy gathering with others to discuss the intersection of spiritual concerns with personal or worldly concerns. Depending on their own life situation, ENTPs may want to concentrate on applying the truths of their beliefs to their personal lives or on examining current societal thinking and structures.

Clouds That Hinder Soulwork

When the gifts of the dominant function of Intuition are violated, or if ENTPs are not affirmed in the soulwork that is most effective for them, their desire to nourish their spiritual side may be dampened. Major factors that can get in the way of ENTP spirituality include:

- Being led by their own intuitive drive to want to know about *all* different types of spirituality.
  "I'm interested in anything spiritual that has helped others. I may not make it my tradition but I don't like to feel that I've overlooked a resource. As an 'information junkie,' I collect spiritual traditions—it's the practicing of the tradition that I tend to neglect."
  DEANNA, 55, PROFESSOR

- Having concerns about how others view their competency.
  "I talk a good game about not caring what others think of me, and in the majority of areas of life this is true. But I never wanted anyone to question my intellect—and this is my spiritual conundrum. I want that absolute freedom from care that my perception of true faith brings, but I have to make myself vulnerable to do that."
  SACHI, 33, CORPORATE TRAINER

- Using a questioning style that makes some people uncomfortable. Out of their quest for truth and understanding, ENTPs seek a level of clarity that can't always be attained in spirituality. Wanting to be witty and challenging, many ENTPs may find themselves by these actions outside the "goodwill" of people who have different styles. Even when they know that their inquiry might be offensive to some, they may still question out of their need for clarification—quite a dilemma.

• Not finding the time for soulwork. With all of the areas for exploration ENTPs find through their Intuition, they tend not to make space for spirituality unless it becomes compelling.

The Second Gift for ENTPs: Introverted Thinking

ENTPs have introverted Thinking as their **auxiliary function.** The gifts of introverted Thinking include using objective criteria to find solutions to problems, clarify principles, and search for truth.

While ENTPs often begin their spiritual journey through the stimulation of the outer world and its myriad of possibilities and perplexities, their auxiliary function of introverted Thinking offers the gift of reflection and logical analysis. Through introspection, they can choose objectively among the options they see, define for themselves what is true and relevant, and bring their intellect to bear on their spiritual insights and experiences.

ENTPs tend to have many irons in the fire at once. To critically examine which avenues are best for their soulwork, they may need to seek solitude and quiet time in order to engage their inner Thinking function. They can then develop a system of prioritization and purpose to determine which of their many interests have the most merit.

Giving time to reflection also allows ENTPs to develop some discipline for their soulwork. They can use this time for meditation, organized study, or writing. This helps them confront their principles to determine what is true.

"My most helpful spiritual director brought a group of us together weekly to teach us how to 'reflect'—no easy matter for someone who wants to constantly be part of the action. Even though the director moved away, our group still meets. I need the encouragement of others to pull back and clarify what I believe."

PAIGE, 51, ATTORNEY

Thus, the auxiliary function of introverted Thinking provides balance: While extraverted Intuition identifies endless challenges and adventures, introverted Thinking points ENTPs toward logical choices, bringing their soulwork from the world at large to their private realm. This helps ENTPs to focus their spirituality on their own principles and needs.

The Third Gift for ENTPs: Feeling

Not as much is documented or agreed upon about how the third, or tertiary, function expresses itself in any of the 16 types.* The **third function** for ENTPs is Feeling. The domain of the Feeling function includes weighing values; discerning what is important for themselves, others, and community; and determining the impact of decisions on people.

For all of the 16 types, the third function tends to evolve later in life, typically after the first two functions are clearly developed. The age at which ENTPs pay attention to their Feeling function may depend on the amount of experience they have using their Feeling function to make decisions and influence others. Without this orientation, given the emphasis in most educational tracks on logical decision-making, ENTPs may find that it takes considerable concentration and energy to use their Feeling function while making decisions. However, as they seek to enrich their spirituality, ENTPs may consciously use their third function, Feeling, to:

- Tailor their soulwork to improve their relationships with people and with their Creator; and
- Further refine their priorities, clarify their values, and then reflect if the way they are living their lives is congruent with their values.

---

*Whether the third function is extraverted or introverted is not well documented in theory or practice. We therefore suggest that people observe how they use it in both the outer (extraverted) and inner (introverted) worlds at different times to see which is most helpful.

ENTPs in the Storms of Life

The Least Accessible Gift for ENTPs: Introverted Sensing

For all of the 16 types, the fourth function is called the **inferior function** because it is the most difficult to use consciously and effectively. The inferior function can be a source of irritation and oversights that can threaten meaning and purpose, competency, relationships, or even careers—but at its best it can be a source of rest or richness in the storms of life, in moving toward deeper spirituality, or in exploring issues as we age. For ENTPs, the inferior function is introverted Sensing.

◈

For all of us, life delivers events and circumstances that we cannot control—even the most fortunate of us eventually have to deal with the relinquishment of relationships, work situations, or dreams. And as we age, the human condition demands that we face the diminishment of our own abilities and eventually our lives. While our soul-work may help us prepare for and weather these storms, knowing our psychological type can help us understand how these storms will affect us and where we might intentionally seek refuge.

The dominant extraverted Intuition function of ENTPs provides some natural coping skills. ENTPs are resourceful, optimistic, and see numerous positive possibilities for themselves and others in almost any situation. Generally, life's problems are perceived as adventures and sometimes even relished for the challenge they evoke.

The auxiliary function of introverted Thinking also provides some help. By moving away from outer distractions, ENTPs can find the space to resurrect their inner guidelines, logical principles, and systems of procedures and rules. This pause for reflection before making decisions allows their Thinking function a chance to be heard.

"The situation with my daughter and her boyfriend was so crazy that it was driving me wild. I decided to get away for the day, so I rented a rowboat. I found a secluded inlet where no one could see me and spent sev-

eral hours just being still to sort things out and decide on a course of action."

JEFF, 50, SALES EXECUTIVE

ENTPs can also access their introverted Thinking by setting aside time for meditation, prayer, or reading. Learning to say "no" and sticking with it can give ENTPs this quiet time and perhaps the opportunity to complete those projects they're always wanted to finish.

When the Storms Overwhelm

However, the storms of life often swell beyond our natural capacity to cope. While life's tragedies strain all of us, no matter how intense our soulwork and regardless of our psychological type, the stormy times for ENTPs can be intensified if the circumstances include any of the following factors:

- When they continue to attack the problem long after others would admit defeat. Many ENTPs have little experience with anything they can't conquer using their own power. Because of their dauntless ingenuity and energy, ENTPs often manage to avoid some of life's setbacks and therefore sometimes don't recognize the severity of their dilemma.
- When they need to deal with emotion-laden, personal issues. ENTPs prefer to avoid showing the emotional side of themselves or to experience that vulnerability in others.
  "In order to get my son the help he needed, I had to sit across from him in a court of law and describe in detail the problems he had. As I watched the tears begin to stream down his face, my voice broke and I was unable to continue. I never cry, but that day I couldn't get hold of myself. The experience brought me a new sense of my soul as I realized how profoundly and deeply my feelings were affected."

JAVIER, 54, EXECUTIVE

- When they are asked to follow standard operating procedures that truly get in the way of what they are trying to accomplish or that violate one of their core principles.

- When they feel they are being unfairly challenged, especially in areas where they perceive they have a corner on truth. ENTPs are typically quick learners who see patterns in masses of information. Because they often become experts in their given areas of interest, they can be particularly unnerved when others question their competency or uncover details they may have overlooked.

In the most despairing moments, all types can be caught by overuse of their strengths, relying too much on their dominant function. The worst time for ENTPs is when they are forced to give up, admitting that their resourcefulness and genuine optimism cannot handle the crisis. They have overused their dominant Intuition by relying on their ability to generate options. In giving up, ENTPs feel not just a sense of loss, but that personally they have somehow lost.

"For the first few years of dealing with our child's health issues, we kept the matter pretty much to ourselves. I read every book I could find until it seemed that sometimes I knew more than the specialists. When the doctors began to hint that there were no further options, I felt as if I had somehow betrayed my daughter. If I'd put more energy into other strategies or moved our family to be nearer to a research hospital, etc. My mind kept dwelling on what I could have done to find a cure for her—a pretty futile task."

SHARI, 48, LOBBYIST

"As I struggled with the loss of my spouse, I pulled inward and isolated myself—almost at the expense of long-established friendships and mental health. Normally I'm a very healthy person, but I developed stress-related health problems. I realized I was turning into a profound negative thinker. I thought I'd never find another person to love me and with whom I could share my thoughts and dreams. It finally dawned on me that even if I never remarry, the support and encouragement I needed from others could be found in friendships. I no longer care to solve issues by myself—and I don't have to."

AARON, 60, MARKETING MANAGER

Clues that ENTPs are being overwhelmed:	• Overeating, sleeping, excessive exercise, and overindulgence in other sensory pursuits
	• Avoiding any challenge to their course of action or understanding of events
How to help ENTPs:	• Remind them to find time for solitude and introspection
For self-help:	• Pay attention to the facts of the situation, not the ramifications, and conduct a logical analysis of who needs to do what by when
	• Analyze physical needs to determine whether changes in sleep, diet, exercise, or lifestyle are needed

The Gifts of the Inferior Function—Rest and Richness

Even though using one's inferior function can be stressful, an irony of psychological type is that *a path to serenity and rest is to intentionally use the inferior function.* For the ENTP, the inferior function of Sensing is opposite the dominant function of Intuition. Therefore, its *conscious use* requires shutting down what is most natural and easy—the Intuitive function, which may have gotten out of control while trying to cope with the storm.

For ENTPs, pursuing activities that use their inferior function, introverted Sensing, forces them to stop looking for possibilities, suspend their creativity, and focus. Through introverted Sensing, ENTPs can get in touch with their own concrete needs and the realities of the moment. Ways to intentionally engage the introverted Sensing function include:

• Practicing meditation or other solitary disciplines to pay attention to the interior world. Mindful meditation can provide benefits without adding yet another burdensome activity to a hectic schedule. Time alone in reflection or prayer with concentrated attention on breathing and thought patterns can be a balm to the often-dispersed ENTP.

- Using images of nature to calm the soul. While some ENTPs seek solitude outside, others imagine favorite places. One ENTP quiets herself by picturing in her mind a storm-swept lake, the feel of the biting wind, the sounds of crashing waves, the smell of rain, and then gradually imagines the storm subsiding until the lake is as still as glass.
- Engaging in exercise, massage, and other types of bodywork can help ENTPs relax, appreciate their physical strengths and limitations, and regain balance.

In soulwork for each type, richness, depth and development come through the inferior function. As useful as it is to understand the inferior function for the storms of life, it provides more benefits as we seek to grow.

In the first half of life we define ourselves, both in work and relationships, through our dominant and auxiliary functions. In the second half of life, the gifts of our inferior function can aid us as we seek to become all that we can be. When we don't take advantage of this natural development of our psychological type, we can become stuck.

Midlife also gives clarity to the brevity of our lives. This compels many of us almost unconsciously to seek richness from unfamiliar experiences as well as to complete the psychological tasks we may have bypassed at an earlier age. As we journey toward wholeness and completion, we can open ourselves to new avenues that are outside of our routines by relinquishing the control our dominant function exerts. Adding spiritual practices that incorporate the attributes of our inferior function can give our soulwork new dimension and zest.

The first two functions, Intuition and Thinking, give ENTPs a creative vision of possibilities and a set of principles that guides their soulwork as well as their lives. However, to continue to grow, ENTPs require the spiritual richness of introverted Sensing. They need to pay attention to the impact of spirituality on their health and daily needs.

This involves:

- Structured time for spiritual discipline to reflect on what is happening in the present moment;
- Using the five senses—what can be seen, heard, touched, smelled, or tasted—to enrich spirituality;
- Applying soulwork to practical, personal needs; and
- Reflecting on or participating in the continuity of traditions or rituals that have stood the test of time.

ENTPs become reacquainted with their spiritual nature as they find meaning in things they'd previously overlooked. While they may continue any of their favorite methods of soulwork, renewal may come from the spiritual pathways that are naturally the domain of ISTJs and ISFJs.

- *I've dedicated two mornings a week to quiet reading and journaling. It's become quite a necessity and is of such high priority that I'm thinking of adding one more time each week.*
- *I enjoy going back over my childhood and early adult years to reflect on how my spiritual life has developed. This practice reminds me where I've been and how that influences what is meaningful for me today and why.*
- *I keep coming back to believing that God is that voice within that I "hear" when I'm in a soul-filled setting or sanctuary; when I'm in that place between sleep and wakefulness; and when I'm still enough to listen. My quietude does bring me blessings!*
- *The trappings of my spiritual life are now important. Give me something that I can see, smell, or touch! I like candles, music, and other things that call my senses to notice what is spiritual. I've overused deep symbolism—I'm beginning to see simple things as miracles. Just lying in the grass and feeling its softness frees my mind of analysis and brings out my emotions of gladness and gratitude at the splendor of what actually is.*
- *I may be back where I started. I want to enjoy the stage I'm at and just not think about the journey anymore. I was in a leadership meeting*

last week and the question was, "What is it that we are supposed to 'get' in our spiritual community?" A good friend, the quietest person there, said, "It is about joy." I hope my own journey takes me there.

I am thankful for

My energy and enthusiasm for life's challenges
My creative and innovative vision
My ability to see patterns and find solutions
The way I can synthesize divergent ideas

In the storms of life, I can find shelter by

Prioritizing my many options and concluding which best meet my life principles
Cutting out distractions and allowing space for reflection and solitude
Paying attention to and living within those rules and guidelines that I know are important to me

To honor myself and my pathway to God, I can

Seek answers, question the pat solutions, and discover the spiritual truths of this world
Pay attention to *what is* and value reality for the evidence and richness it brings to my spiritual journey
Dedicate time for my spiritual practices and life

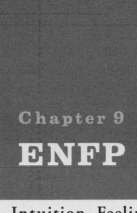

Chapter 9
ENFP

Extraversion, Intuition, Feeling, Perceiving

Finding spirituality in
the outer world of
activities and
possibilities for people

General Description: ENFPs tend to be enthusiastic, inspiring, and charismatic initiators of change who value exploring possibilities for growth and development. Energetic and perceptive, ENFPs often anticipate what people will want in the future. They enjoy variety, newness, and flexibility. Creativity, novelty, and insight are key values.

THE GREATEST GIFT FOR ENFPs:
EXTRAVERTED INTUITION WITH FEELING
Generating numerous ideas and finding abundant resources; finding enjoyment in an infinite variety of interests; aligning passion and creativity in the processes of discovery, learning, and living.

THE ENFP ROLE IN COMMUNITY:
Inspiring others to reach their fullest potential; building generous and open communities to help in the advancement of worthwhile causes and the shepherding of human aspirations.

Extraverted Intuition is the **dominant function** for ENFPs, the function that develops earliest in life, is most comfortable to use, and is easiest to access. Using the dominant function is the natural avenue for each type to pursue soulwork—this is where the soul resides. In other words, for soulwork to be meaningful, the ENFP's dominant extraverted Intuition must be satisfied.

◆

ENFP Spirituality: Atmospheres for Soulwork

Spirituality for ENFPs is broad, open, and deeply personal, reflecting the role of their dominant function, extraverted Intuition. Generally, this love of the spiritually enriched life begins early. ENFPs enjoy exploring the inexplicable and therefore are attracted to soulwork, even if the path they choose is neither typical nor traditional. Because of their affinity for the unseen, many ENFPs find the concept of a Higher Power to be an essential one, but its form may take on many aspects—God, Mother Earth, Jesus of Nazareth, the "spark within," etc. In their curiosity, they often search for as much information as they can find on different religions, spiritual traditions, or philosophies.

ENFPs may craft their own fluid belief system created with information from many sources. ENFPs pursue their spirituality by engaging in discussion with people who hold similar views and values, but may also branch out to dialogue with those with very different traditions and understandings. Their spirituality responds to new and changing insights, like a mobile that changes direction with varying movements of air. While others may see this as fickle, they shouldn't be fooled. The tenets of the ENFP's spirituality may change with new input, but it is generally supported by a bedrock of values centered on personal development and service.

Many ENFPs see soulwork as an avenue for self-discovery. If they are affirmed in their own identity, ENFPs often act to encourage others, especially through speaking, preaching, teaching, or performing.

They want people to experience the joy, love, serenity, or excitement they have garnered from their faith. This encouragement for themselves and others may come from a wide variety of paths ranging from organized religion to support groups, academic classes, writing or journaling, or time spent in nature.

Openness in faith and practice is crucial. Because their dominant function is extraverted Intuition, ENFPs generally seek some sort of spiritual community, whether a small group or an organization, to enhance their soulwork. ENFPs often flourish spiritually in environments where there is an atmosphere of harmony and support as well as an acceptance of the mysteries of faith. When evaluating a specific spiritual expression, they need to know that individual perspectives are valued. ENFPs often find that spiritual growth comes more readily when it is safe to be vulnerable to themselves, others, and God. Their most spiritual times tend to be inspired by their interactions with other people or stimuli from the world around them.

"When I joined the Al-Anon 12 Step Program, I found such a serenity that I felt compelled to reach out to people who struggle with addictions and the accompanying loss of hope. By following the Al-Anon philosophy of putting my issues into God's hands—you know, 'Let go, let God'—I realized a peace I never thought possible."

BARBARA, 53, PUBLICIST

"As a child, my spirituality was connected with my desire to help others. My imagination allowed me to put myself in the shoes of people who struggled in poverty. I wanted to be a part of efforts to help them—either in person or by leading 'crusades' to save the world from strife and hunger. Now I believe my insights and concerns for people are the gifts of God that enable me to look beyond myself. While I'm not the far-off crusader of my childhood dreams, through my profession, I restore one person at a time."

NAN, 62, THERAPIST

Spiritual Paths Using Extraverted Intuition

Whether soulwork is new to ENFPs or they desire to enrich their spiritual practices, pathways that allow for discovery and insight are most rewarding. Some of the methods or techniques that ENFPs use include:

- Seeing the hand of God in art, literature, music, or in random acts of kindness—any artistic or generous endeavor can be the catalyst that fuels their soulwork.
- Engaging their imagination through guided imagery, listening to stories, exploring symbols, drama, or other creative pursuits to develop new perceptions for their personal spiritual quest.
- Helping others and experiencing connection through personal and spiritual growth. Many ENFPs pursue careers in counseling, ministry, human resources, or social work, where they can directly help people in need or influence organizations to serve people better.
- Reading, discussing, or hearing compelling theology, insights, or poetry from a wide variety of sources—both spiritual and secular—that provide new points of view.

  "Because I'm curious, open, and a 'possibility person,' I love the whole idea of exploring those aspects of my life that I can't see or touch. The idea of God and the mysteries of the universe are very encouraging to me and fuel my imagination. Some people say they 'found religion' or they've 'got it.' To me, the spiritual path is a lifelong journey. There's always more to discover."

  GABRIELLE, 28, SOCIAL-SERVICES WORKER

- Traveling, absorbing other cultures and traditions, or departing from their everyday schedules in order to rekindle their creativity, try different experiences, and explore new territory.

Clouds That Hinder Soulwork

When the gifts of the dominant function of extraverted Intuition are violated, or if ENFPs are separated from community, their instinctive pursuit of soulwork can be hindered. Major factors that can get in the way of ENFP spirituality include:

- Being pulled by too many facets of life. ENFPs often struggle to balance their physical, emotional, and spiritual needs, since their extraverted Intuition constantly beckons with the possibility of some new treasure. Busyness then interferes with their need for soulwork. Given this, making room for regular spiritual practices is difficult.
- Becoming bored by familiar spiritual practices. ENFPs may find that their minds wander and soulwork loses its appeal.
  "Rote readings, liturgies, or prayers make me feel fidgety. I often tune out traditional language and predictable practices because they fail to touch any deep chord."
  NEIL, 42, MARKETING REPRESENTATIVE

- Burning out through over-involvement. ENFPs may readily volunteer to support causes or new spiritual practices, beliefs, or leaders. Often before they realize it, ENFPs become overextended, guilty, and worn-out as they try to meet all their commitments. Things begin to slip through the cracks. ENFPs may then need to withdraw or resign to bring their lives back under control, only to start the process over again.
- Knowing they may find many conflicting systems of belief. ENFPs may avoid a typically spiritual life because they may not want to face the potential for conflict and apparent incongruities of their own beliefs and those of others.

The Second Gift for ENFPs: Introverted Feeling
ENFPs have introverted Feeling as their **auxiliary function.** The gifts of introverted Feeling help them to sort through the many ideas and possibilities they see to find the most important ones, those that clearly match their deeply held and internalized values.

Pulling back from their active lifestyle to reflect can add depth to ENFPs' soulwork. This space and time spent alone allows them to find the balance that their introverted Feeling function can provide. Many ENFPs use journaling, prayer, or meditation to determine their own needs and priorities. These disciplines offer an internal sense of support or an inner awareness that they are not alone.

"I find that God shows up when I most need to listen and grow—something I have a hard time doing. However, I'm the type of person who finds it easy, if not imperative, to see the connections among all things and understand how God might be acting in my life."

SHANNON, 44, PSYCHOLOGIST

ENFPs often use their quiet time to decide what is most important to them. By focusing their soulwork on making these judgments, they can develop a rationale for reducing or eliminating some of the activities that crowd their lives. This time to reflect brings new awareness of their inner emotional state.

Thus, the auxiliary function of introverted Feeling provides balance for the ENFPs' Intuition, giving them a better understanding of what will provide the most meaning and value to themselves and others from all the choices their extraverted Intuition envisions.

The Third Gift for ENFPs: Thinking

Not as much is documented or agreed upon about how the third, or tertiary, function expresses itself in any of the 16 types.* The **third function** for ENFPs is Thinking. The domain of the Thinking function includes logical argument, cause-effect reasoning, objectivity, and a search for clarity.

---

*Whether the third function is extraverted or introverted is not well documented in theory or practice. We therefore suggest that people observe how they use it in both the outer (extraverted) and inner (introverted) worlds at different times to see which is most helpful.

For all of the 16 types, the third function tends to evolve later in life, generally after the first two functions are clearly developed. However, many ENFPs are assisted early on if they choose one of the many educational tracks that emphasize logical reasoning and decision-making, the domain of Thinking, their third function. Thus, many ENFPs benefit from being able to reach logical conclusions about matters that are important for them when they *consciously* try to do so. As they seek to enrich their spirituality, many ENFPs use their third function, Thinking, to:

- Evaluate the spiritual traditions or faith systems to which they were exposed by taking an objective look at their own beliefs, seeking consistencies, logical proofs, or evidence of truths; and
- Participate in intellectually rigorous work to establish what is just and fair, right or wrong, and true or false as they work to establish their own spiritual criteria and standards.

ENFPs in the Storms of Life

The Least Accessible Gift for ENFPs:
Introverted Sensing

For all of the 16 types, the fourth function is called the **inferior function** because it is the most difficult to use consciously and effectively. The inferior function can be a source of irritation and oversights that can threaten meaning and purpose, relationships, competency, or even careers—but at its best it can be a source of rest or richness in the storms of life, in moving toward deeper spirituality, or in exploring issues as we age. For ENFPs, the inferior function is introverted Sensing.

For everyone, life delivers events and circumstances that we cannot control—even the most fortunate of us eventually have to deal with the relinquishment of relationships, work situations, or dreams.

And as we age, the human condition demands that we face the diminishment of our own abilities and eventually our lives. While our soulwork may help us prepare for and weather these storms, knowing our psychological type can help us understand how these storms will affect us and where we might seek refuge.

The dominant extraverted Intuition function of ENFPs provides some natural coping skills. ENFPs scan the horizon for insights of all kinds to bring to bear on the situation. Their natural optimism keeps them buoyed up, unless the storm unleashes its full fury. Additionally, they usually have many friends, affiliations, and supportive resources that they can call upon for assistance.

The auxiliary function of introverted Feeling also provides some help. While their natural tendency may be to overextend themselves, ENFPs can seek some solitude to give their introverted Feeling auxiliary function a chance to be heard. Going on a retreat, if only to spend a few quiet hours in nature, may give ENFPs time to reflect on how the situation is affecting them. When life is particularly hectic, even if it is difficult to schedule, a longer retreat might be necessary.

Many ENFPs find that the storms of life are the impetus for adding structure or discipline to their soulwork. They may turn to reading, prayer, or meditation more regularly. Reviewing past journal entries serves to remind ENFPs where they have stumbled before, what helped them, and how they have grown.

"When my business failed, I couldn't sleep past five in the morning. I started using that time for journaling and meditation. I know that 'still, small voice' speaks to me only when I stop the chase, quiet down, and listen. Now, even though such discipline on my part is a challenge, life seems easier when I start my day with the grounding that comes from listening for God."

DEVON, 43, CONSULTANT

Cutting back on activities, amusements, or other external pulls is another way to slow the pace and create a space for soulwork. Learning to say "no" to the requests of others—particularly hard for ENFPs because they may seek to be all things to all people—can also supply some time, even if it is only for rest.

"When I learned that others would respect my needs and still love me, I felt a great sense of relief about saying 'no.' I discovered that many requests can be satisfied by other people or resources. Giving myself time and nourishment makes it even more viable for me to offer spiritual and emotional support to others."

SARA, 50, SALES MANAGER

When the Storms Overwhelm

However, the storms of life often swell beyond our natural capacity to cope. While life's tragedies strain all of us, no matter how intense our soulwork and regardless of our psychological type, the stormy times for ENFPs can be intensified if circumstances include any of the following factors:

- When the problems cause them to focus primarily on the facts involved in order to make immediate decisions. Because ENFPs' attention is oriented toward the big picture, they would rather procrastinate than attend to the unvarnished reality and details of an impending or immediate crisis.
  "I was just about to leave on a pilgrimage when I found out I was diabetic and needed to immediately start a restricted diet. Deciding whether or not to go put me in a real quandary because I wasn't sure that the foods I needed would be available. I changed my mind several times over—my body seemed at war with my soul. I was depressed, totally locked in by the reality of my illness. My despair at being diabetic and its reality of a possible reduction in my activities took me by surprise."
  SONJA, 51, HUMAN-RESOURCES PROFESSIONAL

- When they lose track of the important while trying to cope with the urgent, ENFPs can become stressed when they realize how much there is to do and how little time or energy they have to do it. If a crisis requires a barrage of activity, they may get caught up in the frenzy and not give time to their souls. Feeling frazzled, and, in times of loss, bereft of opportunities, can lead ENFPs to a loss of purpose.

- When a loss of a personal relationship seems inevitable or final.

  "As I worked to launch a new business endeavor, I was so busy with all the details that I lost my grip on what was going on around me. I failed to recognize an attempt by a junior partner (who was probably jealous) to mar or perhaps even destroy my professional reputation. Because I care so much about relationships, I was shocked to find that my colleague could operate from such different premises. For a while I had to fight cynicism, but now I realize this was a hugely important experience for me, opening a path for deeper soulwork."

  JIM, 38, EXECUTIVE COACH

- When they are forced to face a tragedy *alone*, either physically or emotionally. ENFPs can find being alone with their problems depressing. While most ENFPs have circles of support, those who are without close family or friends to fully share their burdens can be set back.

In the most despairing moments, all types can be caught by overuse of their strengths, relying too much on their dominant function. The worst time for ENFPs is when all options seem to be closed and all resources are exhausted—a "no way out" situation or a lose-lose scenario. The finality and certainty of some life events challenge ENFPs' sunny optimism and "all things are possible—only believe" attitude. When these dark times come, ENFPs can become obsessed with finding the newest, latest, or most attractive spiritual options or resources. However, when even *these* possibilities do not work, many ENFPs reach bottom and stop striving for an answer. In the worst storms, a totally different approach to soulwork may be their only refuge.

"My mother's death was the worst experience I've ever had of loss. Because I was an only child, my single mother and I grew to rely on each other to surmount all of life's challenges. As a single adult, after my own brief marriage, I grew even closer to my mother because of our similar experiences

with divorce. *The suddenness of her unexpected death was overwhelming—she had always been there for me but then she was gone. It was so final; I had no control; and there were no other possibilities. In the intervening years, however, I've learned that suffering has a purpose. I am cognizant of the little daily enjoyments of relationships with others—the times I used to take for granted."*

NAOMI, 50, SALES TRAINER

"Looking back, I can't believe I was so oblivious to how overly committed I was, but it took a major auto accident to bring me to my senses. The accident was a direct result of trying to be two places at the same time, skidding out in the snow by driving too fast. Lying in the hospital after reconstructive facial surgery, I had a lot of time to introspect. No career was worth the time I'd been spending away from my family, friends, and God. I vowed to make some changes in my priorities. I wrote down my values and commitments. Now every few months I review these to see whether my life is on track with these values."

CALLIE, 37, CONSULTANT

Clues that ENFPs are being overwhelmed:	• Depression, loss of positive outlook • Frequent incidents involving obsessing, frustrations with typically overlooked details, or preoccupation with health concerns
How to help ENFPs:	• Suggest that they find time and space for reflection and rest
For self-help:	• Take time for physical needs—good food, exercise, massage or other body, sensual, or health-related experiences • Set limits—say no

The Gifts of the Inferior Function—Rest and Richness

Even though using one's inferior function is stressful, an irony of psychological type is that *a path to serenity and rest is to intentionally use the inferior function.* For the ENFP, the inferior function of Sensing is opposite the dominant function of Intuition. Therefore, its *conscious use* requires shutting down that which is most natural and easy, the Intuitive function, which may have gotten out of control while trying to cope with the storm.

For ENFPs, pursuing activities that use their inferior function, introverted Sensing, forces them to concentrate, focus, and determine the current reality of their lives right now. Ways to intentionally engage the introverted Sensing function include:

- Giving regular time to soulwork through meditation, yoga, or other pursuits that require mental absorption and therefore help clear the mind of clutter and chatter.
- Pampering the body with massage, relaxing baths, regular and strenuous exercise, or other practices where the focus is on physical needs.

  "I've learned that occasionally taking a sick day sometimes keeps me from getting really sick. Using my 'day off' to rest can reenergize me in a way that sticking to the task cannot."

  DENYS, 51, SMALL-BUSINESS OWNER

- Concentrating on the immediate impact of the situation: emotions, health, fatigue, etc. In assessing what is *really* happening, not what they want to have happen, ENFPs can take necessary steps to reduce their stress.

  "I need to take time to pay attention to my body and how it is responding to my situation. Tapping into this sort of information brings incredible insights about how I truly feel about a given person, job, or situation—if I get a headache after an encounter with someone, I use that data to determine what in the relationship is stressful to me."

  ROSA, 60, ADULT EDUCATOR

In soulwork for each type, richness, depth, and development come through the inferior function. As useful as it is to understand the inferior function in the storms of life, it provides more benefits as we seek to grow.

In the first half of life we define ourselves, both in work and relationships, through our dominant and auxiliary functions. In the second half of life, the gifts of our inferior function can aid us as we seek to become all that we can be. When we don't take advantage of this natural development of our psychological type, we can become stuck.

Midlife also gives clarity to the brevity of our lives. This compels many of us almost unconsciously to seek richness from unfamiliar experiences as well as to complete the psychological tasks we may have bypassed at an earlier age. As we journey toward wholeness and completion, we can open ourselves to new avenues that are outside of our routines by relinquishing the control our dominant function exerts. Adding spiritual practices that incorporate the attributes of our inferior function can give our soulwork new dimension and zest.

The first two functions, Intuition and Feeling, give ENFPs a vision of future possibilities and a set of values to determine what is most important. To continue to grow, ENFPs need the spiritual richness of introverted Sensing. They need to pay attention to the impact of soulwork on their lives *right now*.

INTROVERTED SENSING SOULWORK

This involves:

- Structured time for reflective spiritual discipline to focus on depth and clarity of understanding;
- Using the five senses—what can be seen, heard, touched, smelled, or tasted—to enrich spirituality;
- Applying soulwork to practical, personal needs; and

- Reflecting on or participating in the continuity of traditions or rituals that have stood the test of time.

ENFPs can become reacquainted with their spiritual nature as they find meaning in things they previously overlooked. While they may continue with their favorite methods of soulwork, renewal may come from the spiritual pathways that are naturally the domain of ISTJs and ISFJs:

- *My nurturing now often comes from the sensory world—feeling the rain on my face, the wind blowing my hair, touching a sculpture, studying a painting, experiencing physical movement through dance or exercise, and seeing or tasting colorful foods.*
- *Alone during prayer, I often become flooded with joy for my own physical being. I breathe, I feel my own body and become concretely aware of the beauty and mystery of life—I am alive!*
- *Preparing the Sabbath meal in the traditional way gives me a sense of the rhythm of my weeks—something which I otherwise would not have noticed in my busy life. Small disciplines practiced routinely bring me contentment in a way my haphazard practices did not. The discipline of the Sabbath arrangements and its meaning for our family make me focus on one thing—seeing God in the events of life.*
- *Each morning I remind myself of the upcoming events of just this day. Remaining in the present—paying close attention to myself, the situation, and others—while letting the past go and the future take care of itself has opened a special kind of serenity for me.*
- *Previously, my soulwork energized me for helping others. Now I use some of that time to practice yoga. I've realized that honoring my physical body in all its wonder is a significant way of doing soulwork.*

I am thankful for

My enthusiasm for all the wonderful possibilities that exist
in the world
My imagination and insights
My resourcefulness and optimism
My emphasis on striving to be all I can be

In the storms of life, I can find shelter by

Quieting down, removing the busy distractions from my life
Allowing myself to rest to nurture my soul
Focusing on what is truly of value to me

To honor myself and my pathway to God, I can

Give free reign to my imagination as I find creative options
for soulwork
Develop my own spiritual philosophy from the many
avenues I explore
Carve out small amounts of time alone for reflection or
prayer to listen for the inner voice that comes from God

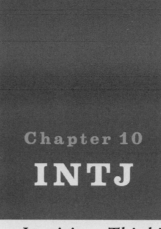

Chapter 10

INTJ

Introversion, Intuition, Thinking, Judging

Finding spirituality
in the inner
world of ideas
and insights

General Description: INTJs tend to be strong individualists who seek novel, logical ways to look at the world. They are visionaries who work hard to attain big-picture goals. With their clear sense of direction, they are tireless and determined in developing hypotheses, ideas, and principles. They see how all the parts fit together, creating new models.

THE GREATEST GIFT FOR INTJs:
INTROVERTED INTUITION WITH THINKING
Creating visions of the future; using reason and objectivity to design methods, strategies, and structures for conceptual understanding—building paradigms based on intellectual acumen.

THE INTJ ROLE IN COMMUNITY:
Challenging traditions, breaking new ground, and questioning the status quo; adding an independent outlook in their endeavors to fashion a better world.

Introverted Intuition is the **dominant function** for INTJs, the function that develops earliest in life, is most comfortable to use, and is easiest to access. Using the dominant function is the natural avenue for each type to pursue soulwork—this is where the soul resides. In other words, for soulwork to be meaningful, the INTJ's dominant function, introverted Intuition, must be satisfied.

◈

INTJ Spirituality: Atmospheres for Soulwork

INTJ spirituality reflects a desire to learn, know, and improve, along with a need to test "the rules and the fools" of traditional spiritual thought or the unrefined backwaters of faith. INTJs search for intellectual stimulation, striving to understand spiritual concepts to build a moral base to guide their decisions about the other areas of their lives. They may engage in in-depth study, deep dialogue with experts, or contemplation in settings that encourage thoughtfulness. Being in this type of environment feeds their dominant introverted Intuition and can provide them with sudden, moving insights into the workings of the Universe. They can become frustrated when others seem comfortable with a more superficial understanding of life's mysteries.

For INTJs, a likely path for soulwork is actively dialoguing with God about prospects for the future. They tend to be systems thinkers by nature, seemingly clairvoyant about what might come to pass, comfortable with the unknown and the exploration of possibilities. Many INTJs find that solitude is important to them for this purpose.

"If I let my mind go, I come up with new insights about our universe and our Creator. I can't put into words how I know, nor can I provide detailed proof, but when I act on these precognitions, the results prove their accuracy."

LINDSAY, 44, CONSULTANT

Spirituality flourishes for INTJs when they are accountable for higher purposes. They enjoy putting their ingenuity to work on efforts of significance using an academic and scholarly perspective. Their worldview can set them apart from "here and now"-oriented people. Complex issues are considered, often with the goal of solving complicated societal concerns. This forward-thinking perspective is valuable to others for the direction it provides. When INTJs commit to a spiritual community, they often become decisive leaders who influence others through the power of their ideas. They can become determined—some might even say stubborn—in the pursuit of a dynamic future vision. Often, their spiritual moments occur when they develop their own new thoughts about universal questions.

"I enjoy working on projects, often alone, that require ingenuity and improvisation—involved issues that have the potential of getting to the root of problems. I often sense that God is trying to talk directly to me as I focus on the task—this is where I can do something of purpose with my life. I interpret my ideas, insights, and perceptions as spiritual messages that are meant to guide me or at least be taken into consideration. I don't tell others about my feeling of being 'chosen' by God, but it radically changed my thinking. I sometimes sense a prophetic calling—trying to bring spirituality and God-centered principles to the ills which face our modern world."

AUBREY, 55, WRITER

"The concept of guilt was instilled early. My spiritual tradition painted a picture of an angry, judgmental God watching me, waiting for the inevitable 'slipups' to occur that would place me in eternal hell. Then about the seventh grade my independent streak began to show. I set out to learn all I could about God and finally concluded that my beliefs were a worthwhile form of insurance: It was better to err on the side of accepting a myth that had no factual basis than to dismiss it and come up short on Judgment Day. My rational mind weighed the consequences and chose the path with the most to gain. 'I believe' . . . what? I still wasn't sure.

"Then in midlife I realized there seemed to be a force guiding my life.

In those quiet moments of solitude when I would shut down my 'throttle' and allow the thought to penetrate my mind, I recognized a spiritual being outside of myself. To me, God is hopeful, not like the punitive figure of my childhood."

NAOMI, 49, CORPORATE TRAINER

Spiritual Paths Using Introverted Intuition

Whether soulwork is new to INTJs or they desire to enrich their spiritual practices, pathways that develop and deepen their insights are most rewarding. Some of the methods or activities include:

- Practicing traditional contemplative disciplines such as meditation, study, prayer, and reflection to encourage their own creativity and discernment. Many INTJs feel most aware of their spiritual nature when pursuing philosophical topics or questions about the larger meaning and purpose of life.
- Engaging actively in debate and dialogue with knowledgeable others about possibilities for society and the best ways to match current knowledge with new, more effective direction. INTJs often serve on long-range planning task forces where they can influence matters and work toward making them happen.
- Spearheading or assisting with projects that require in-depth research. For one INTJ, rewriting the traditional liturgies of her spiritual community to make them more applicable to modern-day circumstances was one of the most meaningful avenues to soulwork she'd experienced.
- Designing, planning, and then producing educational materials on spiritual topics that can be used by others to deepen their beliefs.
- Making space for periods of intense solitude, primarily in outdoor settings or other sanctified places.
  "Once a year I get a combined birthday/anniversary gift—an entire week to be alone at a small retreat center. Each person stays in a private cabin. Throughout the week we can meet with a spiritual director or simply walk the grounds to renew our minds. The first year, I felt guilty about spending so much time away from the family, but

now I know that the entire family benefits from the rejuvenating experience the week is for me."

ANYA, 41, NONPROFIT MANAGER

Clouds That Hinder Soulwork

When the gifts of the dominant function of introverted Intuition are violated, or if INTJs are not affirmed in their strengths, the attraction to the infinite variety of viewpoints and intellectual possibilities for soulwork may be weakened or even extinguished. Major factors that can get in the way of INTJ spirituality include:

- Preferring to work out their own beliefs by themselves or with a trusted other. Many INTJs find it hard to accept a preestablished system or conventional model of spirituality.
  "I sometimes joke that I'm on a lifelong quest for the ultimate, integrated theory of what it is to be human—who we are, how we're made, and how we ought to relate to each other and the world. My personal spiritual experience makes it necessary to include God in the picture, but I can't see our spiritual lives as separate from nor opposed to our physical existence."

KAY, 55, UNIVERSITY PROFESSOR

- Being "at odds" with the idea of a higher power. Some INTJs find the concept of God difficult, especially if their conceptualization is one of an aloof and imperious God who controls or punishes people. In this context, some INTJs may view spirituality as a crutch for the timid and fearful.
- Developing deep but narrow interests, many of which are more pressing than spirituality and respond better to logical thinking. The spiritual aspect of INTJs' lives may be ignored, overlooked, or postponed. INTJs may prefer to stay neutral on the topic until they find the motivation or make the time to give soulwork their *own* deep scrutiny.
- Feeling reluctance to share their innermost selves with others. Privacy and reserve characterize some INTJs, especially in personal matters.

"What I regret as an INTJ is that, whatever my personal perception and interpretation of God, it is a very private matter. I find it difficult to share with others, even my children, and I realize that they are left to come to their own conclusions."

JASON, 35, FINANCIAL ANALYST

The Second Gift for INTJs: Extraverted Thinking

INTJs have extraverted Thinking as their **auxiliary function**. The gifts of extraverted Thinking include using reason and objectivity to assess their insights and determine courses of action to achieve goals, using logical principles.

While INTJs often begin their spiritual journey on their own, mulling over its inherent intricate complexity and intellectual challenges, their auxiliary function of extraverted Thinking may foster a desire to join with others in some form of community, be it a small group or a formal spiritual organization. This gives them opportunities to be open about their spiritual nature and to receive input from others while exploring or determining spiritual truths.

"I used to be pretty adept at 'doing my will in God's name'—I'd envision the entire solution to a problem and expect other people to implement it without a whole lot of debate. Now I try to get their input while I'm still in process. This is never easy, but I don't feel a need to control the whole operation anymore."

NATHAN, 56, MINISTER

Extraverted Thinking also helps INTJs to organize and evaluate their spiritual knowledge and insights. They often reach conclusions by looking at the pros and cons of different alternatives. INTJs tend to seek spiritual communities that emphasize adult education. They enjoy teaching, coaching, or leading others in learning about faith matters. Drawing on their own insights and wealth of scholarship, they can be inspiring teachers, especially with those who engage in the process at a similar intellectual level.

Thus, the auxiliary Thinking function offers balance: While introverted Intuition provides endless insights, extraverted Thinking allows INTJs to bring their gifts to the world at large, working to realign their inner convictions or conquer the problems of life.

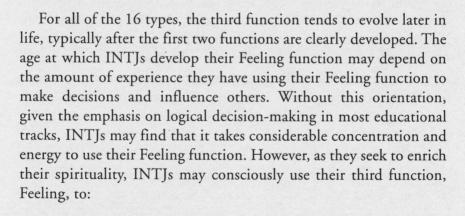

The Third Gift for INTJs: Feeling

Not as much is documented or agreed upon about how the third, or tertiary, function expresses itself in any of the 16 types.* The **third function** for INTJs is Feeling. The domain of the Feeling function includes weighing values; discerning what is important for themselves, others, and community; and determining the impact of decisions on people.

For all of the 16 types, the third function tends to evolve later in life, typically after the first two functions are clearly developed. The age at which INTJs develop their Feeling function may depend on the amount of experience they have using their Feeling function to make decisions and influence others. Without this orientation, given the emphasis on logical decision-making in most educational tracks, INTJs may find that it takes considerable concentration and energy to use their Feeling function. However, as they seek to enrich their spirituality, INTJs may consciously use their third function, Feeling, to:

- Tailor their soulwork to improve their relationships with people and with their Creator; and
- Further refine their priorities by clarifying their values, and then reflecting to determine if the way they are living their lives is congruent with these values.

---

*Whether the third function is extraverted or introverted is not well documented in theory or practice. We therefore suggest that people observe how they use it in both the outer (extraverted) and inner (introverted) worlds at different times to see which is most helpful.

INTJs in the Storms of Life

❖

For all of us, life delivers events and circumstances that we cannot control—even the most fortunate of us eventually have to deal with the relinquishment of relationships, work situations, or dreams. And as we age, the human condition demands that we face the diminishment of our own abilities and eventually our lives. While our soul-work may help us prepare for and weather these storms, knowing our psychological type can help us understand how these storms will affect us and where we might intentionally seek refuge.

The dominant introverted Intuition function of INTJs provides some natural coping skills. INTJs often call on their inner resourcefulness, imagination, and determination to carry them through. Their affinity for the challenge of complex issues also serves them well.

The auxiliary function of extraverted Thinking also provides some help. Using their extraverted Thinking function, INTJs may ask a competent, wise person whom they trust to listen to them with a logical or problem-solving mindset to ferret out the issues, which then need to be addressed in priority order.

"For many years, I didn't think I had any friends—it didn't come naturally to me to be friendly or to seek others out. Now I have a mentor whose brilliance I truly admire and respect who lets me talk, think, analyze, and

express myself, then asks a few cogent questions which gets me through all the muddle and back on track."

JACKIE, 45, SMALL-BUSINESS OWNER

Giving themselves lots of space, privacy, and time out from the fray can also restore the equilibrium of INTJs. A weekend (or longer!) retreat providing solitude, reflection, and meditation will engage their Thinking function and restore INTJs both emotionally and physically.

When the Storms Overwhelm

However, the storms of life often swell beyond our natural capacity to cope. While the tragedies of life strain all of us, no matter how intense our soulwork and regardless of our psychological type, the storms for INTJs can be intensified if the circumstances include any of the following factors:

- When they have to work with too many details that don't fall into logical frameworks. This situation may cause INTJs to feel out of control or to become too detail-bound.
- When unexpected events derail their appropriate and carefully perfected strategies.
  "I had worked so carefully to ensure that we had tended to every aspect in the age discrimination suit our company faced. We had concrete proof that the person we had laid off had not performed well for several years and there was no pattern of similar firings. Our case went out the window when the person who had filed the suit died of a sudden stroke. Being right no longer mattered, but the chaos that followed his death went on for months."

VERN, 61, OPERATIONS OFFICER

- When they are forced to extravert too much. Without alone time to reenergize, INTJs can quickly become bogged down. They may feel so pulled to do things that they have no time to consider the best course of action or the impact they are having on others.

The pressure of so many external activities can be especially frustrating to INTJs.

- When they can't adjust their internal models of the situation. INTJs can lose their objectivity either by being so distracted by the outer world that they have no time to reconsider their plans or by isolating themselves so much that they are closed to new information.

In the most despairing moments, all types can be caught by overuse of their strengths, relying too much on their dominant function. The worst time for INTJs is when they understand their predicament, account for all of its contingencies, carefully make and follow their plan, and still achieve less than adequate results or responses. They have overused their dominant Intuition by relying on their own ability to control the circumstances and regain mastery in the storm that surrounds them. In the worst storms, a totally different approach to soul-work may be their only refuge.

"I was cultivating my business when two merger opportunities came along. They both were aligned with my very successful enterprise. I went after these two new possibilities with gusto. I became so one-sided that I was a classic candidate for burnout. Other than in my professional roles, I was like a robot. Life then lost its spark—I realized that to keep control in the turbulent international marketplace, I had delegated everything but my work. Almost too late, I discovered that I was missing life! God waited for me to understand my one-sidedness and to open up to the needs of those around me, not just the clients I had served so successfully through my work."

JAMES, 33, ARCHITECT

"My spouse and I discussed our family plans while we were still engaged. Year six of our marriage was to mark the arrival of our first child. That year came and went with no pregnancy. We saw several specialists, followed all of the directions, and worked to manage all the variables. It was only after five additional years of struggling, doing all we knew was possible, that we could accept the reality that infertility was our lot in life. That summer

we began to make the most of each day rather than continue to try to control our future. We bought a boat, took several fishing trips, and volunteered to run a youth group where we could make a difference for the kids."

MEGAN, 35, CORPORATE EXECUTIVE

Clues that INTJs are being overwhelmed:	• Hostility, avoidance, or denial of reality—too much TV-watching, computer games, exercise, or overeating, for example • Obsessing about details
How to help INTJs:	• Provide a listening ear so they can uncover the real issues and calm down
For self-help:	• Accomplish a concrete task to regain a sense of mastery—plant the garden, reorganize the office, paint a room, etc. • Pull back from external activities, avoiding meetings or commitments that aren't essential

The Gifts of the Inferior Function—Rest and Richness

Even though using one's inferior function is stressful, an irony of psychological type is that *a path to serenity and rest is to intentionally use the inferior function.* For the INTJ, the inferior function of Sensing is opposite the dominant function of Intuition. Therefore, its *conscious use* requires shutting down what is most natural and easy—the Intuitive function, which may have gotten out of control while trying to cope with the storm.

For INTJs, pursuing activities that use their inferior function, extraverted Sensing, forces them to stop looking for possibilities and suspend their creativity. Through extraverted Sensing, INTJs can get in touch with the tangible aspects of the situation and begin to focus on what can be done immediately. Ways to intentionally engage their extraverted Sensing function include:

- Engaging in detailed crafts or other projects where following directions is essential. Some INTJs choose needlework, gardening, woodworking, etc.
- Reducing the crisis to the facts—its most basic, elemental, and straightforward needs, then moving forward with efficient action.
- Pursuing physical activities such as running, biking, energetic volleyball games, or other sports. Being with people and being a bit wild and crazy can free the soul and later provide fresh inspirations.

In soulwork for each type, richness, depth, and development come through the inferior function. As useful as it is to understand the inferior function for the storms of life, it provides more benefits as we seek to grow.

In the first half of life we define ourselves, both in work and relationships, through our dominant and auxiliary functions. In the second half of life, the gifts of our inferior function can aid us as we seek to become all that we can be. When we don't take advantage of this natural development of our psychological type, we can become stuck.

Midlife also gives clarity to the brevity of our lives. This compels many of us almost unconsciously to seek richness from unfamiliar experiences as well as to complete the psychological tasks we may have bypassed at an earlier age. As we journey toward wholeness and completion we can open ourselves to new avenues that are outside of our routines by relinquishing the control our dominant function exerts. Adding spiritual practices that incorporate the attributes of our inferior function can give our soulwork new dimension and zest.

Through their first two functions, Intuition and Thinking, INTJs naturally see things from unusual perspectives. They are also able to establish principles that help them choose priorities. However, to continue to grow, INTJs need the spiritual richness that comes from extraverted Sensing. They need to pay attention to the impact of spirituality on their lives *right now.*

This involves:

- Experiencing the sacred in what is immediate and real, not in possibilities and the ideal;
- Finding support for one's spiritual path or evidence of the Creator in the details of creation, such as the beauty of rock crystals or the birth of a child;
- Applying spiritual teachings to daily, practical purposes; and
- Enjoying the straightforward gift of being alive.

INTJs become reacquainted with life as they find meaning in things they previously overlooked. They learn to notice "God in the details" and take time to enjoy life's small, tangible, and concrete pleasures. While they may continue many of their favorite methods of soulwork, renewal may come from the spiritual pathways that are naturally the domain of ESFPs and ESTPs:

- *I have a clearer picture of myself and a more realistic assessment of my strengths and needs. A series of health problems taught me the importance of my own physical—not just my intellectual—being. I take more time to savor those days when my legs work well, my stomach's not churning, and my body feels good all over.*
- *Whereas I've always found pleasure in gardening, I now view it as one area of life where I have some fun. Yes, there is the challenge of envisioning just how it should be planted and what the season might bring, but I now take just as much delight in nurturing each flower individually and seeing how the whole process works out.*
- *I've decided to spend time exploring the world by actually going on (instead of just planning for others) an international loaned-executive program. I want to see how the strategies I developed from afar turn out in practical terms. I now enjoy working beside others as we dig wells and I teach new irrigation techniques.*
- *In my late forties I am noticing that all the detailed side of life such as household repairs and maintenance is less of a strain or heroic effort than it used to be. I rather enjoy tackling the mundane necessities.*

- *I have a sense of being in the right place at the right time doing the immediate thing that most needs doing for another person. The simple act of reaching out brings meaning and purpose to my actions.*
- *I used to think of exercise as work—something that I had to do that was distasteful. Now as I walk briskly, I enjoy the feel of the breeze, the coordination of my muscles, and the delight of being alive.*

I am thankful for

My keen insights and inspirations

My love of challenges and complex problems requiring elegant approaches

My ease with systems, strategies, and structures

My determination and drive to perfect my ideas

In the storms of life, I can find shelter by

Developing a plan, then loosening control and accepting the outcome

Inviting logical feedback from a respected and trusted colleague

Giving myself ample time for play and rejuvenation

To honor myself and my pathway to God, I can

Satisfy my intellect with prayer, study, or retreat

Observe the little things right now—the momentary pleasures that can enrich my life when I take time to notice

Put my mind to work for greater purposes that serve my spiritual philosophy

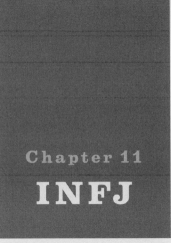

Chapter 11
INFJ

Introversion, Intuition, Feeling, Judging

Finding spirituality
in the inner
world of ideas
and possibilities

General Description: INFJs often have creative and independent ideas for dealing with complex issues and are adept at getting systems to work for people. They tend to focus on long-term possibilities for humankind. INFJs seek life paths that allow them to mirror their integrity, build on their inner ideals, and use their inspirations for the common good. Others can count on them to follow through.

THE GREATEST GIFT FOR INFJs:
INTROVERTED INTUITION WITH FEELING
Seeing life, people, relationships, or the potential of others in a discerning fashion and envisioning innovative solutions to problems.

THE INFJ ROLE IN COMMUNITY:
Contributing future-oriented ideas; understanding the feelings and motivations of others; finding creative ways for people to accomplish tasks while making the process enjoyable.

Introverted Intuition is the **dominant function** for INFJs, the function that develops earliest in life, is most comfortable to use, and is easiest to access. Using the dominant function is the natural avenue for each type to pursue soulwork—this is where the soul resides. In other words, for soulwork to be meaningful, the INFJ's dominant function, introverted Intuition, must be satisfied.

INFJ Spirituality: Atmospheres for Soulwork

In environments where their dominant Intuition is nurtured, spirituality comes easily to many INFJs. With a firm trust of their Intuition, they readily connect with the less tangible areas of life and therefore instinctively work out their own spiritual philosophy. INFJs are most interested in seeking answers to big questions that are significant to their worldview. For example, one INFJ looks for spiritual answers to explain his debilitating health problems. Others call on their spiritual awareness to form a framework through which they make decisions about every aspect of their lives. They often believe there is a God or a power greater than humanity.

INFJs need to work out their own answers to spiritual questions and may study topics in depth. While they enjoy listening to qualified experts or participating in discussions, if INFJs need answers to a particular question, they are more likely to go to a library or bookstore, read several sources, and then come to their own conclusions.

"I spent an extended period of my life (about fourteen years) questioning the existence of God. What other people told me didn't really matter—I needed to build my own arguments. I came to a more complete understanding of what and who God is (as well as what and who God is not!)."

TIM, 52, ATTORNEY

Soulwork for INFJs typically begins in solitude. Contemplative practices such as meditation or prayer come readily, for prayer to many INFJs is simply a space for musing about ideas, searching for input, or gaining wisdom from their Creator to carry themselves through situations with integrity. They often enjoy reading and tend to see lessons for themselves in secular as well as religious writings. Many INFJs use writing to express their spirituality, either privately or to communicate their insights to help others find clarity. Through these efforts, INFJs achieve greater clarity for themselves and are better able to focus their own lives. Their most spiritual moments often come through flashes of intuition—a sense of suddenly knowing something is true for them, perceiving clearly a path they should follow or a plan they should make.

"When I was a teenager, my friends thought I was spiritual just because I was a bit more serious than they were and tended to think about things like the meaning of life. However, when people suggested that I should seek a religious vocation, I didn't want to hear about it. My interest in the spiritual side of life was equal to, not greater than, my other interests.

"Then one day a group of my friends were joking about what life in a seminary might be like. The others were pretty negative, but I pointed out some of the positive aspects of that path. Two hours after this chance discussion I decided to apply to seminary. I have never regretted my choice!

"I realize now that I had an intuitive flash: seminary was right for me. These insights are how I experience things authentically. I don't always work my ideas through—I simply know. That doesn't mean I don't analyze for understanding, but for me the insight comes first. Later, I study to validate what I know to be true. Images and ideas are often a better source of understanding and proof than the most concrete knowledge I can discover."

PAUL, 51, PRIEST

"Perhaps it's because of a very dark childhood, but I struggled for years to find any spiritual connection. Certainly the concept of a loving God is a foreign one. Instead, I was able to meld my own philosophy after a series of dreams in which my grandmother and great-grandmother seemed to reach out to me in love and encouragement, as if we are somehow a part of each other. Spirituality comes alive for me when I picture the interconnectedness of creation. If you've seen a cobweb glistening with golden dew in the morning sunlight, you have a visual image of what I mean. These invisible threads that link the natural world give us our connectedness

and transmit love and care. When these threads are destroyed, people and the earth wither."

CATHERINE, 30, WRITER

Spiritual Paths Using Introverted Intuition

Whether soulwork is new to INFJs or they desire to enrich their spiritual practices, pathways that develop and deepen insights are most rewarding. Some of these methods include:

- Setting aside time for writing down thoughts. INFJs journal to capture hopes and aspirations, use diaries to record events and insights, or write out their prayers, dreams, meditations, or other reflections as aspects of their soulwork.
- Considering artistic endeavors or contemplating works of art as legitimate soulwork. Many INFJs who play musical instruments, paint, or sculpt, lose track of time. These expressions allow for reflection on themes of spirituality, relationships, wholeness, or hope.
- Engaging the imagination. INFJs often create spiritually oriented stories, teaching materials, plays, poetry, or other unusual ways to communicate insights to others. Some INFJs gain new understanding by imagining themselves as specific people in the great stories of their spiritual traditions.
- Conducting independent studies of intriguing topics. INFJs may retreat with a stack of books to an inspiring place and indulge in the luxury of in-depth analyses of topics that feed the soul.
- Helping others find innovative solutions to problems. Coming up with the right focus on an issue or the best way to assist others often fosters their own deep spirituality as they use their talents this way.

Clouds That Hinder Soulwork

When the gifts of the dominant function of introverted Intuition are violated, or if INFJs are not affirmed in their strengths, the instinctive connection with God may be weakened or even extinguished. Major factors that can get in the way of INFJ spirituality include:

- Being in disharmonious circumstances. INFJs tend to idealize people and situations. They want everyone around them to honor commitments, strive to get along, appreciate individual contributions, and help outcasts. If they cannot find a spiritual community that is as committed and mature as they can envision, they may choose to stay away.
- Experiencing cruelty. When this happens, INFJs tend to have difficulty developing a spiritual philosophy.

"Spirituality was not a part of my upbringing; my father considered children a nuisance and ignored us. . . . I had very little experience with compassion and never contemplated whether love acted as a force in our universe. Then as a young adult I was accidentally introduced to God! About the only place my sweetheart's father would let me take her was to a religious service that an out-of-town revivalist was leading. If I'd known in advance what happened at those gatherings, I never would have gone. Between the hymns, the hand clapping, and the heightened emotionalism, I nearly crawled under the seats to escape. But—when the singing stopped and the invited speaker began to talk, the message rang true. I wonder if soulwork would ever have had any pull for me without that evening's experience. I had a lot to learn about the spiritual side of life, but I've never wavered in the essence of my belief."

FRANK, 70, RETIRED BUSINESSMAN

- Being in atmospheres that do not allow for examination of beliefs. While INFJs may intuitively connect with soulwork, many also need to go through a rational process of questioning and study to validate a belief and value system. Soulwork without this process may lack meaning for them.
- Having frustrations with their own lack of perfection. INFJs often fall short of their own expectations for pursuing spirituality, for being actively and directly involved with others, or for sharing their ideas for improving programs or projects. In addition, INFJs

are often hesitant to speak up, even when they clearly see solutions to problems that would aid others. They don't want to "toot their own horns" to be appreciated for the expertise they can contribute.

"After many years of trying to pray 'perfectly,' it suddenly occurred to me that I had never prayed 'well.' My ideal was shattered, but bit by bit I came to understand that while I hadn't met the ideal described in books, my prayer style was all right with God. I quit trying to follow pathways others had prescribed for me. I know now that many people of my type dislike formula, regular or repetitive prayers. My style is spiritual and my prayers work best for me."

EVELYN, 56, COUNSELOR

The Second Gift For INFJs: Extraverted Feeling

INFJs have extraverted Feeling as their **auxiliary function**. The gifts of extraverted Feeling include being aware of the reactions, needs, and values of others, discerning what is of most importance, and reaching out to people.

While INFJs tend to begin their spiritual journey in solitude, their auxiliary function of extraverted Feeling often fosters a need for some sort of community setting, whether a small group or a large organization. They frequently have a deeply felt desire to encourage others in soulwork so that everyone can reach their full potential. To fulfill this desire, they may form or lead small groups, teach, or help create new programs or opportunities.

While many INFJs may be hesitant to share their spiritual journey with people other than close friends or in one-to-one situations, they enjoy meaningful discussions that help them mold their own beliefs.

"I choose my study companions and experiences carefully. I get frustrated by pat answers or any format that doesn't allow me to put forth my own conclusions or add to what the leader or materials are saying. I'd rather take the text to a quiet spot and try to figure out what it means to me and my own circumstances. However, being in a group inspires me in a way soli-

tude can't provide. That's worth my time even if I don't necessarily learn anything new."

PERI, 36, EDITOR

Thus, the auxiliary function provides balance: While introverted Intuition discerns the possibilities, extraverted Feeling points INFJs toward appropriate action, bringing their soulwork from their private realm into their relationships with others and the world at large.

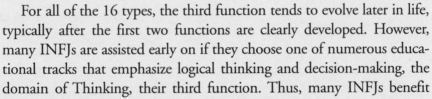

The Third Gift for INFJs: Thinking

Not as much is documented or agreed upon about how the third, or tertiary, function expresses itself in any of the 16 types.* The **third function** for INFJs is Thinking. The domain of the Thinking function includes logical argument, cause-effect reasoning, objectivity, and a search for clarity.

For all of the 16 types, the third function tends to evolve later in life, typically after the first two functions are clearly developed. However, many INFJs are assisted early on if they choose one of numerous educational tracks that emphasize logical thinking and decision-making, the domain of Thinking, their third function. Thus, many INFJs benefit from being able to reach logical conclusions about matters that are important for them when they *consciously* try to do so. As they seek to enrich their spirituality, many INFJs use their third function, Thinking, to:

- Evaluate the spiritual traditions or faith systems to which they are exposed by doing an objective study of their own beliefs, seeking consistencies, logical proofs, or evidence of truths; and
- Participate in intellectually rigorous work to establish what is just and fair, right or wrong, and true or false as they work to establish their own spiritual criteria and standards.

Whether the third function is extraverted or introverted is not well documented in theory or practice. We therefore suggest that people observe how they use it in both the outer (extraverted) and inner (introverted) worlds at different times to see which is most helpful.

The Least Accessible Gift for INFJs: Extraverted Sensing

For all of the 16 types, the fourth function is called the **inferior function** because it is the most difficult to use consciously and effectively. The inferior function can be a source of irritation and oversights that can threaten meaning and purpose, relationships, competency, or even careers—but at its best it can be a source of rest or richness in the storms of life, in moving toward deeper spirituality, or in exploring issues as we age. For INFJs, the inferior function is extraverted Sensing.

◆

For all of us, life delivers events and circumstances that we cannot control—even the most fortunate of us eventually have to deal with the relinquishment of relationships, work situations, or dreams. And as we age, the human condition demands that we face the diminishment of our own abilities and eventually our lives. While our soul-work may help us prepare for and weather these storms, knowing our psychological type can help us understand how these storms will affect us and where we might intentionally seek refuge.

The dominant introverted Intuition function of INFJs provides some natural coping skills. INFJs believe that the future can be made better, giving them an inherently optimistic bent that may help them to weather the small storms fairly well. Additionally, since INFJs tend to weave spirituality into their everyday lives, they can readily access spiritual resources in times of loss.

The auxiliary function of extraverted Feeling also provides some help. INFJs often find that talking through their thoughts and experiences with others helps them understand how they have been affected. However, while they may not want advice and are seldom open to it when struggling, they can experience the gifts of their extraverted Feeling by talking with someone who can empathize or listen attentively.

"I felt like there was a wall between me and my coworkers, as if my presence and problems didn't even show a blip on their radar screens. After

obsessing with the matter too long, I finally talked with a person I could trust who just listened as I poured out my feelings. As I described my dilemma, I gained relief from my pent-up emotions and could see a way out of the situation."

CORINNE, 27, ADMINISTRATOR

Some INFJs seek release for their emotions, losing themselves in the most sentimental old movies or books in order to allow their emotions to flow. Others find it therapeutic to use their extraverted Feeling to become aware of the needs of those around them. One INFJ who had recently been widowed found that she could set aside her own grief by concentrating on the impact of her husband's death on their children, his business partners, and their friends.

When the Storms Overwhelm

However, the storms of life often swell beyond our natural capacity to cope. While life's tragedies strain all of us, no matter how intense our soulwork and regardless of our psychological type, the stormy times for INFJs can be intensified if the circumstances include any of the following factors:

- When their natural tendency toward perfection is triggered. INFJs may deepen their own sense of loss by holding themselves accountable for things beyond their control. When others are involved, INFJs may berate themselves for not being supportive enough, not finding the right things to say or do, or not owning up to their own part in failures.
- When they are forced to monitor too many details, a task that requires them to use their inferior function, extraverted Sensing. They may overlook crucial facts (always a weakness) or spend too much time on unimportant items.
  "Despite our daughter's illness, I thought I was in control of my workload; after all, I had an assistant to take care of all of the administrative details. However, the day before a retreat for two hundred fifty teenagers, I discovered I had given my assistant the wrong dates. The kids were coming that very evening, but the facilities were

reserved for the following night! With that one small mistake that nearly resulted in disaster, I realized how stressed I was."

JOSH, 38, WRITER

- When other people are too full of doom and gloom, dragging the INFJ down along with them.
- When they are expected to extravert too much. If INFJs spend too much of their time in the company of others, they may find themselves exhausted.

  "The week of my 72-year-old father's wedding was difficult. Every minute was booked with appointments, chauffeuring, and family responsibilities. Friday evening found me on the couch with my third bowl of popcorn, unable to rise or contemplate greeting another relative or friend."

BOB, 55, TEACHER

In the most despairing moments, all types can be caught by overuse of their strengths, relying too much on their dominant function. The worst time for INFJs is when they realize that no matter how hard they try to come up with a solution, the problem is beyond their influence or command. They have overused their dominant Intuition by envisioning too many possibilities, trying to resolve things alone, researching information, and pursuing their more solitary spiritual path. When these dark times come, INFJs can further isolate themselves, convinced that the whole world is against them. In the worst storms, a totally different approach to soulwork may be the only refuge.

"When my illness was diagnosed, I thought I could handle my own needs. After all, I had studied meditation, I knew which spiritual readings would comfort me, and I took the time to do these things. The results? Nothing. I was still as frightened as before. I felt as if my carefully crafted soulwork was a failure. This was also the point at which my true healing began, because I finally shared with my spouse my fears about the choices I was facing. I learned that in despair, help can come to me through other people. My own resources can only go so far."

JACKIE, 45, INDUSTRIAL PSYCHOLOGIST

"We knew that my dad was dying, so each time I visited him I pulled myself together, wanting to say good-bye in a way that showed my love. However, seven days later as he lingered and I left his room yet another time, I finally gave up. I told God, 'There's no way I can go back into that hospital alone. I'll fall to pieces and that won't be fair to my father.' It's tough to describe what happened next, but apparently when I relinquished my hope and control, I opened the door for God to help me. That night I dreamed about my father's first moments in heaven. God listed all of the gifts Dad had given me. I awoke with a new sense of peace that carried me back to his sickbed and lasted through the funeral."

LYLE, 31, CONSULTANT

Clues that INFJs are being overwhelmed:	• Unnatural pessimism • Too much time or energy is spent on activities such as watching TV, overeating, obsessive exercising, "mindless" shopping, etc.
How to help INFJs:	• Divert their attention from the crisis at hand, giving them a chance to act as if everything is normal
For self-help:	• Take stock of all work-related responsibilities, temporarily handing off the detail-oriented ones • Allow others to handle anything important that requires extended analysis or precise paperwork—tax returns, medical forms, etc.

The Gifts of the Inferior Function—Rest and Richness

Even though using one's inferior function is stressful, an irony of psychological type is that *a path to serenity and rest is to intentionally use the inferior function.* For the INFJ, the inferior function of Sensing is opposite the dominant function of Intuition. Therefore, its *conscious use* requires shutting down what is most natural and easy—the Intuitive function, which may have gotten out of control while trying to cope with the storm.

For INFJs, pursuing activities that use their inferior function, extraverted Sensing, forces them to stop looking for possibilities and suspend their creativity. Ways to intentionally engage the extraverted Sensing function include:

- Giving full attention to pursuits where following plans or directions to the letter may be necessary. Examples are wallpapering, painting, jigsaw puzzles, and intricate craft projects such as needlepoint or electronics kits.
- Engaging in physical pursuits such as biking, aerobics, or swimming, where the emphasis is on body movements, speed, techniques, and awareness of the here and now.
- Concentrating on the facts of a situation—what was actually said, what really happened. Ignoring the implications and possible outcomes for a bit allows the Intuition to rest. The same rest can come through time spent in the outdoors.

In soulwork for each type, richness, depth, and development come through the inferior function. As useful as it is to understand the inferior function for the storms of life, it provides more benefits as we seek to grow.

In the first half of life we define ourselves, both in work and relationships, through our dominant and auxiliary functions. In the second half of life, the gifts of our inferior function can aid us as we seek to become all that we can be. When we don't take advantage of this natural development of our psychological type, we can become stuck.

Midlife also gives clarity to the brevity of our lives. This compels many of us almost unconsciously to seek richness from unfamiliar experiences as well as to complete the psychological tasks we may have bypassed at an earlier age. As we journey toward wholeness and completion, we can open ourselves to new avenues that are outside of our routines by relinquishing the control our dominant function exerts.

Adding spiritual practices that incorporate the attributes of our inferior function can give our soulwork new dimension and zest.

The first two functions, Intuition and Feeling, give INFJs a vision of future possibilities, their own specially crafted spiritual understanding, and a set of values to determine what is most important. However, to continue to grow, INFJs need the spiritual richness of extraverted Sensing. They need to pay attention to the impact of spirituality on their lives *right now.*

EXTRAVERTED SENSING SOULWORK

This involves:

- Finding the spiritual in what is immediate and real, not in future possibilities and the ideal;
- Finding support for one's spiritual path or evidence of the Creator in the details of creation, such as the beauty of rock crystals or the birth of a child;
- Applying spiritual teachings to daily, practical purposes; and
- Enjoying the straightforward gift of just being alive.

INFJs become reacquainted with the spiritual as they find meaning in the small everyday realities they previously overlooked. While they may continue many of their favorite methods of soulwork, renewal may come from the spiritual pathways that are naturally the domain of ESTPs and ESFPs:

- *I am energized by exploring, whether near home or on vacation. A camera or journal in hand helps me appreciate the small wonders I used to pass right by. Recently I realized that I had never really looked at a* single *flower before. I was focusing on the overall effect of a bouquet, not realizing the intricate design of each individual blossom with its stamen, petals, and filaments. Now at least once a day I try to find beauty in life's details instead of in the big picture.*
- *I had always thought that routine prayers were meaningless, but lately I find a certain comfort in reciting centuries-old litanies. Some are so complete, capturing in a few lines what it has taken me years to express to God.*

- *All my life, beautiful weather simply prepared my heart to worship God and called me to gather for services. But last Sunday, my soul said, "No, let's visit God at the park, not in a building," and I did!*
- *In one of our last conversations before my mother died, the two of us took turns naming our favorite food, song, lake, and so on. I'd never really bothered with those little things before. Now I understand the true gift of knowing those specifics about her. I feel a special connection with Mother every time I eat scones with currant jam.*
- *I always thought that square dancing was for older people until I was "coerced" into filling in for a friend's sick spouse. I had such fun stomping, shuffling, and do-si-do-ing that I then "coerced" my partner to join us the next time. Now we're avid dancers and look forward to the simple pleasures of being with others and the magic that happens when everyone follows the caller.*

I am thankful for

My creativity, which allows me to envision different solutions
My optimism in trying circumstances
My ability to help people recognize their potential
The way I can communicate to others

In the storms of life, I can find shelter by

Realizing that it is okay to seek help
Finding a listening ear so that I can discern my feelings
Assessing the details and tasks, giving away what I cannot handle

To honor myself and my pathway to God, I can

Find creative ways to engage my imagination
Create space for myself to be alone with my thoughts, prayers, or musings
Notice the spiritual in the details of creation

Have confidence in the truth,
although you may not be able
to comprehend it, although you
may suppose its sweetness to be
bitter, although you may
shrink from it at first. Trust in
the Truth . . . Have faith in the
Truth and live it.

— BUDDHA,
DHAMMAPADA

Thinking
Spirituality

Thinking Types find satisfying soulwork through:

- Living the spiritual life through the intellect
- Gaining spiritual insight by observation, study, or debate
- Appreciating the beauty of wisdom and the clarity of teachings
- Seeing applications for standards of accountability and structures for fairness and order
- Learning through exploration of the "thorny" questions of life
- Working to establish universal principles and truths
- Evaluating the logic, effectiveness, and justice of spiritual practices or beliefs

Preferred Extraverted Thinking Soulwork (ESTJ and ENTJ)

- Prayer/meditation as a search for answers, truths, and guiding principles and explanations
- Soulwork through debate and discourse
- Active spiritual life, in the midst of duty and a quest for effectiveness
- Service through working to change structures that seem ineffective, corrupt, or unfair

Preferred Introverted Thinking Soulwork (ISTP and INTP)

- Prayer/meditation by discussing with God principles and ethics
- Soulwork through integrating observations and rational thought
- Reflective spiritual life, in the course of inquiry, study, and wrestling with difficult issues
- Service through determining systems for actualization of improvements

Suggestions for Thinking Soulwork

1. In the Buddhist tradition, the ten perfections are generosity, virtue, doing without, wisdom, energy, forbearance, truthfulness, resolution, love, serenity. Choose one of these and answer the following questions:

- How would you define it?
- What happens when you live your life by this perfection?
- What happens when you fail to do so?

- If you were to make changes in your life to come closer to this perfection, what would they be?
- What would be the outcomes or results?

2. Kahil Gibran said, "I have learned silence from the talkative, toleration from the intolerant, and kindness from the unkind; yet strange, I am ungrateful to those teachers." [1]

- What is (are) the paradox(es) in the above quote?
- When have you found these paradoxes to be true?
- What were the costs/benefits of learning in this fashion?
- Record some examples in your life where the statement has been true or false. What/who were your teachers?
- What are the other areas in your life where you could use a teacher?

3. *From the cowardice that dare not face new truth*
   From the laziness that is contented with half truth
   From the arrogance that thinks it knows all truth,
   Good lord, deliver me.
   —Prayer from Kenya[2]

   To what topics could you apply your gift of Thinking? Select an interesting global or personal issue. Examples might be urban sprawl, societal responsibility toward education, allocation of resources, or something within your own sphere of influence. Evaluate the causes and effects of the situation and the pros and cons of different approaches or solutions. How have truths that were honored in the past been violated? As you ponder the issue, how are you called to work toward an answer?

4. **For the discipline of study:** As you read or hear about a topic, gather the facts and meanings. Devote the majority of your study time to discerning the correctness of what you have read. Is it true? Even if it's true, is it right or wrong? Positive or negative? Then, consider the impact of your deliberations on yourself or others.

5. **For the discipline of meditation or prayer:** Consider a single precept or dogma of your spiritual tradition and meditate/pray about the implications of following or not following it and your rationale for your choice.

6. **For the discipline of simplicity:** Simone Weil said, *"The danger is not lest the soul should doubt whether there is any bread, but lest, by a lie, it should persuade itself that it is not hungry."*[3] How could your need for clarity and truth block you from trying any of the "simple" forms of soulwork? Your need to be competent or right?

7. **For the discipline of celebration:** Find your own way to acknowledge those times when justice prevails, truths are made clear, or reason and logic result in an elegant solution or outcome. Some examples to stimulate your thoughts of celebration: Reward your colleagues when everyone pulls their own weight. Do something special with your child when he or she holds to a principle. Revel in the concise and logical writing of a favorite author. Set aside time to appreciate the techniques and splendor of Bach organ cantatas. Take time to laugh hard at the cleverness of comedy or the absurdities of fools. Make a covenant with God about a change in your soulwork or guiding principles and mark each successful anniversary (perhaps weekly at first!) of the keeping of that covenant.

8. Choose a spiritual concept such as truth, love, wholeness, joy, justice, or fairness.

   - What are its attributes?
   - How can you tell when it exists?
   - How does this concept work effectively with people, organizations, or the world? How does it work ineffectively?

Ponder this information as tangible evidence of these intangible forces. How does your understanding of these concepts deepen?

9. Find two or three people who share your willingness to include objective analysis or even doubt as part of soulwork. Meet regularly to discuss a sacred text, a secular book, or a current issue. Begin by pointing out everything that is *wrong* with the opinions presented by the authors or text and then move toward finding those aspects with which you can agree.

10. Indulge in the study of a scientific subject or aspect of natural history that interests you—either through reading or by direct observation. What principles are in operation? What explanations can you discover? How might these principles and explanations help you understand your own experiences and the choices you face?

11. To bring rest to the work of the mind, consider something that simply *cannot* be explained logically by what is currently known: the vastness of the night skies, the infinite varieties of bird species, or the precise balance of elements that makes life on Earth possible. Observe the power of a thunderstorm or the crashing of the ocean's pounding surf. Watch a butterfly come out of its cocoon. Set out honey for ants and wait for the army to communicate the feast. Ponder the infiniteness and boundaries of your intellect to understand the world.

12. Consider what you *know* to be true about an aspect of spirituality. For example, you might list what you know to be true about:

   - The strength of forgiveness
   - The power of making peace
   - The Golden Rule and other spiritual precepts
   - The Creator and the connectedness of the Universe

   Where are the consistencies? How can you use this information to reconcile the inconsistencies in situations around you? Apply this same process to the platitudes and slogans from the secular world (e.g., "Nice folks finish last . . . ") in order to find your own truth.

13. Take a risk. Venture into an area of spirituality where you have no previous experience and are therefore not an expert. For example: Study the role of liturgical dance (you don't have to actually *dance*), offer to teach children in your spiritual community, or take a course in counseling or other matters of the heart. Sometimes by opening yourself to areas where you have no established competency, you can relinquish a possibly too-tight rein of control—spooky but adventurous.

14. Set aside time to listen to music that frees your mind from analysis—instrumentals or songs with words in a language you don't speak. Perhaps record several of these on a single tape so that you can have uninterrupted music for soulwork while relaxing in a sacred spot.

15. Reconsider your spiritual life through the lens of truth. Strive for honesty as you pray about your hopes, fears, doubts, and blessings. Perhaps use the moral codes of your faith (Ten Commandments, Golden Rule, Five Precepts) to reexamine whether your actions are guided by your principles. Where might change need to occur?

16. What major question(s) hinders your soulwork? Evil in the world? The injustices you see? The mythical or unproven aspects of the spiritual tradition in which you were raised? The lack of true compassion in people who claim to be spiritual? Sort through and identify the key source of discord or resistance, then work through this issue, either in discussion with people who have explained it to their own satisfaction, through reading, or through your own thoughtful meditation.

17. George Fox, founder of The Religious Society of Friends (Quakers), implored us, *"Do rightly, justly, truly, holily, equally to all people in all things; and that is according to that of God in everyone, and the witness of God, and the wisdom of God, and the life of God in yourselves."*[4] Try each day to perform one act that restores justice, applies fairness, or does right by another. Perhaps it is as simple as instruct-

ing your children that whoever cuts the pie chooses their slice last; or bringing to management's attention a policy that is unfair; or finding an opportunity to return a favor or kind deed.

18. In what situations do you feel inadequate, incompetent, or ill at ease? What seems to be a theme in your complaints? Think about these areas with a critical yet compassionate eye. How could these be areas where you might learn more about the workings of your soul?

Embrace your:

> Truth
> Logic
> Knowledge
> Linear Focus
> Clarity

Chapter 12

ESTJ

Extraversion, Sensing, Thinking, Judging

*Finding spirituality
in the outer world
of principles
and action*

General Description: ESTJs tend to be decisive, to-the-point, and practical organizers who value accomplishment and closure. They use logical analysis to guide their actions. They enjoy being in charge, directing others, and providing structure while monitoring their own and the group's commitments. They are forceful and systematic.

THE GREATEST GIFT FOR ESTJs:
EXTRAVERTED THINKING WITH SENSING
Uncovering truth and seeking justice through objective and efficient problem-solving, moving quickly toward accomplishing practical and necessary tasks.

THE ESTJ ROLE IN COMMUNITY:
Leading people and processes toward tangible accomplishments and goals in a responsible, methodical way in order to make the most of a situation, task, or plan.

> Extraverted Thinking is the **dominant function** for ESTJs, the function that develops earliest in life, is most comfortable to use, and is easiest to access. Using the dominant function is the natural avenue for each type to pursue soulwork—this is where the soul resides. In other words, for soulwork to be meaningful, the ESTJ's dominant function, extraverted Thinking, must be satisfied.

ESTJ Spirituality: Atmospheres for Soulwork

ESTJs approach their soulwork in a manner similar to how they approach the other areas of their lives: pragmatically and purposefully. They often look to spirituality to build a moral foundation for themselves and their families, to widen their social circles, or to provide important traditions and rituals. These goals may lead them to join a spiritual community or other environment that addresses these issues. Then, if they see tangible and direct evidence of the beneficial effects of soulwork, ESTJs may logically work to deepen their own belief system.

"Somewhere during the past years my faith went from something I did to something that was meaningful. My spirituality provides friends on whom I can count for support, a vehicle to serve others, a sense that I'm a part of something bigger than myself, and a connectedness to others worldwide. Overall, I've concluded that it's logical to believe."

SUSAN, 48, PURCHASING AGENT

For ESTJs, spirituality allows them to be a part of a force larger than themselves in order to correct injustices and solve problems. Their outward, goal-oriented leadership—running committees, chairing service projects, or otherwise being responsible to their community—is often motivated spiritually. ESTJs tend to find the most meaningful expressions of soulwork when helping others who, in their eyes, deserve their assistance.

"I once was down on my luck and several friends provided me with money and part-time work. Now I feel it's 'give-back time'—it's the fair and right

thing to do. We must be here for a purpose and I want to believe that my life counts. I want to leave the world in better shape than I found it. Sometimes the way to do that is on my own and sometimes it's with my spiritual community. Regardless, when we need to raise money for a disabled child or natural disaster relief effort, I'm there—often front and center."

DAN, 51, TAX ACCOUNTANT

Fueled by the drive of their dominant function, extraverted Thinking, to seek clarity, ESTJs often perceive the variety of spiritual traditions and practices as systems in conflict. Therefore, no matter what system they choose, ESTJs grasp onto the core principles that provide concrete, direct evidence that there is merit in living by those principles. They often look to and uphold the moral codes, dogmas, or doctrines of their faith as objective standards of conduct for themselves and others. While to the outside world, ESTJs may appear established in a belief system, their inner spirituality is often an ever-deepening aspect of their lives.

"It's not a deliberate process, nor is it as organized as the rest of my life. While I pursue private soulwork to gain more understanding of my spirituality, too much pressure to explain all these inner thoughts or share on a personal level is difficult for me. Many people don't suspect or know just how spiritual I am because I'm uncomfortable with the unknown aspects of it."

MARISSA, 52, SMALL-BUSINESS OWNER

"After I got married, there were peaks and valleys in my spirituality. Between building a career, a house, and a family, life was very full. However, one day while we were driving home from preschool, my daughter asked, 'Why does that building have a "t" up on top?' I realized then that I would be derelict in my duty if my children did not receive spiritual instruction. I began to analyze my own faith. What did I believe? Just what were the pros and cons of involvement and what system could speak to real issues in a direct and honest way?

"It took some soul-searching. I concluded that it was more reasonable to have a faith than not. Before, I think I saw spirituality as an insurance *policy against the ebbs and flows of life. Now I understand how it adds meaning and purpose to all I do."*

MEG, 38, OPERATIONS MANAGER

Spiritual Paths Using Extraverted Thinking

Whether soulwork is new to ESTJs or they desire to enrich their spiritual practices, pathways that aid them in developing principles that apply to real-life issues are often most rewarding. Some of these methods and activities include:

- Determining moral and ethical standards, using established traditions or religious systems as a base.
  "I struggle with capital punishment and gender issues. They can seem black and white. We need a right and wrong, but when you're dealing with people, those areas get pretty gray. Still, I want a standard to compare against—and the right to voice my informed opinion."

  HENRY, 53, SERVICE-AGENCY DIRECTOR

- Attending structured programs or classes that provide clear examples, practical applications to life experiences, or otherwise deal with "hard issues": parenting, family building, career enhancement, medical ethics, etc.
  "The goals for my spiritual life have to be as conquerable as the goals in other areas of my life. I need a course to complete, a book to finish reading, a specific plan for spiritual growth so I know when and if I've met my goal."

  GRETA, 36, HOMEMAKER

- Incorporating soulwork into everyday occurrences (e.g., reading the newspaper, exercising, or commuting).
  "As I read the morning paper, I literally count my blessings and consider if I should apply my skills to any of the problems the news describes."

  DUSTIN, 56, ATTORNEY

- Taking leadership roles such as administrators, managers, or committee chairs of projects where a tangible task is to be accomplished or a problem solved. ESTJs tend to enjoy experiences where many come together to do what no one could do alone.
- Going to retreats, rallies, or other large spiritual gatherings to understand the effects of soulwork on each others' lives.

Clouds That Hinder Soulwork

When the gifts of the dominant function of extraverted Thinking are violated, or if ESTJs are not affirmed in their strengths, the desire to use soulwork to develop their life-guiding purposes may be weakened or even extinguished. Major factors that can get in the way of ESTJ spirituality include:

- Not seeing any material benefits from spirituality.
  "I find it very easy to ignore the call of my spiritual side. Bills demand to be paid, work projects must be completed, and I devote a considerable amount of energy to community service through my men's club. I do my part and follow my principles in so many aspects of life that I wonder if soulwork is necessary."
  TED, 51, EXECUTIVE

- Desiring proof to ascertain their spiritual reality.
  "There are no facts, nothing is certain. Part of me believes in heaven, yet part of me wonders whether there really is anything beyond our life here. This knowledge gives me a zest for making this life count. However, as I'm learning and growing more in my faith and getting older, I'm more drawn to sort out what I truly believe."
  WILLIAM, 45, VICE PRESIDENT, ADMINISTRATION

- Being asked to depart radically from the tried and true in spiritual practices or disciplines. ESTJs prefer to stay with what's already known and tend not to want to tamper with important truths or traditions.
  "Our spiritual community went to a Friday instead of Saturday format for evening prayers. What a surprise to me and an annoyance to

boot. I find evening prayers on Saturday night as a way to wrap my week and begin anew. I'm not happy with the change and am considering leaving for another community that better fits my schedule."

JOEL, 31, SCHOOL PRINCIPAL

- Observing a violation of accepted codes of conduct, either by those in leadership positions or by a change in the rules. ESTJs may hesitate to support any group that fails to be fair or to hold its leader accountable.

The Second Gift for ESTJs: Introverted Sensing

ESTJs have introverted Sensing as their **auxiliary function.** The gifts of introverted Sensing include appreciating the richness of traditions, noticing the fullness of detail in the world around us, and applying soulwork to practical, personal needs.

While ESTJs naturally concentrate on bringing logic to bear on their activities in the outer world, they also need time alone in order to access their auxiliary function of introverted Sensing. In these quiet moments, ESTJs can determine their own practical, spiritual needs and whether the choices they are making are in line with the facts of the situation.

"After putting all my energy for several months toward pursuing an advanced degree, I had to get away by myself to rethink my situation. I realized that I hadn't given enough thought to whether this profession would allow me to live my life by my principles. Was this the right educational track for me? Did my skills match the career requirements? Was it worth the time investment? While I eventually decided that I was on the right path, this pause to reevaluate all the details and facts gave me the confidence I needed to move ahead."

GEORGINE, 25, MBA STUDENT

Introverted Sensing provides ESTJs with a different avenue for soulwork, enriching their spirituality using their five senses. ESTJs might slow their pace enough to notice their body's needs—whether they are succeeding in balancing their diet, rest, and exercise requirements with their often hectic schedules. Monitoring their physical state can also provide them with a mirror to their emotional state.

"I stop myself, quiet down, and look at what hurts. For example, when my stomach gets irritable, I know it's a clue for me to take it easy and determine the real source of my frustration. The answer often comes quickly. Then I can use this information to plan actions to rectify the situation."

CARLA, 28, PROBATION OFFICER

ESTJs can also engage their introverted Sensing function by structuring time for reflective spiritual disciplines. They may choose to follow the suggestions in a book of prayer or design a personal ritual that they use regularly.

Thus, the auxiliary function provides balance: While extraverted Thinking determines truth, introverted Sensing helps ESTJs focus on their internal experiences, needs, and realities. This quiet reflection on the past and present informs their outer world of proactive endeavors.

The Third Gift for ESTJs: Intuition

Not as much is documented or agreed upon about how the third, or tertiary, function expresses itself in any of the 16 types.* The **third function** for ESTJs is Intuition. The domain of the Intuitive function includes focusing on the unseen, the reality of the improbable, and paying attention to insights, imagination, and information relating to future possibilities.

For all of the 16 types, the third function tends to evolve later in life, typically after the first two functions are clearly developed. How well ESTJs can access their third function, Intuition, depends on their

---

Whether the third function is extraverted or introverted is not well documented in theory or practice. We therefore suggest that people observe how they use it in both the outer (extraverted) and inner (introverted) worlds at different times to see which is most helpful.

degree of comfort with and exposure to imaginative, creative endeavors. Family, school, or recreational pursuits may help ESTJs find opportunities for their Intuition in the midst of a largely Sensing world.

As they seek to enrich their spirituality, many ESTJs use their third function, Intuition, to:

- Discover new insights about their spiritual tradition or sacred readings, either through creative-thinking exercises, studying myths and symbolism, or creative exercises with others who enjoy using their imagination; and
- Explore things that cannot be easily explained. In addition to finding answers through what they can tangibly observe or experience, ESTJs may become more willing to consider less rational explanations for things or events that seem to have no explanation.

ESTJs in the Storms of Life

The Least Accessible Gift for ESTJs:
Introverted Feeling

For all of the 16 types, the fourth function is called the **inferior function** because it is the most difficult to use consciously and effectively. The inferior function can be a source of irritation and oversights that can threaten competency, careers, meaning and purpose, or even relationships—but at its best can be a source of rest or richness in the storms of life, in moving toward deeper spirituality, or in exploring issues as we age. For ESTJs, the inferior function is introverted Feeling.

For all of us, life delivers events and circumstances that we cannot control—even the most fortunate of us eventually have to deal with the relinquishment of relationships, work situations, or dreams. And as we age, the human condition demands that we face the diminishment of our own abilities and eventually our lives. While our soulwork may help us prepare for and weather these storms, knowing our psychological type can help us understand how these storms will affect us and where we might intentionally seek refuge.

The dominant extraverted Thinking function of ESTJs provides some natural coping skills. ESTJs often continue on course once they've established a feasible plan, especially if they have previous experience with a problem and a useful structure in place to meet the situational requirements. In addition, they are often able to remain objective about the situation, reserving their energy for the struggle to overcome the odds.

The auxiliary function of introverted Sensing also provides some help. To recover a sense of balance, ESTJs may need to consciously seek out some time alone to assess what their experience has taught them and their own practical needs before starting off again. They may need to "pamper" themselves with time out for exercise, massage, or for indulging. Surprisingly, ESTJs can often unjam their Thinking through a few good nights' sleep or a weekend away in the country.

ESTJs may also be helped by amassing all the specifics in the situation and looking for any new input or facts.

"When my cousin came down with cancer, I was horrified. She was so fit and followed all the rules for healthy living! I asked her what I could do to help and she suggested that I go to the doctor with her. I think it helped me more than her, for I got all the facts directly from the specialist. I didn't have any experience with cancer but I talked to two friends who did. They gave me some concrete data that I could use to help Darlene in fighting back."

MARSHA, 48, SALES MANAGER

When the Storms Overwhelm

However, the storms of life often swell beyond our natural capacity to cope. While life's tragedies strain all of us, no matter how intense our soulwork and regardless of our psychological type, the stormy times for ESTJs can be intensified if the circumstances include any of the following factors:

- When they begin to doubt their ability to cope with the situation. For all types, the storms of life may involve a loss of control. For

ESTJs, who value a regulated approach to life, this loss of control can be especially threatening. Knowing that their logic and problem-solving skills are not able to "best" a problem, they can feel like quitting.

- When they are expected to lead during a crisis but have already reached their "limit." Because ESTJs habitually take charge, others expect them to continue to do so in times of loss. However, ESTJs may want to be taken care of themselves; may seek to withdraw to avoid any emotional displays; or may reluctantly assume, at some personal cost, their normal leadership role.

"Because so much was coming so fast, I knew if I continued, I would start shouting, 'I'm being treated like a robot!' or 'It's not fair; others aren't helping!' I had to get away for a solo bike ride and a good cup of coffee but felt instead like I was shirking my responsibilities."

GWYN, 35, INSURANCE INVESTIGATOR

- When a deeply-rooted principle is disregarded or violated by themselves or others.
- When they in some way may have inadvertently hurt people. In their drive toward accomplishment, ESTJs may have to face up to what others perceive as impatient, cold, or unfeeling actions. This can be debilitating, especially if ESTJs thought they were acting in the best interests of all. In most crises, ESTJs continue to focus on the external problems, giving rather limited time to consolation or support. Sometimes it takes a significant intervention by others or their own conscience before they slow down enough to consider the impact of the situation.

In the most despairing moments, all types can be caught by overuse of their strengths, relying too much on their dominant function. The worst time for ESTJs is when they find their efforts inefficient or useless. They may become so caught up in their chosen, logical plan or decision that they close themselves to new information and ignore the other aspects of the crisis—the long-range, interpersonal, or factual implications. In addition, if they haven't focused on soulwork in the past, ESTJs will most likely overlook the spiritual dimension of their situation.

"When I was fired, my first reaction was shock. I focused on what others had done to cause it—the lack of management planning, the inefficient sales force, etc. As I started my job search, I had to come to grips with the issues where I could be at fault: my business and my interpersonal skills. Only after much introspection did I pinpoint those areas that need development. I was surprised by my emotional response because I had damaged a number of important work relationships. I found an excellent executive coach and started immediately to modify my behavior by considering people and *goals."*

RYAN, 44, MANUFACTURING MANAGER

"My best friend died of a sudden heart attack while we were golfing together. He was my same age, 36. I was temporarily halted in my tracks. What if I had no more opportunities to be with my wife? What if it were my children who were suddenly fatherless? The importance of my career moved to an unprecedented second place as I re-sorted my life's goals. While occasionally I return to my old pattern of overworking (more often than I'd like to admit), taking time to recall Toby's death still serves to remind me to readjust my work habits and consider the meaning and purpose of my life."

TOM, 39, BENEFITS OFFICE,
STATE GOVERNMENT

Clues that ESTJs are being overwhelmed:	• Overemotionalism or hypersensitivity • Concentrating too intently on the task at hand, acting cold and impersonal toward others
How to help ESTJs:	• Offer alternative explanations, new factual information, and practical suggestions
For self-help:	• Pause to reflect on the impact of the situation on self and others • Reconsider the facts and details involved, then adjust strategies to meet the current reality and future goals

The Gifts of the Inferior Function—Rest and Richness

Even though using one's inferior function is stressful, an irony of psychological type is that *a path to serenity and rest is to intentionally use the inferior function.* For the ESTJ, the inferior function of Feeling is opposite the dominant function of Thinking. Therefore, its *conscious use* requires shutting down what is most natural and easy—the Thinking function, which may have gotten out of control while trying to cope with the storm.

For ESTJs, pursuing activities that use their inferior function, introverted Feeling, forces them to consider the storm by looking at its interpersonal aspects while reflecting on questions about what is most important for themselves, others, and society. Ways to intentionally engage the introverted Feeling function include:

- Paying attention to the emotional impact of a situation by setting aside all of its demands and concentrating on the personal meaning of what has happened. Use this affective information as input in the decision-making process.
- Stepping back from the logical implications to consider what effect their selected outcome has on those closest to them. ESTJs often find it rather unnatural to consciously explore these areas. Therefore, they may find it easier to talk things through with an empathetic listener whom they can trust.
- Engaging in reflective recreational opportunities that allow them to express their inner feelings or to contemplate motivations through activities such as painting, writing, reading literature or poetry, or journaling.

In soulwork for each type, richness, depth, and development come through the inferior function. As useful as it is to understand the inferior function for the storms of life, it provides more benefits as we seek to grow.

In the first half of life we define ourselves, both in work and relationships, through our dominant and auxiliary functions. In the second half of life, the gifts of our inferior function can aid us as we seek to become all that we can be. When we don't take advantage of this natural development of our psychological type, we can become stuck.

Midlife also gives clarity to the brevity of our lives. This compels many of us almost unconsciously to seek richness from unfamiliar experiences as well as to complete the psychological tasks we may have bypassed at an earlier age. As we journey toward wholeness and completion, we can open ourselves to new avenues that are outside of our routines by relinquishing the control our dominant function exerts. Adding spiritual practices that incorporate the attributes of our inferior function can give our soulwork new dimension and zest.

The first two functions, Thinking and Sensing, give ESTJs a set of logically determined principles to help with decisions about life, reality, and the practical aspects of any course of action. However, to continue to grow, ESTJs need the spiritual richness that comes from introverted Feeling. They need to pay attention to the impact of spirituality on their values and relationships.

INTROVERTED FEELING SOULWORK

This involves:

- Searching for the personal meaning in spiritual practices;
- Having an inner bedrock of values to determine what is important and then attempting to live in accordance with those values;
- Finding time for solitary and deep soulwork, paying attention to the joys and longings of the spiritual journey; and
- Cultivating close personal relationships—first with self, then with selected others—by sharing feelings and matters of the heart.

ESTJs become reacquainted with the spiritual as they find meaning in things they previously overlooked. While they may continue many of their favorite methods of soulwork, renewal may come from the spiritual pathways that are naturally the domain of INFPs and ISFPs:

- *Spirituality used to help me* do, *but now it helps me* be. *I've learned to take time to pay attention to things that used to be more of a nuisance than a blessing.*

- *For me, God was always "out there." Now I find the visionary writings of people like St. Teresa of Avila and some of the Eastern mystics fascinating.*

- *Until recently I considered journaling unimportant and a waste of good time. However, I've started a process of writing down those things that are truly significant to me. Through this journal, I can be sure that my time goes to what is most important.*

- *I handed my day planner to my assistant and told him to cancel everything. Alone, I allowed myself to grasp how devastated I was by my father's sudden death. All week long, I'd made arrangements, called all of the relatives, held my mother's hand, in short, helped everyone but me. Writing out what I'd say at the funeral allowed my feelings to rise to the top.*

- *I was afraid I'd cry, but I decided if that occurred, I could handle it. I mustered up my courage and told my aging parents how much I loved them. I also went on to delineate what they'd done for me and my appreciation for it all. To my delight and surprise, we all cried, hugged, and felt closer than ever. I was so glad I took the risk.*

I am thankful for

My orientation toward fairness and justice
My sense of order and responsibility
My ability to lead others to accomplish goals
The decisiveness and reasoning I bring to solving problems

In the storms of life, I can find shelter by

Focusing on what truly matters to me, both now and for eternity
Embracing instead of avoiding my emotions, realizing that feelings can enrich my life
Taking time alone to ensure that *all* my needs are met

To honor myself and my pathway to God, I can

Find tangible ways to incorporate the spiritual into my daily
life

Use my organizational gifts to be a part of something that
matters

Value the intangible—my relationships and other areas that
give meaning to life

Chapter 13

ENTJ

Extraversion, Intuition, Thinking, Judging

Finding spirituality
in the outer world
of objectivity
and possibilities

General Description: ENTJs tend to be active, take-charge organizers of processes, people, and plans. They are goal-directed, big-picture focused, and ardent problem-solvers, especially of large and complex issues. They enjoy providing structure and designing strategies to correct systems. ENTJs have high expectations, are persistent, and value fairness.

THE GREATEST GIFT FOR ENTJS:
EXTRAVERTED THINKING WITH INTUITION
Bringing order out of chaos; stepping into voids requiring leadership and vision; energetically mobilizing others to action to meet needs for posterity.

THE ENTJ ROLE IN COMMUNITY:
Long-range planning, future-oriented ideas; calling others to competence; decisive leadership for groups and organizations; bringing intellectual and philosophical insights to spiritual questions.

Extraverted Thinking is the **dominant function** for ENTJs, the function that develops earliest in life, is most comfortable to use, and is easiest to access. Using the dominant function is the natural avenue for each type to pursue soulwork—this is where the soul resides. In other words, for soulwork to be meaningful, the ENTJ's dominant function, extraverted Thinking, must be satisfied.

ENTJ Spirituality: Atmospheres for Soulwork

The ENTJ approach to spirituality is similar to the way they handle everything else in life: vigorous, cerebral, and substantive. Spirituality must relate to the big questions of life and provide stimulation for thought and action. ENTJs are often compelled to challenge traditional thinking, creating openings for further inquiry into our nature, origins, and reason for being.

"For most of my life, 'faith' was in direct opposition to my preferences for logic and clarity. Many of my early spiritual experiences involved opinions, not beliefs. Opinions often shift—they are influenced by emotions and experiences. Beliefs should be deeper than that. One should base beliefs on well-developed frameworks that bear up under logical examination. I have to know not just what I believe, but why."

BARRY, 61, EXECUTIVE COACH

The ability to be about something greater than themselves provides the attraction for spirituality to many ENTJs. Wanting to be a part of solutions for major problems, ENTJs may join in spiritual communities to assist in efforts that no one person could tackle. ENTJs may be found promoting efforts, organizing solutions, and fostering excellence in programs and people.

"Waiting in line at the airport, taking classes in an institution, or being part of organizing a social/community gathering, I recreate 'the way we have always done it' by asking what we are trying to accomplish, acknowl-

edging the obstacles, and then problem-solving creatively. It's just part of how I am made. In my spiritual community, I join with others to brainstorm on all of the issues we could attack—fetal alcohol syndrome, migrant workers, inner-city crime—we choose which ones we can influence, we develop a plan, and then go out and do something about it! I can't do these things alone and therefore appreciate my effectiveness as part of a social outreach unit."

PHYLLIS, 42, FINANCIAL PLANNER

ENTJs often advance logical frameworks for their beliefs and prefer to use their natural skepticism to develop new insights into universal truths. Some ENTJs become scholars of their faith, clarifying and codifying spiritual principles. They tend to identify discrepancies and disputable matters and are frustrated when free exchanges of opinion and information are curtailed. Often their most spiritual moments come when they are allowed to bring their intellect to bear on matters of faith.

"A series of events caught my attention and culminated in my acknowledgment that some force greater than humanity existed in creation. I was on a quest to add purpose to my life, pondering what mattered most to me. Studying quantum physics was most helpful in 'cracking the code' of our cosmos, adding a fresh perspective to our existence. At the same time, I headed a task force to provide meaningful summer experiences for special kids. As I pulled together businesses, churches, synagogues, and foundations, I watched something bigger than the sum of the parts at work. People who usually fought each other tooth and nail down at City Hall were cooperating. Supplies arrived like magic, major obstacles dissolved, and I thought, 'This is God—I may be the leader, but God's hand is on this undertaking.' Understanding even a part of God could take a lifetime, but I'm determined to pursue adding a spiritual dimension to my life."

STAN, 53, HUMAN RESOURCES CONSULTANT

"I knew I had found an environment in which I could be comfortable when the spiritual director told me that instead of worshipping any teachings, she worshiped God. In our study group, we challenge each other not to take

things out of context and to neither make mountains out of molehills nor molehills out of mountains—we strive for an authentic, relevant faith.

"Ministers, rabbis, and spiritual directors should be a part of us, not set apart. They are one aspect of the process of defining our experiences as children of God. They are not the only spokespeople for God. When anyone starts to dictate exactly what another human being should believe, they are exercising control and power, not spirituality. If they cannot be honest about the good and the bad that religious expression brings, I have no time for them."

MARIA, 58, NONPROFIT FOUNDATION DIRECTOR

Spiritual Paths Using Extraverted Thinking

Whether soulwork is new to ENTJs or they desire to enrich their spiritual practices, pathways that allow for logic, skepticism, and intellectual challenge are often most appealing to the ENTJ. Some of these methods may include:

- Rigorous study, debate, and discussion of spiritual issues to clarify the principles of one's faith.
  "I love the traditions in which I was raised, but I tend not to look to them for all the rules concerning right and wrong that many people have about faith. Rather, I try to define the bigger picture of the characteristics of a faith-filled person."

  DEANNA, 36, PERSONNEL MANAGER

- Leading work projects or learning experiences that enable others to accomplish good works or deepen their understanding of God.
  "I have always been 'a part' of the system and see value in what 'the church' has to offer. However, the traditional ways used to reach a wide array of people (including myself) have not been very effective. While out of one side of my mouth I will say that 'church' is not for me (meaning these traditional methods), on the other hand I say, 'If only we did it this way, or in this setting, or with this leadership, etc., it would be more effective.' Somehow I see the bigger picture, understand the underlying purpose, and suggest or develop new strategies to

meet the end goal. I've been able to do this in several capacities within my denomination and it truly brings me joy."

T A N I ,   3 1 ,   MINISTER

- Being in settings of grandeur, whether the cathedrals of civilization or the forests, mountains, or seashores, to foster awareness of the majesty of a higher power.
- Defining their principles, then defining a purpose to ensure they put their efforts toward something that matters.
- Pursuing scientific, philosophical, anthropological, or other schools of thought to uncover new patterns and insights that strengthen or support their beliefs.

  "To me the issue was, if the universe is the answer, then what was the question? I know that some people are shocked when I mention that the most profound spiritual text I've ever read was Stephen Hawking's A Brief History of Time!"

S E T H ,   4 7 ,   SYSTEMS DESIGNER

Clouds That Hinder Soulwork

When the gifts of the dominant function of extraverted Thinking are violated, or if ENTJs are not affirmed in their strengths, their desire to search for truth and find the logical underpinnings of their spirituality may be weakened or even extinguished. Major factors that can get in the way of ENTJ spirituality include:

- Perceiving a lack of purpose in some forms of spirituality. Soulwork may compete for time with the many other activities that have clearer purposes. Therefore, spirituality may be relegated to a low priority in the lives of ENTJs.
- Avoiding situations that bring out emotions, either from themselves or others. Too much talk of love, relationships, and feelings can push ENTJs away from others.

  "Part of it might be that I just don't use some of the language that is common to many spiritual paths. If I say that I'm influenced by the traditions of a given community, agree with its basic theological tenets, and can commit myself to acting on its priorities—well, that is

passionate language for me. I think in terms of purposes and results as I seek my spiritual path, not personal relationships and feeling loved."

PAUL, 44, REAL-ESTATE DEVELOPER

- Seeking the end goals of spirituality so intently that they miss out on the process of becoming more spiritual. While ENTJs can be found at the forefront of many spiritual endeavors, taking the leap of faith from a life of logic to a life of belief can be a difficult step for many.

  "Throughout childhood I constantly heard, 'To whom much is given, much is required.' In my adult life I often find myself questioning, 'Am I really using my talents to the best of my ability?' I tend to get caught up in the doing side of spirituality—the outcomes—and forget to nurture my inner growth."

DREW, 34, MARKETING MANAGER

- Demanding competency from organized religion as they do from the other aspects of their lives.

  "My first Hebrew instructor deserved every bit of the respect he demanded. He was very competent and that made it easy for me to accept his moral stance and teaching. However, his example provides an extremely high benchmark for me to judge other spiritual leaders and movements. When they don't measure up, I can easily become skeptical and question the purpose of belonging or participating fully."

BETH, 26, GRADUATE STUDENT

The Second Gift for ENTJs: Introverted Intuition

ENTJs have introverted Intuition as their **auxiliary function.** The gifts of introverted Intuition include focusing on future possibilities, delving into the unseen, and having insights about the larger issues of life.

Pulling back from their active lifestyle to reflect can add depth to ENTJs' soulwork. This space and time spent alone allows ENTJs to find the balance that their introverted Intuition function can provide. ENTJs often use brainstorming techniques with themselves as they reflect about problems and solutions, working to identify several options to reach a goal. They may clearly define a problem while interacting with others, but then tend to come up with better possibilities for solutions when alone—perhaps during their few solitary daily tasks like commuting, showering, or exercising.

Many ENTJs also find that solitude allows them to pay attention to the insights and hunches they receive through daydreaming, prayer, or meditation, often a needed source of information.

"I've learned to trust my intuition in spiritual matters. When I take the time to meditate over a situation the answer often becomes palpably clear. There's no logic or thought involved—I just know what I am supposed to do or pass on to another person. The rightness of this is confirmed when others tell me that God put me in their life for a reason. Allowing my intuition to guide me helps me past some of the demands of my Thinking function."

KENT, 64, INVESTMENT BANKER

Thus, the auxiliary function provides balance: while extraverted Thinking searches for truth, introverted Intuition points ENTJs toward possible interpretations and applications of their principles and beliefs.

The Third Gift for ENTJs: Sensing

Not as much is documented or agreed upon about how the third, or tertiary, function expresses itself in any of the 16 types.* The **third function** for ENTJs is Sensing. The domain of the Sensing function includes a firm grasp of reality, attention to details, and an enjoyment of present and everyday circumstances—accepting life as it is.

◈

---

*Whether the third function is extraverted or introverted is not well documented in theory or practice. We therefore suggest that people observe how they use it in both the outer (extraverted) and inner (introverted) worlds at different times to see which is most helpful.

For all of the 16 types, the third function tends to evolve later in life, typically after the first two functions are clearly developed. However, many ENTJs are assisted early on in accessing Sensing, their third function, because Sensing predominates in most of the world's cultures and in many early educational curricula and systems. Thus, many ENTJs benefit from being able to understand factual and practical matters when they *consciously* try to do so. As they seek to enrich their spirituality, many ENTJs use their third function, Sensing, to:

- Add nuance to their spirituality by learning the factual, historical, and practical aspects of a belief system; and
- Pay attention to the impact of soulwork on their current situation, noticing the simple things that bring joy to life—being healthy, experiencing the outdoors, or finding satisfaction in day-to-day events.

ENTJs in the Storms of Life

The Least Accessible Gift for ENTJs: Introverted Feeling

For all of the 16 types, the fourth function is called the **inferior function** because it is the most difficult to use consciously and effectively. The inferior function can be a source of irritation and oversights that can threaten competency, meaning and purpose, careers, or even relationships—but at its best can be a source of rest or richness in the storms of life, in moving toward deeper spirituality, or in exploring issues as we age. For ENTJs, the inferior function is introverted Feeling.

For all of us, life delivers events and circumstances that we cannot control—even the most fortunate of us eventually have to deal with the relinquishment of relationships, work situations, or dreams. And as we age, the human condition demands that we face the diminishment of our own abilities and eventually our lives. While our soul-

work may help us prepare for and weather these storms, knowing our psychological type can help us understand how these storms will affect us and where we might intentionally seek refuge.

The dominant extraverted Thinking function of ENTJs provides some natural coping skills. With their natural drive to solve problems, ENTJs usually look for objective, rational, and complex solutions, moving ahead with confidence. In addition, they are often able to remain emotionally detached from the problem, reserving their energy for the struggle.

The auxiliary function of introverted Intuition also provides some help. Allowing time for introspection gives ENTJs a chance to expand upon their opinions and options, considering the interrelation between the parts and the whole. Surprisingly, simply getting several good nights' sleep often brings new ideas, connections, and the optimism needed to confidently change their original course of action.

"Once I recharge, tell me it can't be done and all my energy will go to finding a way to make it happen, bringing others along for the ride. After a period of time, I need to slow down, refocus, and recharge the battery, even for a short, short while—then it's back to high gear again."

ELLEN, 29, HEADHUNTER

When the Storms Overwhelm

However, the storms of life often swell beyond our natural capacity to cope. While life's tragedies strain all of us, no matter how intense our soulwork and regardless of our psychological type, the stormy times for ENTJs can be intensified if the circumstances include any of the following factors:

- When they believe their own lack of competency may have contributed to a poor outcome.
  "As a religious professional I wanted to be competent at all aspects of my work, but providing personal counseling to members of our spiritual community was problematic for me. I took classes only to learn that many counseling sessions were doomed to fail—people often seek

counseling in religious settings because they don't *want to change! I finally learned that competency in this area doesn't necessarily mean that people solve their problems or that I must do it for them."*

ZACHARY, 48, RABBI

- When they or those close to them lose control over their emotions.
  "On the one hand, I knew my spouse should *be frightened and even tearful as we waited for the results of the medical tests. On the other hand, though, I found myself wanting to avoid any interaction with her and the doctors until we could have a rational, unemotional discussion of how to proceed. So I felt cold, guilty, and useless to help."*

SANDY, 38, ATTORNEY

- When their actions are construed by others as treating people like objects or interchangeable parts.
  "I didn't mean to discredit other people, but I was in such a 'just do it!' mode that I moved too quickly past the people part of the process. I had to go back to several of the staff members to double-check how they had interpreted my comments—and it was not an enjoyable experience."

LYNNE, 41, CORPORATE EXECUTIVE

- When a spiritual principle or truth is disregarded or violated. Because of their thoughtful and considered approach to spirituality, when ENTJs choose to commit to a spiritual path or tradition, they can be annoyed when others sweep spiritual principles aside.

In the most despairing moments, all types can be caught by overuse of their strengths, relying too much on their dominant function. The worst time for ENTJs is when their own abilities fail them and a sense of being powerless sets in. They have overused their dominant Thinking by reducing everything to a logical formula and carefully devising a plan—even though many of life's issues are illogical. When these dark times come, ENTJs may quickly become frustrated. In the worst storms, a totally different approach to soulwork may be the only refuge.

"In my mind, our divorce pointed to me as the failure. At the time, I was an executive in charge of an organization that coordinated over one thousand volunteers. All seemed to be going well in my life—until the divorce papers appeared on my desk. I dropped all involvement and contact with people as I sorted through my role in the breakup. I was too close to tears to intelligibly or rationally discuss the situation with anyone."

MANNY, 51, CITY MANAGER

"As a project manager, I was proud of my record—every project under budget, on schedule. However, one day my boss hauled me in. In analyzing employee turnover, my department had one of the highest ratios. The staff claimed that I didn't pay attention to their needs. My first thoughts were disgust—I'd worked to make sure they were some of the highest-paid people in the company, or in the marketplace for that matter. Then I started to blame myself and doubt my effectiveness. It took me quite some time to analyze my own actions and make necessary changes."

TONY, 36, PROJECT-DEVELOPMENT MANAGER

Clues that ENTJs are being overwhelmed:	• A rigid approach to problems and an unwillingness to see other possibilities • Uncharacteristic self-pity, illogical thinking, or emotionalism
How to help ENTJs:	• Encourage them to slow down, put tasks aside, and reflect
For self-help:	• Find a trusted person to provide an outside viewpoint on how others are being affected by the situation • Take stock of those principles held most deeply and see whether they are reflected in outward actions

The Gifts of the Inferior Function—Rest and Richness

Even though using one's inferior function is stressful, an irony of psychological type is that *a path to serenity and rest is to intentionally use the inferior function.* For the ENTJ, the inferior function of Feeling is opposite the dominant function of Thinking. Therefore, its *conscious use* requires shutting down what is most natural and easy—the Thinking function, which may have gotten out of control while trying to cope with the storm.

For ENTJs, pursuing activities that use their inferior function, introverted Feeling, forces them to consider the interpersonal aspects of the storm and to reflect on questions about what is most important for themselves, others, and the larger community. Ways to intentionally engage the introverted Feeling function include:

- Completing a values clarification exercise to determine what matters to them personally. Sometimes this helps ENTJs select efforts that have the most meaning from the many possible challenges they have the ability to tackle.
- Stepping back from the logical implications of a situation to consider the impact their solution has on those closest to them. They might also pay attention to their own feelings and emotional states about the situation and use them as factors in their decision-making.
- Reading novels or journaling to get at issues of character and motivation; painting or writing poetry to express inner emotions; or talking one-to-one with a trusted other about deeply personal matters.

In soulwork for each type, richness, depth, and development come through the inferior function. As useful as it is to understand the inferior function for the storms of life, it provides more benefits as we seek to grow.

In the first half of life we define ourselves, both in work and relationships, through our dominant and auxiliary functions. In the second half of life, the gifts of our inferior function can aid us as we seek to become all that we can be. When we don't take advantage of this natural development of our psychological type, we can become stuck.

Midlife also gives clarity to the brevity of our lives. This compels many of us almost unconsciously to seek richness from unfamiliar experiences as well as to complete the psychological tasks we may have bypassed at an earlier age. As we journey toward wholeness and completion, we can open ourselves to new avenues that are outside of our routines by relinquishing the control our dominant function exerts. Adding spiritual practices that incorporate the attributes of our inferior function can give our soulwork new dimension and zest.

The first two functions, Thinking and Intuition, give ENTJs a set of logically determined principles to help guide decisions about life, envision future possibilities, and arrive at their own specially crafted spiritual understanding. However, to continue to grow, ENTJs need the spiritual richness of introverted Feeling. They need to pay attention to the impact of spirituality on their values and relationships.

INTROVERTED FEELING SOULWORK

This involves:

- Searching for the personal meaning in spiritual practices;
- Having an inner bedrock of values to determine what is important and then attempting to live in accordance with those values;
- Finding time for solitary and deep soulwork and paying attention to the joys and longings of the spiritual journey; and
- Cultivating close personal relationships—first with self, then with selected others by sharing feelings and matters of the heart.

ENTJs become reacquainted with the spiritual as they find meaning in things they previously overlooked. While they may continue many of their favorite methods of soulwork, renewal may come from the spiritual pathways that are naturally the domain of ISFPs and INFPs:

- *Emotions were always sort of an unknown black box for me, so to speak. Now I'm intrigued by the notion that emotions are things we do, not things that just happen to us. They are a valuable part of experiencing all that life has to offer, not something to avoid at all costs.*

- *In Africa, working in solitude on a technical assignment, I had more time than at any other point in my life to reflect on what brings meaning to me. No phones, no TV, no newspapers to provide more information. Without the distractions, I felt the presence of God in a new and very deep way. I realized that I wanted to live for a purpose; if I listened, perhaps my spiritual side could enable me to be a force to improve our world—at least the small part I can influence.*

- *At just the right moment, someone handed me a values exercise. What really* did *matter to me? I had my goals, my mission statement, but suddenly that wasn't enough. The people side of my life wasn't adequately represented. While I value using my talents to the fullest, I also value time with those I love, laughter, and—of all things— leisure!*

- *My crisis made me look at my spiritual life in a new way. No, I couldn't provide intellectual proof—I still consider faith beyond the realm of the evidence. However, there* is *something out there bigger and more competent than I am. In the crisis, I found support and perhaps even tenderness or love from what I term God.*

- *I made myself step back from my big-picture approach for managing those under my care in our spiritual community and developed a computer tickler system so that I could remember them as individuals. I realized I placed a high value on showing I took an interest in their joys and sorrows, so my computer reminded me to send notes for the anniversary of a spouse's death or to check on someone's job search. I don't want you to think of it as a mechanical approach because it enables me to overcome a real weakness.*

I am thankful for

My mind, which sees solutions and strategies where others
see turmoil
My quest for truth and clarity, adding insights to
each endeavor
My commitment to excellence in everything I undertake
The way I lead people toward well-defined goals

In the storms of life, I can find shelter by

Taking time out to explore alternative possibilities and
solutions
Discovering what matters most to me and those I value
Considering the experiences of others and asking for
their help

To honor myself and my pathway to God, I can

Satisfy my need to know—my desire to understand our
universe and ultimately our Creator
Define and accept a logical basis for what I take on faith—be
able to intellectualize this intangible part of our being
Find ways to bring my soulwork to bear on my relationships
with others and with God

Chapter 14
ISTP

Introversion, Sensing, Thinking, Perceiving

*Finding spirituality
in the inner world
of questions
and experiences*

General Description: ISTPs tend to be reserved observers who use logic and reasoning to find expedient and efficient ways to get things done. They value clarity of thought and are adept problem-solvers who seek pragmatic solutions. ISTPs prefer to remain in the background unless there are extenuating circumstances—then they act quickly to come to the rescue.

THE GREATEST GIFT FOR ISTPS:
INTROVERTED THINKING WITH SENSING
Analyzing facts and details in a search for truth; dissolving red tape in the process of finding the best way to get things done.

THE ISTP ROLE IN COMMUNITY:
Contributing quietly behind the scenes; lending a hand when no one else steps forward; offering a wealth of information about their special interests; providing realism to any effort they undertake.

Introverted Thinking is the **dominant function** for ISTPs, the function that develops earliest in life, is most comfortable to use, and is easiest to access. Using the dominant function is the natural avenue for each type to pursue soulwork—this is where the soul resides. In other words, for soulwork to be meaningful, the ISTP's dominant function, introverted Thinking, must be satisfied.

◆

ISTP Spirituality: Atmospheres for Soulwork

ISTPs are independent thinkers and justifiably proud of it. They are acutely aware that there are no easy answers to the big questions of life and question the attempts of others to assume away the dilemmas. For ISTPs, spirituality is about determining what they believe by comparing what they see in the world around them to what they find to be true.

For many ISTPs, choosing their spiritual path is a rational process. ISTPs may not be convinced easily of the merit of soulwork without thorough and convincing arguments. They have a healthy natural skepticism and seek environments where they are allowed to raise doubts. They may examine the pros and cons of a life with or without a set of beliefs and choose the alternative that is the most sensible. ISTPs are also keen observers of people and notice how their spirituality influences their lives. The decisions ISTPs make about different spiritual traditions are often based on this type of evidence; ISTPs look to soulwork as a guide, so their actions reflect their principles.

"My parents were really black and white: you take one path or the other. As a youth I did a quick pro and con analysis and figured that religion would probably do me more good than harm, so I went along with it. Now that I've been involved for years I see much finer nuances than my original logic, but that's initially what got me here!"

TARA, 27, OCCUPATIONAL THERAPIST

Rather than setting aside time for spirituality, ISTPs are more likely to recognize the spiritual in the consistencies and events of everyday life. These often inexplicable times when a sense of order or purpose is present comprise the underpinnings of the ISTP's faith. Typically, ISTPs are aware of forces outside our rational or objective human existence. Common occurrences, such as hearing a child pray, enjoying outdoor activities, or sensing gratitude from another person when they provide help, give ISTPs evidence of God.

ISTPs might commonly be found actively solving problems to express their spirituality rather than in formal worship, study, or practice of other spiritual disciplines. Soulwork has to have practical results in their lives or it loses its value. Applications for soulwork that appeal to ISTPs include providing their children with a spiritual foundation or using social outreach programs as a vehicle to assist others. They are motivated to be involved in more personal spiritual paths when others seem to benefit from them. Soulwork for ISTPs most often has the greatest impact when they rationally work through an issue.

"My beliefs are the product of my mind and the more trappings that are added, the harder it is for me to believe. Take Moses and the burning bush, the parting of the Red Sea—the story starts to sound like any Greek or Roman myth. Embellishments like angels and miracles make me think twice—when I hear things like that, I wonder whether I've placed my faith in another string of legends.

"While these stories can be historical, I realize too that they could also be events inspired by God designed to make us think and ponder the divine aspects of life. In addition, the alternative is atheism, and . . . well, you don't shake off years of attending religious services. My faith is a structure that provides a reality for me as I approach life on a day-to-day basis."

DEBRAH, 49, NURSE

"I find it difficult to be spiritual in the midst of a crowd. Solitude is more refreshing. A few weeks ago I joined others from my spiritual community at a huge gathering. While I enjoyed the opening ritual, I could go for months *without another similar experience.*

"I have to acknowledge my own spiritual path—soulwork happens for

me when I'm out fishing or hiking. The river is my cathedral, a place where I sense the awesomeness of God."

COLLIN, 33, SYSTEMS ANALYST

Spiritual Paths Using Introverted Thinking

Whether soulwork is new to ISTPs or they desire to enrich their spiritual practices, pathways that tap into their search for truth and logical understanding of the world are most rewarding. Some of these methods include:

- Taking time away from a structured spiritual system to define for themselves what spirituality means. ISTPs don't always go willingly to corporate worship or organized learning experiences—there are too many other things they would rather be doing. However, once there, ISTPs are often glad they participated, especially if it's been some time since they attended such events.
- Listening to teaching or spiritual material that is logically presented. ISTPs appreciate stories and anecdotes, but want them to be clearly related to the point being made.
- Attending classes that bring spirituality to bear on parenting, workplace ethics, and other down-to-earth applications. ISTPs don't only want to know what some spiritual giant did; they want to understand the context in which it was done, what a modern-day parallel would be, and how they can utilize the information.
- Meeting with a few people for open discussion of their differing beliefs.

  "In one of my favorite spiritual experiences, we all studied the same subject, discussed information we had learned, and then together assessed what it all meant. I'm more comfortable with spiritual matters that cannot be determined if I've done my best to find the limits of what can be proved. Some people get offended when I ask questions that to me are obvious ones to ask, claiming that I am attacking the core of what they believe. It would be nice if spiritual matters were that clear-cut, but they simply aren't. When I admit what I don't know for sure—only then can I identify what I know to be true!"

BEN, 52, TELECOMMUNICATIONS MANAGER

- Offering tangible, practical help to others. ISTPs can be counted on to fill a need if it seems the necessary thing to do. For most ISTPs, results are the essence of faith—the rest seems like meaningless talk.

"I think of it this way: God and I have a contract. My part is to do what I can for others and God's part is to influence what I do. I don't expect answers for every little problem I face, but I believe that if I am committed to a faithful life, acting on my principles, then God provides direction by guiding my thoughts. I don't have a need to ask for more."

GREG, 27, FORESTER

Clouds That Hinder Soulwork

When the gifts of the dominant function of introverted Thinking are violated, or if ISTPs are not affirmed in their strengths, the role of soulwork may shrink in importance. Major factors that can get in the way of ISTP spirituality include:

- Participating in structured activities that lack substance or practical application. Being in the same place at the same time each week, following a given course of activities, can feel restrictive and stifling to ISTPs. If they rebel at the routines insisted upon by others or religions or cultural norms, their spiritual lives become more accidental or incidental.

- Holding a perception that others have more mystical experiences or direct personal relationships with God and are therefore more spiritual. Rational and often skeptical ISTPs may assume that if their own lives lack these occurrences, their soulwork is not authentic.

- Perceiving a lack of fairness on the part of spiritual people and institutions. When ISTPs provide resources to help others or organizations to be effective, they expect to see evidence that their assistance made a difference. When needs are identified, they expect people who espouse a belief in service to step forward to assist. ISTPs resent having to do it all or to lead efforts where everyone could have voluntarily cooperated but didn't. When they have these unfair experiences with a group, they tend to simply leave.

- Being engulfed by their own emotionalism. ISTPs also resent blatant (or even subtle) attempts of leaders to induce emotionalism or other irrational atmospheres. ISTPs are private people who want to keep their feelings in check.

  "The 'touchy-feely' emotional stuff doesn't work for me. I perceive God as an interconnecting force, not a friend that walks beside me— I simply haven't experienced that. God exists and takes an interest in us, but I don't get hugs from God, nor do I want them. I have my own way of looking at all of this."

  KORI, 63, CATERER

The Second Gift for ISTPs: Extraverted Sensing

ISTPs have extraverted Sensing as their **auxiliary function**. The gifts of extraverted Sensing include experiencing the sacred in what is immediate and real while engaging fully in the active life given to us.

While ISTPs tend to begin their spiritual journey in solitude, their auxiliary function of extraverted Sensing often fosters a need to gather with others, whether in a small group or a large organization. In community, ISTPs want the freedom to seek answers, not accept the "party line." They may question the origins of dogma; ask whether the details of a story are correct; put forth alternative explanations; or seek to reexamine principles to ascertain whether they are universally applicable.

ISTPs prefer a spiritual environment that allows for more than one point of view as they seek out facts and applications through debate and analysis. ISTPs are also drawn to people who can provide concrete examples of ways in which soulwork has helped them—what they did and what happened next.

Extraverted Sensing also allows ISTPs to see the spiritual in the world around them.

"At night, I feel closest to the power that some call God. Gazing at the stars that just hint of the vastness of the universe, I long to understand the one who designed this planet."

BRETT, 28, CARPENTER

Thus, the auxiliary function provides balance: While introverted Thinking provides clarity and a set of principles, extraverted Sensing gives ISTPs an awareness of the workings of the world and a way to act on their principles in practical ways.

The Third Gift for ISTPs: Intuition

Not as much is documented or agreed upon about how the third, or tertiary, function expresses itself in any of the 16 types.* The **third function** for ISTPs is Intuition. The domain of the Intuitive function includes focusing on the unseen; the reality of the improbable; and paying attention to imagination, insights, and information relating to future possibilities.

For all of the 16 types, the third function tends to evolve later in life, typically after the first two functions are clearly developed. How well ISTPs can access their third function, Intuition, depends on their degree of comfort with and exposure to imaginative, creative endeavors. Family, school, or recreational pursuits may help ISTPs find opportunities to develop their Intuition in the midst of a largely Sensing world.

As they seek to enrich their spirituality, many ISTPs use their third function, Intuition, to:

- Discover new insights about their tradition or sacred readings, either through creative thinking exercises, studying myths and symbolism, or by creative activities with others who enjoy using their imagination; and
- Explore things that cannot be easily explained. ISTPs may become more willing to consider less rational explanations for things or events that seem to have no explanation.

Whether the third function is extraverted or introverted is not well documented in theory or practice. We therefore suggest that people observe how they use it in both the outer (extraverted) and inner (introverted) worlds at different times to see which is most helpful.

**The Least Accessible Gift for ISTPs:
Extraverted Feeling**

For all of the 16 types, the fourth function is called the **inferior function** because it is the most difficult to use consciously and effectively. The inferior function can be a source of irritation and oversights that can threaten competency, careers, meaning and purpose, or even relationships—but at its best it can be a source of rest or richness in the storms of life, in moving toward deeper spirituality, or in exploring issues as we age. For ISTPs, the inferior function is extraverted Feeling.

◆

For all of us, life delivers events and circumstances that we cannot control—even the most fortunate of us eventually have to deal with the relinquishment of relationships, work situations, or dreams. And as we age, the human condition demands that we face the diminishment of our own abilities and eventually our lives. While our soul-work may help us prepare for and weather these storms, knowing our psychological type can help us understand how these storms will affect us and where we might intentionally seek refuge.

The dominant introverted Thinking function of ISTPs provides some natural coping skills. Even in crises, they often remain objective and calm about matters, looking to their inner principles to guide their actions. ISTPs are seldom swayed by the opinions of the outer world and can therefore remain quite independent of public approval as they evaluate alternatives.

The auxiliary function of extraverted Sensing lets ISTPs reassess what is really going on and determine the facts and the givens in a situation.

"I had to convince myself that despite the conflicts with my coworkers, I could stay on the job. I did this by calculating the number of years remaining until I could retire, the number of displaced workers I could counsel in those years, and the weeks of vacation that would occasionally allow me to

escape the office. I also decided it was an opportunity to take a more spiritual approach. With those facts in mind, I could rationalize keeping my work life stable. Perhaps God is using this difficult experience to make me stronger or more mature."

ROBIN, 52, JOB-REHABILITATION COUNSELOR

Other ISTPs engage in tasks with concrete results or lots of external activity, where their hands instead of their minds are at work. Examples include skiing, gardening, building, or even housecleaning.

"While I would seldom organize a block party or other social event, I devised a rotating schedule for renting log splitters and teaming together with other families to fill everyone's woodsheds. The gatherings were a lot of fun and had a practical purpose."

JOHN, 37, SMALL-BUSINESS OWNER

When the Storms Overwhelm

However, the storms of life often swell beyond our natural capacity to cope. While life's tragedies strain all of us, no matter how intense our soulwork and regardless of our psychological type, the stormy times for ISTPs can be intensified if the circumstances include any of the following factors:

- When they are unsure how to handle their own emotional response or that of others.
  "There are times when I know that I need time apart from others to recover my composure, yet feel selfish when I withdraw—quite a dilemma."

  RUTH, 39, EMERGENCY-ROOM NURSE

- When a situation doesn't fit their logical view of what should happen or when they can't grasp the reasons behind events, they may become despondent.
  "Given that we'd never had a fight, I was clueless as to why my fiancée broke off our relationship. She left town, giving us no chance

to discuss her reasons. Alone, my mind spun out of control as I tried to analyze the situation. I found myself longing for affirmation from others and for their assessment that it wasn't all my fault."

CHAD, 32, POLICE OFFICER

- When the crisis fills their time with too many work activities, family matters, and other concerns requiring their attention. ISTPs then lose the time alone that their dominant Thinking function requires for reflection and energy.
- When they can't find a way to make things work better or more smoothly in order to get things done. ISTPs pride themselves on their ability to step in when needed and provide an efficient way to handle emergencies or crises. If this is not the case, they can feel useless.

    "My dad should have spent his last days at home but we couldn't reorganize the rooms, order the health-care equipment, and make the other arrangements fast enough. With my medical background, I should have been able to arrange things, somehow."

    LARA, 48, HMO ADMINISTRATOR

In the most despairing moments, all types can be caught by overuse of their strengths, relying too much on their dominant function. Because they often spend much time alone, reworking their thoughts, the worst time for ISTPs may be when they have analyzed the facts and drawn their conclusions of the causes and courses of action, thereby closing themselves off from other perspectives. If they isolate themselves too much, they miss new data that might help them reopen the possibilities. In the worst storms, a totally different approach to soul-work may be the only refuge.

"My parents didn't want to discuss our differing views on the war. Dad thought I was shirking responsibility. No matter how hard I tried, I couldn't get through to them that my decision was based on months of agonizing analysis of the issues and the results I saw—some of my friends were already dead, the bombs were killing more innocent people than enemies, and I thought our government had lied. When my parents wouldn't even listen, I exploded in a way that shattered my mother. I left feeling

that I had lost their love forever. Fortunately, rather than shutting myself off from disagreements that seemed too big to surmount, circumstances forced me back home regularly. I took time to see their position and strengths in a different way. Eventually I made peace with their point of view. Their principles came from their circumstances, my decision from my own."

TOBIE, 49, SOCIAL WORKER

"When my son's personality began to change, I tried to deal with the problem alone—I saw no reason to spill my anxieties to anyone that wasn't involved. After months of drunken threats from my son, disappointments, and mounting evidence of overwhelming dysfunction, police informed me that he was in jail. As he entered alcoholic treatment, I entered a 12-Step program. I quickly learned that I needed the support of others and the spirituality embodied in that program to understand why all of this had happened and to escape from the paralyzing downward whirlpool of self-blame."

LUCIA, 53, DENTAL ASSISTANT

Clues that ISTPs are being overwhelmed:	• Relying too much on logic, perhaps splitting hairs; unwilling to consider new data • Overreacting to the "helpful" suggestions of others
How to help ISTPs:	• Reach out and expressly invite them to participate in an activity, perhaps even assign them a task
For self-help:	• Reassess the facts with supportive others and look for new interpretations • Engage in diversionary activities perhaps so demanding that it's impossible to think of problems

The Gifts of the Inferior Function—Rest and Richness

Even though using one's inferior function is stressful, an irony of psychological type is that *a path to serenity and rest is to intentionally use the inferior function.* For the ISTP, the inferior function of Feeling is opposite the dominant function of Thinking. Therefore, its *conscious use* requires shutting down what is most natural and easy— the Thinking function, which may have gotten out of control while trying to cope with the storm.

For ISTPs, pursuing activities that use their inferior function, extraverted Feeling, requires them to interact with people who may bring new data or new ways of doing things more efficiently. Extraverted Feeling places emphasis on warm and supportive relationships and feelings, seeking harmony whether logical or not. Ways to intentionally engage the extraverted Feeling function include:

- Selecting projects or enjoyable activities that bring them into community with others.
  "I love to cook, but I recently realized that I use my gourmet dinners as a way to relate to other people. I can handle a group of six or eight and we concentrate on the dining experience—the taste, the different textures and aromas. The meal is much more enjoyable when shared with a few others."

  TRENT, 54, ELECTRICAL ENGINEER

- Completing a values clarification exercise, comparing those values with ones held by significant people in their lives, and factoring subjective criteria into decisions.
- Focusing on relationships, being aware of the needs of others, and discovering what is personally meaningful.
  "When I'm stressed I typically seek solitude, but in times of deep loss, I don't want to be alone. I prefer being with those who accept and love me despite my shortcomings. While I know God provides this sort of refuge, I also want assurance with 'skin on.'"

  JOE, 39, FARMER

In soulwork for each type, richness, depth, and development come through the inferior function. As useful as it is to understand the inferior function for the storms of life, it provides more benefits as we seek to grow.

In the first half of life we define ourselves, both in work and relationships, through our dominant and auxiliary functions. In the second half of life, the gifts of our inferior function can aid us as we seek to become all that we can be. When we don't take advantage of this natural development of our psychological type, we can become stuck.

Midlife also gives clarity to the brevity of our lives. This compels many of us almost unconsciously to seek richness from unfamiliar experiences as well as to complete the psychological tasks we may have bypassed at an earlier age. As we journey toward wholeness and completion, we can open ourselves to new avenues that are outside of our routines by relinquishing the control our dominant function exerts. Adding spiritual practices that incorporate the attributes of our inferior function can give our soulwork new dimension and zest.

The first two functions, Thinking and Sensing, give ISTPs a set of logically determined principles to guide their decisions about life, define reality, and note the practical aspects of any course of action. However, to continue to grow, ISTPs need the spiritual richness that comes from extraverted Feeling. They need to pay attention to the impact of spirituality on their values and relationships.

EXTRAVERTED FEELING SOULWORK

This involves:

- Discerning what is of most importance to people in your environment, especially those closest to you;
- Joining with others in community to accomplish tasks that are helpful for individuals and society;
- Reaching out and communicating the warmth and affection felt for others; and
- Focusing on what is positive in spiritual pathways, leaders, and sacred texts, and noting what is worthy of gratitude and appreciation.

ISTPs become reacquainted with the spiritual as they find meaning in things they previously overlooked. While they may continue many of their favorite methods of soulwork, renewal may come from the spiritual pathways that are naturally the domain of ENFJs and ESFJs:

- *Time with those I care about is now equally as important as the solitary moments I've always needed. I've sought help for my tendency to close myself off from others because I don't want to repeat the patterns of my family of origin. I've learned to express my feelings in ways that don't seem manipulative or forced.*

- *I've come to depend on my Wednesday breakfasts with "the guys." All of us are willing to admit the struggles middle age brings. Earlier I wouldn't have cared, but now I want to understand how they are dealing with the issues I also face.*

- *My kids were through with college and I had a small pension for security, so I took an "illogical" job just to have fun. Friends couldn't believe I was working in a home-improvement store, but with all my experience, I can really help the customers—they've started to ask for me by name because they know I'll make sure they have just what they need.*

- *After several friends helped me through a situation of intense grief, the reality of God changed for me. God is no longer an invisible force, but a power in the relationships between people. When there is love and kindness, I can see God in action. God is more real to me than ever before.*

- *As a child, religious holidays meant little more to me than our house being overrun by noisy relatives. Now I look forward to those times when we can all gather in one place. Preparing the special foods and using the table settings that came from our grandmother makes me keenly aware of the connecting love of family.*

I am thankful for

> My efficiency and ability to get things done
> My quiet commitment to lending a hand when needed
> My reasoning, which defines what is
> The practical bent I provide in using systems and
> information

In the storms of life, I can find shelter by

> Reserving time for reflection and analysis
> Finding ways to acknowledge and deal with my emotions
> Reassessing reality, reviewing what can and cannot change

To honor myself and my pathway to God, I can

> Satisfy my logic and my rational side as I determine my
> needs for soulwork
> Reconsider what I value, the relationships and purposes that
> will make my life most meaningful
> Acknowledge the spiritual in my experience—finding the
> consistencies and truths that are manifestations
> of God

Chapter 15
INTP

Introversion, Intuition, Thinking, Perceiving

Finding spirituality
in the inner world
of intellect
and ideas

General Description: INTPs tend to seek out purity of thought and are motivated to examine universal principles. Intensely focused on areas that matter to them, INTPs appreciate elegance and effectiveness in the conceptual realm. Independent, resourceful problem-solvers and theoretical model builders, INTPs relish the life of the mind.

> ### The Greatest Gift for INTPs: Introverted Thinking With Intuition:
> *Synthesizing information into logical systems and structures; analyzing thoughts and ideas; searching for underlying truths and ethics of fairness in order to find the best answers to problems.*
>
> ### The INTP Role in Community:
> *Asking hard questions; calling attention to inconsistencies; clarifying positions and categorizing principles while quietly and deeply exploring issues to provide a blueprint for things in the future.*

Introverted Thinking is the **dominant function** for INTPs, the function that develops earliest in life, is most comfortable to use, and is easiest to access. Using the dominant function is the natural avenue for each type to pursue soulwork—this is where the soul resides. In other words, for soulwork to be meaningful, the INTP's dominant function, introverted Thinking, must be satisfied.

INTP Spirituality: Atmospheres for Soulwork

INTP spirituality is as individual as INTPs are. They run the gamut from deeply-committed religious leaders to atheists. For many, the captivating part of spirituality is its use as an analytical tool or pathway to "the beyond" as they search for the connectedness of the Universe. As one INTP put it, "Yes, the world is complex, but there is some serenity in knowing we share a spiritual force."

Not content to use the definitions of others, INTPs generally take a studied approach to the topic if they find it interesting. On an intellectual level, they understand that full spiritual growth involves recognizing, accepting, and cultivating both logical and illogical experiences. However, their quest for clarity leads them to challenge nonintellectual experiences to arrive at an understanding while recognizing that paradox is at work throughout the spiritual realm.

INTPs often begin their spiritual journey through question or doubt; they then use those doubts to spur their spiritual inquiry. Many INTPs are well-read and conversant about spirituality, but that may not indicate a personal belief system. They might even belong to a spiritual community where they participate in the social outreach programs but disagree with major spiritual tenets. Others could see this as a major inconsistency, but INTPs see things in categories and can tolerate the discrepancy because they have a deeper underlying principle that unites the two.

Soulwork for INTPs might be setting up logical principles and steps to prove different spiritual truths. They use logical explanations, but also work to explain things that do not meet logical criteria. When questioned, INTPs will offer a rationale—and typically a complex one at that—for their approach to the topic. Their spirituality tends to be private, although INTPs may seek community with others in their search for spiritual connectedness. However, some remain on an intellectual level even when they hold roles such as rabbi, teacher, preacher, etc. INTPs are more likely to share well-reasoned arguments or justifications of their position rather than their personal feelings.

"I've come to realize that spiritual truth is not limited to what can be described by logic, but also includes much of just plain, raw life experience. For example, I have always sought truth and had thought that it was something I could grasp with my mind, just as I could reach out and grasp an object on the table. But at one point in my journey I came to the painful realization that in looking at truth this way, I had missed an enormous realm of spiritual understanding. I then came to realize that I needed to start learning the truth that love is. And if love is a kind of truth, then that kind of truth is grasped not with the intellect, but with my experience of relationship and connectedness to others."

AMERY, 58, RESEARCH PSYCHOLOGIST

"I find the contemplative traditions to be the most unifying experience for me. I've been to India, borrowed from zazen, practiced centering meditation, and incorporated many of the principles of Greek Orthodoxy as well as the early Christian church. To broaden my knowledge base, I've read almost all of the sacred texts—the full Bible at least four times, for example—searching for consistencies. I think that people who call themselves spiritual need to examine what's out there and make their own core judgments, just as I've done. It has been a long journey for me to grasp how different people relate to spiritual matters. Now I know that others' spiritual views and experiences are based on their own gifts, which allow them to see and connect with things that I do not."

KANYA, 53, SYSTEMS ANALYST

Spiritual Paths Using Introverted Thinking

Whether soulwork is new to INTPs or they desire to enrich their spiritual practices, avenues that open up intellectual inquiry and reflection are most rewarding. Some of these methods or activities include:

- Reading, collecting, and gathering books and other media on mysticism, spirituality, and religious traditions and practices. Generally, inquiry for INTPs is based on cognitive understanding and critique rather than application for their personal lives. Still, many INTPs find these activities inspiring and uplifting as well as thought-provoking.

  "When others try to tell me that faith is about believing, I point out that there is no sense believing what isn't true. For me, the question as to whether the stories of my religious tradition are true or not is irrelevant. Whether they are myths or fact, what is important is the truth in their meaning and insights into human nature."

  ELLEN, 59, PSYCHOLOGIST

- Attending conferences, taking academic courses, deep discussion in small groups (two to three others) or other intellectual learning opportunities. Topics that blend spirituality, theology, philosophy, archaeology—especially from a systems perspective—may be most appealing. To INTPs, these environments often provide opportunities for knowledgeable discussion where they can "unpack" a spiritual principle, book, or code.

- Finding a spiritual practice that honors their love of reflection and the life of the mind such as meditation, contemplation, or prayer.

  "I know that I expect a great deal from any formal expression of spirituality. While any corporate worship experience must engage my mind, it is also logical that a religious belief system should have a strong sense of feeling. I am disappointed in any gathering that is too cognitive. I want to be inspired and uplifted as well."

  GRANT, 45, MANAGEMENT PROFESSOR

- Structuring their conclusions into logical, ordered models to foster understanding of the spiritual dimension of life.
- Wrestling with the "big issues" of faith, trying to derive explanations or frameworks for discussing experiences that do not meet logical criteria or that defy rational explanations. One INTP said, "We all need to understand what we're buying into and recognize how watered down, emotional, simplistic, or reductionist our faith can be."

Clouds That Hinder Soulwork

When the gifts of the dominant function of introverted Thinking are violated, or if INTPs are not affirmed in their strengths, the drive to pursue soulwork through a search for truth, clarity, and unifying principles may be lost. Major factors that can get in the way of INTP spirituality include:

- Being in the company of those who disregard the intellectual aspects of spirituality. If others, especially the INTP's teachers or guides, fail to rationally analyze or critique their own beliefs, settle for less than truthful conclusions, or try to press their own beliefs onto an INTP (or even onto others, for that matter), then INTPs may dismiss these teachers as spiritually incompetent.
- Focusing on inconsequential, tangential, or minor facets of soulwork as subjects worthy of serious debate—wearing of hats, times of day for specific events, diets, etc.

  "In my study of comparative religions, I was amazed at the universality of symbols of faith such as the roles of food and ritual in building community or the regulations regarding who wears or does not wear specific kinds of headgear. Sometimes I am in awe, other times I want to ask what all of this has to do with the big questions of belief."

  KATHLEEN, 32, COGNITIVE PSYCHOLOGIST

- Wanting to avoid public displays of feelings or emotions. Preferring calmness in self and others, INTPs dislike straying from a cool, dispassionate mindset and therefore avoid sharing in public their deeply private thoughts or emotions.

"I grew up as a preacher's kid. I was constantly mortified when members of my dad's congregation would say, 'Let's hear a witness from the preacher's son!' At the first chance of leaving the charade, I opted for independence and left the community for good."

LEROY, 53, EDITOR

- Being aware of the expectation of many spiritual traditions that one must have a heartfelt or mystical experience in order to be "truly spiritual." The cerebral approach, valid for INTP, is often viewed as invalid and unspiritual by others.

  "I like to hear how you define spirituality, mainly because my definition appears to be very different from the spiritual experiences of others. However, so often when I ask for clarification, I get the implication that I'm not spiritual, which hurts and confuses me."

PATRICK, 28, REPORTER

- Knowing that spiritual people can over-rely on the truism that some things are beyond our human comprehension. While INTPs agree, they might argue that such truisms are still worth thinking about, not buying into "Keep things simple and just believe."

The Second Gift for INTPs: Extraverted Intuition

INTPs have extraverted Intuition as their **auxiliary function.** The gifts of extraverted Intuition include seeing future possibilities and many connections in the outer world, and actively pursuing with others ideas that will improve systems and structures.

While INTPs tend to begin their soulwork in solitude, their auxiliary function of extraverted Intuition fosters a need for some sort of community setting, whether a small group or a large organization. INTPs often find their way to spiritual communities that encourage exploration of broad topics, that search out various "truths" while acknowledging differing opinions and respect skeptical or critical thinking. They want to help organizations and people be as effective as possible using an intellectual, yet determined style that is well-grounded in their principles.

Given these kinds of conditions, and if they can accept a structure for their spirituality, INTPs may feel at home.

"Sometimes I can be captivated by music or ritualistic ceremony when (and only when) I get past my initial suspicions and doubts about the authenticity of it all. If I listen to the words of a teaching or song, I am more likely to criticize it and resist it. I think that's why I prefer readings in Hebrew. It provides the meditation of chant. But when it is in English, I struggle to turn my mind from its debating mode."

ANNE, 65, FINE ARTIST

Intellectual learning opportunities (seminars, discussion groups) that foster creative approaches can also tap the INTP's extraverted Intuition. Exploring traditions and generating numerous spiritual pathways in the company of similarly curious minds can add deeper understanding to the INTP's thinking.

Thus, the auxiliary function provides balance: While introverted Thinking supplies logical frameworks and clarifying principles, extraverted Intuition directs INTPs toward larger world views, new meanings, and relationships. This brings their soulwork from the private realm into activities and relationships with others and the world at large.

The Third Gift for INTPs: Sensing

Not as much is documented or agreed upon about how the third, or tertiary, function expresses itself in any of the 16 types.* The **third function** for INTPs is Sensing. The domain of the Sensing function includes a firm grasp of reality, attention to details, and an enjoyment of present and everyday circumstances—accepting life as it is.

Whether the third function is extraverted or introverted is not well documented in theory or practice. We therefore suggest that people observe how they use it in both the outer (extraverted) and inner (introverted) worlds at different times to see which is most helpful.

For all of the 16 types, the third function tends to evolve later in life, typically after the first two functions are clearly developed. However, many INTPs are assisted early on in accessing Sensing, their third function, because Sensing predominates in most of the world's cultures and in many early educational curricula and systems. Thus, many INTPs benefit from being able to understand factual and practical matters when they *consciously* try to do so. As they seek to enrich their spirituality, many INTPs use their third function, Sensing, to:

- Add nuance to their spirituality by learning the factual, historical, and practical aspects of a belief system; and
- Pay attention to the impact of soulwork on their current situation, noticing the simple things that bring joy to life—being healthy, experiencing the outdoors, or finding satisfaction in day-to-day events.

INTPs in the Storms of Life

The Least Accessible Gift for INTPs:
Extraverted Feeling
For all of the 16 types, the fourth function is called the **inferior function** because it is the most difficult to use consciously and effectively. The inferior function can be a source of irritation and oversights that can threaten competency, meaning and purpose, careers, or even relationships—but at its best can be a source of rest or richness in the storms of life, in moving toward deeper spirituality, or in exploring issues as we age. For INTPs, the inferior function is extraverted Feeling.

◈

For all of us, life delivers events and circumstances that we cannot control—even the most fortunate of us eventually have to deal with the relinquishment of relationships, work situations, or dreams. And as we age, the human condition demands that we face the diminishment of our own abilities and eventually our lives. While our soulwork may help us prepare for and weather these storms, knowing our psychological type can help us understand how these storms will affect us and where we might intentionally seek refuge.

The dominant introverted Thinking function of INTPs provides some natural coping skills. Their rational, analytical approach and ability to find inconsistencies or flaws in reasoning prepare them to meet crises. INTPs are often outwardly cool and objective because they logically accept that every life has its ups and downs. They therefore have a cognitive acceptance of life's tragedies and losses.

The auxiliary function of extraverted Intuition also provides some help. INTPs' natural curiosity and need to explore the truth about things lead them into active involvement with others and life. Questioning and debating their insights with others, getting out of the house or workplace, and traveling are favorite ways for INTPs to engage their Intuition.

"I didn't think I could afford the time to get away from all the problems swirling in my mind. Just when every fiber in my being said, 'Don't go,' a friend dragged me out to play racquetball. Being with others and playing a challenging game removed all the furies of my overwrought mind. Now I know that these activities are essential. Getting the motivation to do it, however, can take all my logical and intuitive resources. After I return I almost never know why I had such a struggle in the first place."

S OPHIE , 49, JUDGE

Many INTPs find that exploring the natural world (especially with others), assaying mountains, sunsets, or waterfalls, can unjam the exaggerated thinking that stress can produce. Looking at how something in nature really works sometimes provides the inspiration for a new path of thought. Additionally, talking with others, taking a group hike with no set destination in mind, or gardening with a Zen-like awareness, can provide a welcome change of habit as well as time for interaction.

When the Storms Overwhelm

Howadowever, the storms of life often swell beyond our natural capacity to cope. While life's tragedies strain all of us, no matter how intense our soulwork and regardless of our psychological type, the stormy times for INTPs can be intensified if the circumstances include any of the following factors:

- When their grief or that of others causes emotional outbursts. Because INTPs approach life in an impersonal and often detached way, such eruptions can cause them even further distress. When one INTP concluded that her principles had been violated, she blurted out with uncharacteristic feeling, "Religion is for the simpleminded! You all should grow up and do your own thinking." She was later embarrassed, but it was too late to retract her comment.

- When their commitments or workload interfere with their need for autonomy and independence. Because INTPs thrive best when they have psychological space, quiet environments, and ample time for reflection, even the day-to-day push of modern life can be contrary to their natural style and can affect their physical well-being.

- When situations or people appear arbitrary or illogical, INTPs may grow despondent, defiant, or develop physical symptoms of stress.

  "There was a terrible battle going on in my spiritual community. I did not take sides, seeing truth in both viewpoints. I tried to keep the dialogue open and to be helpful, only to find that both *sides considered me as the enemy! It was a lose-lose situation overall—and an emotional one at that."*

  PIA, 60, ARCHITECT

- When others fail to grasp their ideas and analysis of the situation, despite careful efforts to communicate.

In the most despairing moments, all types can be caught by overuse of their strengths, relying too much on their dominant function. The worst times for INTPs is when they become rigid in their logical principles. This can lead those closest to them to conclude that INTPs are unaffected by the situation or don't care about people. At the height of a crisis, their seeming aloofness may be their undoing. A cycle often starts with strong feelings of loss or anger that, as they intensify, become even harder for INTPs to express. This generates an enormous well of potentially explosive emotions, which is threatening to INTPs and others who are used to the INTP's consistent calm and logic. Resentment, confusion, or lack of support from others may result. In the worst storms, a totally different approach to soulwork may be the only refuge.

"When my wife decided she wanted a divorce, I was devastated. I guess I appeared my normal reserved and calm self, but inside I felt a lot of pain. Talking with a few close friends helped and I went to a counselor for a while. The intense pain faded after about a year, but I never did really understand why our marriage failed—that was difficult for me. I still find myself analyzing what went wrong. However, I realize now that part of my struggle was losing the option to rework the relationship. I coped by rational analysis, but analyzing the past couldn't bring back the option."

RANDY, 31, COMPUTER PROGRAMMER

"During my crisis period I discovered that 'God is Love' is a simple word definition; appropriately used, the words are interchangeable. There is a basic underlying fact being referred to—the phrase itself, like life, is meaningless. People experience a oneness under varying circumstances. Call it love and you have labeled it, not explained it. However, whatever love is, it is a fact. Invoking it and living with it more often produces a difference perceptible to others.

At midlife, I rebuilt an internal model and learned how to live more consciously with other people externally. 'You are more at peace with yourself; it is no longer upsetting to have you around'—a direct quote from my mother."

ALI, 54, CHEMIST

| Clues that INTPs are being overwhelmed: | • Preoccupation with minor inconsistencies |
| | • Hypersensitivity to perceived slights or to emotional expressions in others |

| How to help INTPs: | • Invite them to join in activities, perhaps assigning them a specific task |

| For self-help: | • Focus on a demanding activity to allow the mind to relax and perhaps reframe the circumstances |
| | • Consider the impact of actions on others and see if a change of mind or heart will bring more closeness with and support from them |

The Gifts of the Inferior Function: Rest and Richness

Even though using one's inferior function is stressful, an irony of psychological type is that *a path to serenity and rest is to intentionally use the inferior function.* For the INTP, the inferior function of Feeling is opposite the dominant function of Thinking. Therefore, its *conscious use* requires shutting down what is most natural and easy— the Thinking function, which may have gotten out of control while trying to cope with the storm.

For INTPs, pursuing activities that use their inferior function, extraverted Feeling, requires them to join with people who may possess new perspectives, organizing methods, or an understanding of human motives and values. Extraverted Feeling places an emphasis on warm and supportive relationships and feelings, seeking harmony whether logical or not. Ways to intentionally engage the extraverted Feeling function include:

• Focusing on relationships, being aware of the needs of others, and discovering what is personally meaningful. Some INTPs find it easier to share life's major hurts with people they barely know (sometimes with a person seated next to them on a bus or airplane).

- Completing a values clarification exercise, comparing those values with ones held by significant people in their lives, and factoring subjective criteria into decisions. For many INTPs, stress is often a critical component of spiritual development. Great emotional upheaval can lead to enhanced spirituality.
- Being with people in purely social and/or recreational activities—group volleyball, team sports, or other personally enjoyable activities.

In soulwork for each type, richness, depth, and development come through the inferior function. As useful as it is to understand the inferior function for the storms of life, it provides more benefits as we seek to grow.

In the first half of life we define ourselves, both in work and relationships, through our dominant and auxiliary functions. In the second half of life, the gifts of our inferior function can aid us as we seek to become all that we can be. When we don't take advantage of this natural development of our psychological type, we can become stuck.

Midlife also gives clarity to the brevity of our lives. This compels many of us almost unconsciously to seek richness from unfamiliar experiences as well as to complete the psychological tasks we may have bypassed at an earlier age. As we journey toward wholeness and completion, we can open ourselves to new avenues that are outside of our routines by relinquishing the control our dominant function exerts. Adding spiritual practices that incorporate the attributes of our inferior function can give our soulwork new dimension and zest.

The first two functions, Thinking and Intuition, give INTPs an intellectual spirituality based on their logical reasoning and awareness of future possibilities. However, to continue to grow, INTPs need the spiritual richness of extraverted Feeling. They need to pay attention to the impact of spirituality on their relationships with others and with their Creator.

This involves:

- Discerning what is of most importance to people in your environment, especially those closest to you;
- Joining with others in community to accomplish tasks that are helpful for individuals and society;
- Reaching out and communicating the warmth and affection felt for others; and
- Focusing on what is positive in spiritual pathways, leaders, and sacred texts, and noting what is worthy of gratitude and appreciation.

INTPs become reacquainted with the spiritual as they find meaning in things they previously overlooked. While they may continue many of their favorite methods of soulwork, renewal may come from the spiritual pathways that are naturally the domain of ESFJs and ENFJs:

- *We had breakfast together, just my daughter and me. We discussed our possible move to another city and how it might affect her high school years. Later, she told me that she had been amazed by my intense interest in her concerns. "Dad, whether we move or not, I know now that you care and consider the effects on me. That counts for a lot."*
- *I spent years proving or disproving every tenet of my faith, seldom letting the message sink in. "Feeling" God's love was a foreign concept. Then one day my spiritual director asked, "Do you think God loves you?" "Yes, all my analyses add up to that." "But do you really believe that?" He suggested that I catalog the times I had felt the love of others and how many times I had hurt those who love me. I then realized the power of God's love for me. That was the beginning of my new spiritual relationship with God—at the age of forty-five! I found the deepest and most powerful encounters when I recognized the value of my inner feelings.*
- *After our father died, I gathered my siblings together. We set aside all of our logical analysis about the benefits of selling the family cabin and discussed how we felt about it! Even though we may only use the*

cabin a few weeks of the year, we realized that the memories and traditions were too strong to sever. Sharing it might be a hassle, but we won't sell the cabin!

- *Pre-midlife, evaluating the emotions of others in order to show the appropriate response seemed manipulative. This was a useful analytical tool—internally modeling others to get information about their likely behavior. I can now provoke or permit empathy, after I've analyzed the situation intellectually. Part of my soulwork now is learning to occasionally give my emotions free rein—perhaps even shed tears.*

- *Whereas early on my major change points nearly always began at a place of trying to disprove other ideologies, now I find that times of great stress and emotional upheaval lead to enhanced spirituality.*

I am thankful for

My skepticism, which for me is a tool for getting at truth
My love of wrestling with complex issues, which challenge
and exercise my intellect
My curiosity that propels my search for truth
My understanding of the principles that regulate the universe

In the storms of life, I can find shelter by

Focusing on the big picture and looking for new possibilities
Using others as a sounding board to clarify my values
Assessing the impact of the situation on those around me

To honor myself and my pathway to God, I can

Pursue and analyze those areas where I doubt
Honor my need for precision, enlightenment, and wholeness
Explore the ways my soulwork can benefit my relationships
with others

So many gods, so many creeds,

    So many paths that wind

    and wind,

When just the art of being

    kind

Is all this sad world needs.

— ELLA WHEELER
WILCOX,
*THE WORLD'S
NEED*[1]

Feeling
Spirituality

Feeling Types find satisfying soulwork through:

- Living the spiritual life through avenues for personal meaning
- Enjoying the heartfelt longings and emotions of the spiritual journey
- Appreciating the beauty of relationships with others and the Creator
- Seeing applications for defining personal values, finding meaning, and individual and community growth
- Learning through understanding the motivations, inspirations, and examples of others
- Working to discern what is important for self, others, and community
- Evaluating the impact of soulwork on the inner and outer life

Preferred Extraverted Feeling Soulwork (ESFJ and ENFJ)

- Prayer/meditation with and for the needs of people and community
- Soulwork through meaningful interpersonal relationships
- Structured spiritual life, which is a basis for commitment to others
- Service through involvement with people; organizing to meet group needs

Preferred Introverted Feeling Soulwork (ISFP and INFP)

- Prayer/meditation through silent petitions for others and the longings of one's heart
- Soulwork through a personal relationship with God or Creator
- Spontaneous spiritual life, as a result of observations or insights
- Service through defining values systems, interpersonal ideals, and modeling integrity and compassion

Suggestions for Feeling Soulwork

1. "The noble-minded dedicate themselves to the promotion of peace and the happiness of others—even those who injure them" (Hindu teaching). What are the values of this statement? How do you relate to the values found in this teaching? If you were to espouse the values expressed in this statement, what kinds of conflicts might arise? When and how would these values be ineffective for you or others?

2. As you read this prayer by St. Francis of Assisi, make it your own petition. To what situations does it apply in your life? On which aspect (faith, joy, understanding, etc.) do you most want to concentrate now? How will you do that?

> *Lord, make me an instrument of your peace.*
> *Where there is hatred, let me sow love,*
> *Where there is injury, pardon;*
> *Where there is doubt, faith;*
> *Where there is despair, hope;*
> *Where there is darkness, light;*
> *Where there is sadness, joy.*
> *Divine Master, grant that I may not so much seek*
> *To be consoled, as to console,*
> *To be understood, as to understand,*
> *To be loved, as to love,*
> *For it is in giving that we receive;*
> *It is in pardoning that we are pardoned;*
> *It is in dying that we are born to eternal life.*[2]

3. Make a notebook of prayers by collecting poems, sacred readings, or meaningful quotes. Offer them as prayers, either for yourself or for others. Examples might be: "And this is my prayer, that your love may overflow more and more with knowledge and full insight to help you to determine what is best, so that in the day of Christ you may be pure and blameless."[3] (Philippians 1:9-10)

> *Let me not wander in vain.*
> *Let me not labor in vain.*
> *Let me not mingle with the prejudiced.*
> *Let me not leave the company of the virtuous.*
> *Let me not fly into anger.*
> *Let me not stray off the path of goodness.*
> *Let me not seek for this day or for the morrow.*
> *Give me such a wealth, O Almighty!*

PATTINATAR, TENTH CENTURY[4]

4. **For the discipline of study:** Reflect on your interpersonal relationships and those of others. Look to the facts, meanings, and truths, but devote the majority of your study time to the impact and implications of those relationships. What are the values and motivations of each individual? What controls them? What helps them? What lessons are there for your life?

5. **For the discipline of meditation or prayer:** As you meditate or pray about your own needs or those of others, listen for ideas of what you might be able to do for them. Are you being called to serve beyond the very real need for prayer? If so, record your ideas and actions. Then at a later time, look back on whether you were to act beyond prayer or not. How have you and others benefited from your prayers or actions?

6. **For the discipline of simplicity:** Take a hard look at your possessions, activities, serving roles, and forms of soulwork.
   - Which feed your soul?
   - Which prevent you from experiencing the things you value more?
   - Which do you try to do so "perfectly" that they block your joy?
   - Which truly add to your spirituality?

7. **For the discipline of celebration:** In addition to birthdays, anniversaries, and holidays, take time to honor and enjoy important relationships. Make sure you tell others how they have encouraged you. Ponder how empty your life would be without specific people. Then find ways to celebrate and give thanks for these people. Find time to spend with them. Send a card. Write out a prayer specifically for them (and let them see it). Give a gift to charity in their name or otherwise honor them and their relationship to you.

8. Ask someone you trust to comment on your spirituality by offering concrete and specific examples. What do they see as your strengths as a spiritual person? How can your gifts be developed further? Rejoice in having these attributes and consider what forms of soulwork might use them.

9. Nurture a special relationship for the purpose of mutual spiritual growth. You might meet regularly, correspond, study together, share difficulties and joys, or simply hold each other accountable for meeting spiritual goals.

10. Consider learning from inspiring (but not necessarily spiritual) literature, films, biographies, or magazines as legitimate soulwork. Choose titles with admirable characters and compare their motivations, struggles, and triumphs with your own. How can you apply the authors' messages to your own life?

11. Make two lists: the things you *have* to do for other people and the things you do for others that bring *you* joy. If your first list is too long, put a star by those tasks that someone else ought to do, a check by those that you feel inadequate in handling, and a diamond by those where you struggle to love the people you serve. What patterns arise? Is your life in balance? Evaluate all these tasks to see how they fit with your personal values and needs. What changes could be made?

12. Feeling types sometimes forget to place themselves on their list of people to be served. Find time in your soulwork for self-care: reaffirm your gifts, allow yourself to exercise and eat healthfully, take a nap—and affirm for yourself that this is indeed soulwork. Notice the energy you have for your mind and your body as you work to be a better steward of *you*. Remember at times to allow others the chance to serve you.

13. What styles of music or specific songs speak to the longings of your heart? Record onto one tape several songs that are inspiring to you so that you can hear, uninterrupted, music that reminds you of the joys of your spiritual walk.

14. What are the ways you can bring harmony to your interactions with people so that they will want to know the secrets of your soulwork or perhaps strive to model themselves after you?

15. By declaring yourself a spiritual person, you may place yourself in situations of conflict. Clarify the values you wish to see reflected in your life. How does your spirituality support your values or the way you live your life? What value conflicts do you expect because of your spirituality? How can your being open to those conflicts inform and enrich your spirituality? Ponder or journal on the changes you want to make to bring your life more into line with these values.

16. Pause often to reflect on the ways in which you have been able to love your neighbor as yourself. Where can you add courtesy and kindness to the processes of your workplace, home, or spiritual community? Give thanks for the moments when you were open to others' needs.

17. Ponder the fact that you are created and of value just as you are. What does this imply for your life? What about the lives of others? How is that value encouraged, supported, or nourished?

18. Reflect on your past relationships. How have they aided your soulwork? Where have they hindered your spirituality? What key learnings have you obtained in these relationships?

Embrace your

Values
Authenticity
Empathy
Memories
Compassion

Chapter 16
ESFJ

Extraversion, Sensing, Feeling, Judging

Finding spirituality
in the outer world
of people and
experiences

General Description: ESFJs tend to be organized, structured, and responsible in achieving their goals for meeting day-to-day needs. They are reliable, straightforward, outgoing types who enjoy managing others, working harmoniously to complete tasks in a timely fashion. ESFJs typically are tactful, caring leaders who focus on building good relationships.

THE GREATEST GIFT FOR ESFJS:
EXTRAVERTED FEELING WITH SENSING
A deliberate yet compassionate approach to life; adeptness in interpersonal endeavors; discerning the specific needs of self and others; radiating warmth and friendship.

ESFJ ROLE IN COMMUNITY:
Making people feel welcome and valued by understanding what matters for the welfare of the community; emphasizing cooperation and tolerance in serving others.

Extraverted Feeling is the **dominant function** for ESFJs, the function that develops earliest in life, is most comfortable to use, and is easiest to access. Using the dominant function is the natural avenue for each type to pursue soulwork—this is where the soul resides. In other words, for soulwork to be meaningful, the ESFJ's dominant function, extraverted Feeling, must be satisfied.

◇

ESFJ Spirituality: Atmospheres for Soulwork

ESFJs often see soulwork as an authentic way to bring love and caring to the world, both for themselves and for others. Through their dominant function, extraverted Feeling, ESFJs often notice when people are experiencing fulfillment, happiness and joy, or hurt, neglect, and rejection. Through their spirituality, they may strive to assist people in learning to value themselves and others. With their natural desire to help and serve, ESFJs are often drawn to the concept of a Creator who provides support, encouragement, and strength, no matter what life brings. With this understanding, spirituality often becomes the ESFJ's steadfast rudder in times of need.

ESFJs often notice the sacred in the actions and choices of others. In their efforts to live with honesty and integrity, ESFJs usually appreciate the day-to-day small, loving gestures they witness as evidence of a loving God. They may also enrich their soulwork by asking others how they reached decisions about specific spiritual issues. In these observations and discussions, either one-on-one or in small groups, ESFJs find tangible, factual ways to illuminate their own soulwork. Even though many ESFJs accept the creeds or teachings of their faiths, they often feel a desire to reexamine or redefine these teachings until they fit their personal experience and needs.

"For me, prayer is about action. Why pray if it doesn't lead to practical acts of love? When I am working for others, I am praying. When I am praying, I am working for others. At times I confess that I am so others-focused that

I forget that I need to pray for myself and to nurture my own soul as well so I can continue to grow in love and wisdom!"

DANA, 57, VOLUNTEER COORDINATOR

ESFJs often engage in meaningful disciplines for soulwork or participate in regular rituals or services. Many ESFJs enjoy their early experiences in religious communities, chalking up perfect attendance records, developing friendships, and enjoying those traditions that serve as a bridge from the past to the present generation.

"I attend morning prayers at our spiritual community as often as I can. Some of my friends wonder why it doesn't get tiresome for me. Along with the ritual that feeds my soul, I know I'm dedicating a portion of my day to my faith and participating in a ritual as many generations of women have as well."

ELAINE, 67, RETIRED

For ESFJs, spirituality is often a pathway to nurture self-esteem in themselves and in others. ESFJs work diligently to create climates where each and every person is accepted and included. Most ESFJs project a friendly, caring persona that adds an atmosphere of hospitality to the endeavors they undertake. ESFJs may seek roles in organizing events, educating children, or greeting people in ways that help them feel welcomed and appreciated. Fostering acceptance, cooperation, and harmony are important values for most ESFJs. Their most spiritual moments often come as they are able to experience emotional healing, or even well-being, in themselves or in others.

"At one time, I needed others to be strong for me, providing guidance for my choices. I thought other people were more capable than I was, so I relinquished some responsibility for myself. Then I joined a book club in my neighborhood. Even though we discussed secular novels, the themes gave us a chance to share at a deep, spiritual level. As I met with these other women regularly to discuss fictional heroines, I was encouraged by their examples to explore my own talents. I found that I have leadership abilities, I'm gifted at organizing events—and everyone seems to feel at home when I arrange things. Looking back, I was like an ostrich with its head in

the sand, hiding from the unknown when I had all the capabilities to deal with it and didn't know it."

KRISTELL, 29, OFFICE MANAGER

"I used to think of God as my organizing force—the source of the rules I should apply to my life. This structure appealed to me because I so wanted to do the 'right thing.' I now realize that I placed God in the role of my judge. Since I couldn't possibly live up to the expectations I placed on myself, I was sure that I fell short in the eyes of God as well.

"It took a devastating experience to convince me otherwise. My life was so shattered that I doubted God's existence. One of my best friends stuck by me through this period of grief and depression. Gradually, the actions of this friend brought me to an accurate understanding of love. Slowly, I realized that God acts in the same way. God wants and accepts my devotion despite my flaws or my emotional state. Although the rules still act as my guide, I now see them as a source of wisdom for my life, not a list of my duties and shortcomings."

VALERIE, 42, DIETICIAN

Spiritual Paths Using Extraverted Feeling

Whether soulwork is new to ESFJs or they desire to enrich their spiritual practices, pathways that provide structure and avenues for helping people (including themselves) mature and grow spiritually are most rewarding. Some of these methods include:

- Participating in organized learning opportunities, especially when fellowship abounds, diversity of viewpoints is welcomed, a spirit of generosity prevails, and each person's individual experiences and stories are validated.
- Talking with friends about spiritual experiences, learning about the basis for their life choices, the concrete ways God acts in their lives, and the ways soulwork comes alive for them.
- Working together in groups or communities to help or enable people to find and appreciate more of the good in life.

"I gladly took on rearranging and stocking the children's resource room at our place of worship. I knew that my approach would make it easier for volunteers to quickly find what they needed—and I even provided things they didn't yet know they'd need! Having everything in its place makes it much easier for the volunteers and makes people more willing to give of their time."

RENEE, 26, TEACHER

- Making time for special, regular spiritual practices. ESFJs might design their own ritual of daily quiet time, engage in a form of meditation, regularly attend services, or meet with certain friends as a method of soulwork.
- Defining spiritual concepts and values from their own personal experience and that of people they admire, and learning what each means for their soulwork.

Clouds That Hinder Soulwork

When the gifts of the dominant function of extraverted Feeling are violated, or if ESFJs do not experience warmth, acceptance, or harmony, their desire for soulwork may be diminished. Major factors that can get in the way of ESFJ spirituality include:

- Having a spiritual concept of shame or one of God as judge. ESFJs set high standards for themselves and may fall into the trap of thinking, "God has a yardstick and no matter how hard I try, I can't measure up." They also set high standards for others and become disappointed when people act all too human.
- Experiencing emotionally manipulative forms of spirituality. ESFJs can be vulnerable to such tactics themselves as they search for concrete evidence of love—either from God or from other people in a spiritual community. However, once "burned," ESFJs are often superior judges of manipulation and artifice, especially as it relates to the emotional domain, and can often quickly spot this kind of "fakery."

"I've learned by experience what to look for and what's genuine. Now I'm a pretty strong barometer for others and myself whenever there is

manipulation or game-playing. I can point out and label it for what it truly is—an attempt to win a point by using emotional subterfuge."

GRIFFIN, 45, PEDIATRICIAN

- Being so intent on meeting the self-worth needs of others that they overlook their own needs. Sometimes ESFJs become so expert in their role as teacher, spouse, counselor, or caregiver that they fail to see any value in themselves outside of these roles.

- Desiring to promote harmony so much that it keeps them from acknowledging when conflict or disagreements are actually happening. Externally, ESFJs may proceed as if nothing has occurred, even when deep hurt resides inside, by sitting on their feelings, thinking, "You shouldn't feel that way." The eventual realization of the conflict or that people have been hurt can cause ESFJs to feel an eruption of doubt, grief, or anger. These circumstances can lead even the most devout to experience a crisis of faith.

   "I took a leadership role in a volunteer recruitment effort because I so believed in its purpose. However, things went wrong and my hopes for harmony were dashed by constant bickering and second-guessing. Now I realized how I stuffed it—I should have spoken up at the first hint from my inner feeling that certain people were acting in ways that would defeat everyone's efforts."

   TED, 33, RETAIL MANAGER

- Sticking with one religious or spiritual tradition out of loyalty. Accordingly, ESFJs may not examine other, perhaps more appealing, faiths. They may overlook the faults in their own tradition and not be constructively critical when necessary, until they reach spiritual maturity.

The Second Gift for ESFJs: Introverted Sensing

ESFJs have introverted Sensing as their **auxiliary function.** The gifts of introverted Sensing include appreciating the richness of traditions, noticing and remembering both internal and external details, and applying soulwork to practical, personal needs.

While ESFJs often need regular contact with other people, they also need time apart from others in order to access their auxiliary function of introverted Sensing. In these quiet moments, ESFJs can review their experiences, look at current reality, and determine their view of spirituality based on this information. They can also use it to inform their decision-making by asking what the facts say and finding the basis for value judgments.

Introverted Sensing also provides ESFJs with a different avenue for soulwork, a delight in spiritual discovery by using their five senses.

"I see the variety of fish in the zoo aquarium and take note of all the different colors, designs, and textures of the marine life. God created all of this— no combination of random forces could have produced such delightful results."

JESSA, 41, SUPPORT-GROUP FACILITATOR

ESFJs can also engage their introverted Sensing function by structuring time for reflective spiritual disciplines. They may choose to engage in time-honored practices such as following the suggestions in a book of prayer or designing a personal ritual that they use regularly.

Thus, the auxiliary function provides balance: While extraverted Feeling brings an awareness of the needs of people, introverted Sensing helps ESFJs find practical applications of soulwork for their own lives.

The Third Gift for ESFJs: Intuition

Not as much is documented or agreed upon about how the third, or tertiary, function expresses itself in any of the 16 types.* The **third function** for ESFJs is Intuition. The domain of the Intuitive function includes focusing on the unseen, paying attention to imagination, insights, and information relating to future possibilities.

---

*Whether the third function is extraverted or introverted is not well documented in theory or practice. We therefore suggest that people observe how they use it in both the outer (extraverted) and inner (introverted) worlds at different times to see which is most helpful.

For all of the 16 types, the third function tends to evolve later in life, typically after the first two functions are clearly developed. How well ESFJs can access their third function, Intuition, depends on their degree of comfort with and exposure to imaginative, creative endeavors. Family, school, or recreational pursuits may help ESFJs find opportunities for their Intuition in the midst of a largely Sensing world.

As they seek to enrich their spirituality, many ESFJs use their third function, Intuition, to:

• Discover new insights about their tradition or sacred readings, either through creative thinking exercises, studying myths and symbolism, or by creative activities with others who enjoy using their imaginations; and

• Explore things that cannot easily be explained. In addition to finding answers through what they can tangibly observe or experience, ESFJs may become more willing to consider less rational explanations.

ESFJs in the Storms of Life

The Least Accessible Gift for ESFJs: Introverted Thinking

For all of the 16 types, the fourth function is called the **inferior function** because it is the most difficult to use consciously and effectively. The inferior function can be a source of irritation and oversights that can threaten relationships, careers, meaning and purpose, or even competency—but at its best can be a source of rest or richness in the storms of life, in moving toward deeper spirituality, or in exploring issues as we age. For ESFJs, the inferior function is introverted Thinking.

For all of us, life delivers events and circumstances that we cannot control—even the most fortunate of us eventually have to deal with the relinquishment of relationships, work situations, or dreams. And as we age, the human condition demands that we face the diminishment of our own abilities and eventually our lives.

While our soulwork may help us prepare for and weather these storms, knowing our psychological type can help us understand how these storms will affect us and where we might intentionally seek refuge.

The dominant extraverted Feeling function of ESFJs provides some natural coping skills. For ESFJs, the storms of life may initially serve as a call to action, especially if others are involved. Being quick to provide emotional support, ESFJs often know what might most help other people. Also, they tend to have friends with whom they regularly share their spirituality and therefore can look to these trusted people for solace in times of crisis.

The auxiliary function of introverted Sensing also provides some help. ESFJs need time alone to pull back and determine, in a factual and common-sense manner, just what is happening to *them*. Their introverted Sensing can serve to remind them to take good care of themselves in order to surmount the chaos around them.

"To outsiders who are used to my normal bubbly self, my withdrawal might seem almost depression-like. However, I simply get to a point of over-commitment where I realize I'm not doing anyone any good. I take stock of my own needs and indulge in some restoring activities—hot tub soaks, my favorite foods, catering to my own tastes for a time. Then I feel recharged and am able to turn outward again."

ALIZA, 52, FULL-TIME VOLUNTEER

Other ESFJs put their auxiliary function to use on detail-oriented projects that require precision. They may work on cross-stitch, calligraphy, model-building, automotive work, organizing belongings, or balancing their checkbook.

Introverted Sensing can also help ESFJs reassess the facts and realities of the storm they are facing to get basic data about what needs to be done, by whom, and by when.

When the Storms Overwhelm

However, the storms of life often swell beyond our natural capacity to cope. While life's tragedies strain all of us, no matter how intense our soulwork and regardless of our psychological type, the stormy times for ESFJs can be intensified if the circumstances include any of the following factors:

- When they are asked to compromise their values.
- When the storm results in conflict and ESFJs feel responsible or blamed, especially by people close to them. If major disagreements erupt over decisions that must be made, if values are compromised, or even if interpersonal niceties are completely tossed aside, ESFJs may become discouraged, disappointed, and stressed.
- When they are not supported emotionally. With all the help they give to others, when ESFJs themselves need to be encouraged, nourished, or cared for and it is not forthcoming or is presented in an unsuitable way, they may feel slighted, or at the worst, deserted.
- When their careful efforts to organize structures or events fail to prevent others from being hurt. ESFJs may experience feelings of guilt, betrayal, or deep injustice in extreme situations.
  "Even though I couldn't help the people involved, I felt I should have been able to ward off the problem. I was so upset with myself that I refused every offer of help from friends and family. I shoved away the support when I needed it the most."
  VICTOR, 37, NURSE

In the most despairing moments, all types can be caught by overuse of their strengths, relying too much on their dominant function. Often in crises, ESFJs try to keep everyone happy and everything going. The worst time for ESFJs is when they continue reaching out to others, performing all of their usual and many roles. They may use up their reserves by not listening to their souls crying for rest. It may take a major insight or new information before they can again focus on what is truly important to them. In the worst storms, a totally different approach to soulwork may be the only refuge.

"With the perspective of the passing of time, I realize how my lack of self-confidence made me vulnerable to an unhealthy relationship. For three years I tried everything to please my boyfriend. I guess I had a wacky sense of loyalty

and follow-through. Then one morning after we'd had a terrible fight, I realized that I was actually frightened of him. I started listing out the details of our relationship. The good times and beneficial facts did not outweigh the problems. For the first time, I thought about making this person the father of my children—and immediately walked to a pay phone to call my own parents. It took me a long time to sort out my feelings and define for myself what I needed in a relationship, but I made the effort to do so."

KENDALL, 29, X-RAY TECHNICIAN

"I was so stressed by the start of school, our cross-country move, and my new job that I became quite moody and irritable. Then one morning while walking my daughter to school, we stopped at a traffic crossing and she instinctively reached for my hand. At that moment I tangibly felt God's presence and gifts to me as well as my need to slow down. I called a new friend for lunch, drove the long way home in order to rethink my priorities, and resumed my normal, appreciative perspective within a few days of allowing myself those moments for reflection."

RAE ANN, 36, HOMEMAKER

Clues that ESFJs are being overwhelmed:	• Excessive criticism of themselves and others or withdrawal from group activities and camaraderie • Overanalyzing problems—consulting too many "experts," reading too many "expert" sources
How to help ESFJs:	• Encourage them to take care of themselves, volunteer to cover some of their responsibilities
For self-help:	• Indulge in self-care, eating the proper foods, resting, and exercising • Seek a change in routine or start a new project that's enjoyable and fun

The Gifts of the Inferior Function—Rest and Richness

Even though using one's inferior function is stressful, an irony of psychological type is that *a path to serenity and rest is to intentionally use the inferior function.* For the ESFJ, the inferior function of Thinking is opposite the dominant function of Feeling. Therefore, its *conscious use* requires shutting down what is most natural and easy— the Feeling function, which may have gotten out of control while trying to cope with the storm.

For ESFJs, pursuing activities that engage their inferior function, introverted Thinking, allows them to set aside their emotions and view the situation from a more objective standpoint. Ways to intentionally engage their introverted Thinking function include:

- Talking through the situation with an impartial third party. Since logic is not a strong suit for ESFJs, hearing someone else's views of the pros and cons or the causes and implications of their actions often brings about a feeling of calm.
- Analyzing the experiences of other people. Some ESFJs consciously consider the points of view and motivations of several fictional characters or friends and try to determine the logic these people used. In departing from their appreciative style, ESFJs may come to new understandings to augment their people-oriented experiences.
- Working puzzles or playing games that engage the mind in more intellectual ways.

In soulwork for each type, richness, depth, and development come through the inferior function. As useful as it is to understand the inferior function for the storms of life, it provides more benefits as we seek to grow.

In the first half of life we define ourselves, both in work and relationships, through our dominant and auxiliary functions. In the second half of life, the gifts of our inferior function can aid us as we seek to become all that we can be. When we don't take advantage of this natural development of our psychological type, we can become stuck.

Midlife also gives clarity to the brevity of our lives. This compels many of us almost unconsciously to seek richness from unfamiliar experiences as well as to complete the psychological tasks we may have bypassed at an earlier age. As we journey toward wholeness and completion, we can open ourselves to new avenues that are outside of our routines by relinquishing the control our dominant function exerts. Adding spiritual practices that incorporate the attributes of our inferior function can give our soulwork new dimension and zest.

The first two functions, Feeling and Sensing, give ESFJs a set of values, a depth of understanding of people, and a commonsense style of meeting their own and others' needs. However, to continue to grow, ESFJs need the spiritual richness of introverted Thinking. They can work toward a deeper, objective, logical examination of their spiritual journey, taking a new interest in the world of the mind rather than the heart.

INTROVERTED THINKING SOULWORK

This involves:

- Choosing one's spiritual path through an objective process of examination;
- Raising doubts in order to bring clarity to an issue;
- Searching for universal principles; and
- Defining categories and standards to apply to spiritual issues.

ESFJs can become reacquainted with the spiritual as they find meaning in things they previously overlooked. While they may continue many of their favorite methods of soulwork, renewal may come from the spiritual pathways that are naturally the domain of INTPs and ISTPs:

- *After identifying specific examples of how I have experienced each concept, I defined for myself what words such as love, truth, and wisdom meant. I looked at how these concepts were used in different con-*

texts, how they applied to different areas of my life, and made the new meanings part of my experience.

- *I made a matrix of the roles I play and the burdens I place on myself. I looked at who really has the responsibility for each outcome. This helped me reduce my list of 'shoulds' and 'oughts' as well as the number of roles I have to play.*

- *I learned that spiritual issues need to be evaluated beyond black versus white or good versus bad. There is a continuum upon which people and events can be placed. There are gray areas!*

- *The prove/disprove approach to theology now fascinates me, whereas I once found it irrelevant to the 'real' purpose of faith—building relationships. Now I can better reach out to others because my beliefs are more grounded.*

- *In the past I only wanted to make personal applications of my tradition's sacred texts. Now I study them from a textual criticism standpoint. I use different colored markers, look for repeated words or phrases, consider how usage changes from passage to passage, and determine new insights based on what I find—very different from comparing my own life to the lives of people of long ago!*

I am thankful for

My ability to befriend and care for people
My warm and enthusiastic manner
Being in tune with feelings of others and knowing what is important in life
The way I invite others in so we can all join in serving the common good

In the storms of life, I can find shelter by

Finding space and quiet time to reflect on the facts of the situation
Realizing my personal limitations and what is beyond my control
Assessing what I value, what is most important for my own life, before choosing to serve

---

To honor myself and my pathway to God, I can

- Develop a few intimate "spiritual friendships" that allow for deep conversations and examination
- Celebrate myself, others, and the beauty in the universe as expressions of the Divine
- Explore what my logical mind can add to my heartfelt pathways

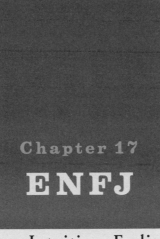

Chapter 17
ENFJ

Extraversion, Intuition, Feeling, Judging

*Finding spirituality
in the outer world
of possibilities
for people*

General Description: ENFJs tend to be lively and friendly communicators who seek to inspire others to work together toward the development of people or the institutions that serve them. Warm, interpersonally aware, caring, and cooperative, ENFJs listen to aspirations and then create, organize, and structure processes to meet them.

THE GREATEST GIFT FOR ENFJs:
EXTRAVERTED FEELING WITH INTUITION
*Seeing the positive in people and situations as well as the possibilities
for improvement; articulating their own needs and the desires of
others, helping all to grow into wholeness.*

THE ENFJ ROLE IN COMMUNITY:
*Generating enthusiasm, building camaraderie, communicating with
zest and commitment, motivating and leading people and
organizations toward the community's mission and core values.*

Extraverted Feeling is the **dominant function** for ENFJs, the function that develops earliest in life, is most comfortable to use, and is easiest to access. Using the dominant function is the natural avenue for each type to pursue soulwork—this is where the soul resides. In other words, for soulwork to be meaningful, the ENFJ's dominant function, extraverted Feeling, must be satisfied.

ENFJ Spirituality: Atmospheres for Soulwork

ENFJ spirituality is more prophetic, poetic, and people-centered than theological. With extraverted Feeling as their dominant function, ENFJs find soulwork a natural area for exploration that complements their quest for personal growth and development, and that of others. ENFJs tend to develop a spiritual philosophy that is deeply meaningful and motivates their life's work. Seeing worth and dignity in all people—themselves included—ENFJs strive to communicate the significance of each human life and the gifts that soulwork offers.

"I enjoy seeing people grow and develop to be all they can be. I believe that I'm doing God's work when I am contributing to this nurturing of people's uniqueness and individuality. The activities that attract me most are those that encourage others to see themselves as God sees them—worthy of love and approval. If more people received affirmation for who they are, everyone's life would be so much better!"

SALLY, 58, PSYCHOTHERAPIST

ENFJs flourish spiritually where there are encouragement, support, and caring activities that develop relationships. For most ENFJs, harmony among people is of utmost importance and soulwork is a vehicle to bring about congenial and empathetic relationships. As extraverts, ENFJs often seek a spiritual community, whether a small group or formal organization. They are attracted to groups that listen to their members before making decisions. For many ENFJs, being a part of a spiritual community is a way to improve people's welfare and that of the world at large.

ENFJs have a spiritual leadership style that is more prophetic than pragmatic or programmatic. Often, they can envision just how a process or organization can best serve people. With that acumen, ENFJs frequently find themselves in formal or informal roles such as teacher, mediator, facilitator, speaker, leader, or writer. They enjoy creating or designing new programs. Then, when the task is well in hand, they may turn the endeavor over to others, eager to begin something new. In addition, ENFJs hold accountable the spiritual organizations to which they belong to make deeds congruent with ideals.

"As a member of my spiritual community's governing board, I was surprised by a request for funding to refurbish our building. Our worship center was structurally fine, although the color schemes were outdated. Spending our limited resources this way would put a crimp on our stated mission of providing innovative programs for children. I reminded the board of its prior commitment to children and suggested that until we'd met our goals there, we should postpone the redecorating. Later, people thanked me for restating our vision."

RAUL, 45, PUBLIC SPEAKER

ENFJs readily volunteer, lead, and assist efforts that have an educational, benevolent, or spiritual purpose. In doing this "good work," they contribute energy and enthusiasm to such a degree that others may find it hard going without them. Often their most meaningful soulwork comes through working to make the world a better place.

"I view spirituality as an intersection between God and us and between me and others. I've had many experiences where I've felt prompted to carry out a certain deed on behalf of others, only to find out later how well my deed matched their need. You can't get me to argue about the existence of God because to me it's irrelevant—something about my philosophy of spirituality obviously brings results. As I see it, I long ago entered into a covenant

with God; this covenant is an ongoing force in my life. When I hear and respond to what God is telling me, I can live through whatever life throws my way."

NOEL, 68, RETIRED CORPORATE TRAINER

"Some people misunderstand my soulwork because it takes place outside of organized religion. There's a simple reason: Any time I join a spiritual community, I end up in charge of something! I have to pick and choose where I put my energy to work and right now I believe I can do more good with people who have no *relationship with a God or Higher Power.*

"I am a deeply spiritual person—my soulwork is what I do *as I seek to help other people through my volunteer work. I've found joy in it all, from organizing fundraising drives to sitting with a child who flew from halfway around the world to have heart surgery. Life is about helping others and making a difference. I can't abide people who think of themselves first. I work to make my organization serve people, not process them."*

JANITA, 49, HOSPICE ADMINISTRATOR

Spiritual Paths Using Extraverted Feeling

Whether soulwork is new to ENFJs or they desire to enrich their spiritual practices, pathways that allow for personal meaning and insights are most rewarding. Some of these methods and activities include:

- Discussing their spiritual journey, perhaps in a formal, organized learning setting with an atmosphere that allows them to develop personal relationships, to feel safe, and to share their hopes and concerns with others.

   "For me, building relationships with people is the *most important purpose in life. I can easily nurture my soul by gathering with others who share my values and beliefs, especially when we've had the chance to connect on a personal level and gain a sense of shared history. I appreciate the encouragement of others who think that our efforts can*

make things better for humankind. That may sound overly altruistic to some people, but my spirituality and sense of hope are intertwined."

LARA, 40, TEACHER

- Participating in retreats, study or support groups, classes, or seminars that involve interaction with others as well as time for introspection. Many ENFJs enjoy being part of the leadership for these enrichment experiences, putting to work their creativity, organizational skills, and ability to discern what others need.
  "Our community saw a huge increase in people in the midst of job transition. When I conveyed to the staff at my spiritual community how people in job transition might benefit from a support group, they provided the financial resources and space for me to launch the program."

RENALDO, 28, MIDDLE MANAGER

- Helping others in their search for wholeness. As Extraverts, ENFJs often find meaningful soulwork by working with people to ensure their well-being in a way that maximizes human potential. They may work with people individually or choose to communicate the precepts, values, and mission of their spiritual community via public speaking or teaching.
- Choosing study methods or small group experiences that provide discipline and structure. With their tendency to fill their schedules, many ENFJs seek a regular time and space for soulwork. They may do this through their own personal time using a set format for prayer or meditation, or through a learning experience where a spiritual director or mentor chooses the exercises and provides the avenue for study and learning.
- Bringing about congruence between ideals and action, both personally and for groups or communities. ENFJs often seek communities that are inclusive yet tolerant of paradox—even seeking paradox as a gateway to growth.

Clouds That Hinder Soulwork

When the gifts of the dominant function of extraverted Feeling are violated, or if ENFJs are not affirmed in their strengths, the instinctive desire to connect with others in a spiritual quest may be weakened or even extinguished. Major factors that can get in the way of ENFJ spirituality include:

- Being in atmospheres that are devoid of harmony or that are at odds with their values system. ENFJs whose relationships, either personal or within their spiritual community, are negative may struggle to find meaningful paths for soulwork, especially if they see no way to change the dynamics.

    "I put my whole heart into my commitments or else I wouldn't be involved in such a dedicated way. I also strive for warm and pleasing relationships with others. When I've given of myself that way, I expect to stay unless *the person or organization crosses one of my deeply held values or beliefs. Then—well, I can really turn a cold shoulder."*

    WENDY, 35, FAMILY-PRACTICE PHYSICIAN

- Being overcommitted—taking the weight of the world on their shoulders and then experiencing a lack of appreciation for their efforts. Burnout can result for ENFJs, especially if they are so driven that they take little time for rejuvenation.
- Struggling with a spiritual concept of shame or of God as judge. The standards that ENFJs set for soulwork and their responsibilities toward other people may then be so high that they continually fall short.
- Losing patience when spiritual traditions become too bureaucratic and people are overlooked in the process. ENFJs may become frustrated if they lack opportunities to participate in or control those factors of the spiritual community that affect the common life. They may take a public stand or go elsewhere if they perceive that the needs of some people are being ignored.

    "When I am part of a passive group, my mind tends to brainstorm ways to improve things. I came up with several suggestions to make our community gatherings more appealing for both the young fami-

lies and older members who attend. However, the leadership did not allow people to express their ideas, nor did they attempt to be flexible. I finally quit attending as the complaints of those around me increased. Now I lead a small study group that really appreciates my efforts and preparations."

FLORIAN, 52, ACTOR

The Second Gift for ENFJs: Introverted Intuition

ENFJs have introverted Intuition as their **auxiliary function.** The gifts of introverted Intuition include focusing on future possibilities, delving into the unseen, and gaining insights about the issues of life.

Pulling back from their active lifestyle to reflect can add depth to ENFJs' soulwork. This space and time spent alone allows them to find the balance that their introverted Intuition function can provide. When interacting with people, ENFJs may be acutely aware of how others are responding to situations or ideas. However, in moments of solitude, they may then be better able to generate numerous possibilities or options that give new insights on the issues or interactions they face.

"Being with God in a silent, connecting way leads me to my own thoughts. These often help me deepen my faith and add to my awareness of myself, other people, and my spiritual journey. While I prefer to pray with others, praying alone, perhaps while walking, can help me discover new ideas."

JENNIFER, 41, MINISTER

Using both their gifts of extraverted Feeling and introverted Intuition allows many ENFJs to move toward *whole* personhood—in keeping with the ENFJ theme of personal growth and development.

"I use my intuition to find patterns and deeper meanings in the spiritual books I read. These patterns help me understand what is happening in my own life—I especially find helpful those connections I glean when I'm

reading about others who've come up against and then surmounted similar obstacles. However, to do this, I have to quiet down, allowing myself plenty of uninterrupted time for the nuances to flow."

IAN, 24, ARTIST

Thus, the auxiliary function provides balance: While extraverted Feeling gives ENFJs awareness of others, introverted Intuition helps them focus their soulwork on their insights and aspirations for themselves, others, and causes they hold dear.

The Third Gift for ENFJs: Sensing

Not as much is documented or agreed upon about how the third, or tertiary, function, expresses itself in any of the 16 types.* The **third function** for ENFJs is Sensing. The domain of the Sensing function includes a firm grasp of reality, attention to details, and an enjoyment of the present and everyday circumstances—accepting life as it is.

For all of the 16 types, the third function tends to evolve later in life, typically after the first two functions are clearly developed. However, many ENFJs are assisted early on in accessing Sensing, their third function, because Sensing predominates in most of the world's cultures and in many early educational curricula and systems. Thus, many ENFJs benefit from being able to understand factual and practical matters when they *consciously* try to do so. As they seek to enrich their spirituality, many ENFJs use their third function, Sensing, to:

- Add nuance to their spirituality by being aware of the factual, historical, and practical aspects of a belief system; and
- Pay attention to the impact of soulwork on their current situation, noticing the simple things that bring joy to life—being healthy, experiencing the outdoors, or delighting in day-to-day events.

---

*Whether the third function is extraverted or introverted is not well documented in theory or practice. We therefore suggest that people observe how they use it in both the outer (extraverted) and inner (introverted) worlds at different times to see which is most helpful.

ENFJs in the Storms of Life

> ### The Least Accessible Gift for ENFJs:
> ### Introverted Thinking
>
> For all of the 16 types, the fourth function is called the **inferior function** because it is the most difficult to use consciously and effectively. The inferior function can be a source of irritation and oversights that can threaten relationships, meaning and purpose, careers, or even competency—but at its best can be a source of rest or richness in the storms of life, in moving toward deeper spirituality, or in exploring issues as we age. For ENFJs, the inferior function is introverted Thinking.

For all of us, life delivers events and circumstances that we cannot control—even the most fortunate of us eventually have to deal with the relinquishment of relationships, work situations, or dreams. And as we age, the human condition demands that we face the diminishment of our own abilities and eventually our lives. While our soulwork may help us prepare for and weather these storms, knowing our psychological type can help us understand how these storms will affect us and where we might intentionally seek refuge.

The dominant extraverted Feeling function of ENFJs provides some natural coping skills. Their network of friends, optimistic outlook, and responsive approach to interpersonal issues serve ENFJs well. In addition, because ENFJs tend to be masters of both the written and spoken word, they usually know how to approach others when they themselves need help.

The auxiliary function of introverted Intuition also provides some help. ENFJs may find that quiet time alone, if only for a few hours in retreat from their external obligations, allows them a mental space to come up with new insights and fresh possibilities.

Some ENFJs use solitude, perhaps journaling or meditating, to gain a different perspective on how a given situation affected them and what additional interpretations might be made of what actually occurred.

"As I journal, I visualize that God is looking over my shoulder, gently showing me my blind spots and reassuring me about the areas where I am on target. I stop judging myself and listen for God's voice to direct me in the situation."

TANYA, 51, HOME ECONOMIST

When the Storms Overwhelm

However, the storms of life often swell beyond our natural capacity to cope. While life's tragedies strain all of us, no matter how intense our soulwork and regardless of our psychological type, the stormy times for ENFJs can be intensified if the circumstances include any of the following factors:

- When their core values are violated. ENFJs seek congruency between expressed and acted-upon ideals and are deeply shaken when their important beliefs are compromised, misapplied, or ignored.
- When ENFJs perceive a problem as their fault. Stress often results and may bring about a strong physical reaction.
  "I noticed I developed hives just about the time our missions team started to fight over which project would be funded first. I was not expecting the intensity of conviction so many team members had for very different projects. It was a painful experience both emotionally—and as I now see—physically, too!"

ANDREW, 55, NON-PROFIT EXECUTIVE

- When a situation is contentious.
  "I hate it when people don't get along. I want to mediate, reduce, or deflect conflict—unless the situation involves a healthy search for each party's growth. Intellectually, I know people can have legitimate differences and I want to help them work it out. Sometimes when a conflict is so severe that it breaks up a friendship or a group, I feel guilty or useless because my efforts did not produce a positive outcome! I still find it hard at a gut level to accept hostilities."

APRIL, 64, RETIRED CAREER COUNSELOR

- When ENFJs or those they care about are belittled, misunderstood, or patronized, they can feel angry or despondent. Because ENFJs see human relationships as *the* most important aspect of life and because their values often include a sense of meeting people at least halfway, ENFJs can be particularly upset when relationships have a competitive up-down, in-out, or me-vs.-you manner.

In the most despairing moments, all types can be caught by overuse of their strengths, relying too much on their dominant function. The worst time for ENFJs is when they focus too intently on restoring cooperation and harmony, sometimes to the point of enmeshment. ENFJs tend to worry about receiving the disapproval of people they admire, or even of God. They may therefore hold back from contributing their own special ideas. Thus, their aversion to conflict sometimes robs them of working to change patterns in themselves or others, or to intervene in situations and add their own valid point of view.

"My friends expected me to be angry when I was diagnosed with cancer. I think they wanted me to throw a tantrum about how unfair this disease was, but that just isn't the way I am. I wanted to use my energy for more positive thoughts. What finally beat me down, though, was the bureaucracy related to the chemotherapy treatments. 'Go here, sit there, fill out this form, wait three hours'—and different nurses each time, drab waiting rooms, with no effort made to be there emotionally with the frightened patients. That caused me to explode. I can stand being sick, but not being treated like a nameless body!"

EVA, 45, PUBLIC RELATIONS

"I had worked so hard to understand the positions of each of the members of my committee that I was shocked when two of them accused me of self-serving motives in planning our next gathering. My every word, my every action, had been for the reconciliation of everyone. That night as I talked the situation over with my spouse, I even considered resigning as chair rather than cause any more disharmony. Fortunately, my spouse provided a more objective view of what had happened."

NORIKA, 27, OFFICE ASSISTANT

| Clues that ENFJs are being overwhelmed: | • Exhibiting hostility to others or trying too hard to "make" people get along |
| | • Avoiding customary interests or being sidetracked by poor logic |

| How to help ENFJs: | • Review their contributions, offer support as needed, and appreciate what they tried to do to make things go well |

| For self-help: | • Set aside some roles and responsibilities in order to find time for reflection, rest, and a reordering of priorities |
| | • Try a change in schedule or routine and allow time for self-care |

The Gifts of the Inferior Function—Rest and Richness

Even though using one's inferior function is stressful, an irony of psychological type is that *a path to serenity and rest is to intentionally use the inferior function.* For the ENFJ, the inferior function of Thinking is opposite the dominant function of Feeling. Therefore, its *conscious use* requires shutting down what is most natural and easy—the Feeling function, which may have gotten out of control while trying to cope with the storm.

For ENFJs, pursuing activities that use their inferior function, introverted Thinking, allows them to set aside their emotions and view the situation from a more objective standpoint. Ways to intentionally engage the introverted Thinking function include:

• Talking through the situation with an impartial third party. Since logic is not a strong suit for ENFJs, hearing someone else's views of their actions often brings a calming influence.
• Doing a pro/con analysis of each current responsibility, then gathering input from someone who cares. Use this exercise to clarify which tasks are too taxing, no longer necessary, or better done by others.

- Playing strategy-oriented board games or ones that involve mystery. ENFJs often find that such activities allow them to be with friends without having to discuss and deal with the problems they are facing! Other ENFJs complete crossword puzzles or cryptograms, thereby reducing their stress.

In soulwork for each type, richness, depth, and development come through the inferior function. As useful as it is to understand the inferior function for the storms of life, it provides more benefits as we seek to grow.

In the first half of life we define ourselves, both in work and relationships, through our dominant and auxiliary functions. In the second half of life, the gifts of our inferior function can aid us as we seek to become all that we can be. When we don't take advantage of this natural development of our psychological type, we can become stuck.

Midlife also gives clarity to the brevity of our lives. This compels many of us almost unconsciously to seek richness from unfamiliar experiences as well as to complete the psychological tasks we may have bypassed at an earlier age. As we journey toward wholeness and completion, we can open ourselves to new avenues that are outside of our routines by relinquishing the control our dominant function exerts. Adding spiritual practices that incorporate the attributes of our inferior function can give our soulwork new dimension and zest.

The first two functions, Feeling and Intuition, give ENFJs a set of values and an ability to envision ways to be helpful. However, to continue to grow, ENFJs need the spiritual richness of introverted Thinking. They need to work toward a deeper examination of their spiritual journey, taking a new interest in the world of the mind in addition to the world of the heart.

INTROVERTED THINKING SOULWORK

This involves:

- Choosing one's spiritual path through an objective process of examination;

- Raising doubts in order to bring clarity to an issue;
- Searching for universal principles; and
- Defining categories and standards to apply to spiritual issues.

ENFJs become reacquainted with the spiritual as they find meaning in things they previously overlooked. While they may continue many of their favorite methods of soulwork, renewal may come from the spiritual pathways that are naturally the domain of ISTPs and INTPs:

- *One of my new missions in life is to educate our legislature about the needs of single fathers. However, rather than being at the forefront of this lobbying effort, I'm doing the behind-the-scenes research. I'm amazed at how much I enjoy reading court cases in order to find legal precedents to support our positions.*
- *I realized that as I was approaching sixty I had a tad less energy than I did as a forty-year-old. I've always had a full calendar and I love being with people, but now I need some time to do just what I want—even to be alone. In order to get that time, I took out my yearly schedule and listed all of my commitments. I then assigned a higher numeric value to those things which met three conditions: no one else could do them, they gave me the greatest joy, and they allowed me to learn. By using a logical analysis for elimination, I found some time in my schedule just for me.*
- *I've taken to studying with an objectively oriented friend. We get into long discussions about our beliefs and she presses me to clarify my statements, forcing me to search for the true meanings of my faith.*
- *I'm more inclined to want an academic approach to spiritual learning experiences. Before, I wanted to know how the sacred texts applied to my life and relationships. Now I'm just as interested in alternative explanations for the origins of certain stories and their cultural context. Understanding these things allows me to better explain them to others.*
- *I've done a lot of work around my need for harmony. Sometimes it simply isn't logical for people to agree. With this truth now firmly ingrained, I can embrace the fact that disagreement is sometimes healthy and can even be a starting point for transformation. I'm much freer to concentrate on the issue at hand than the squabbling among the people around me.*

I am thankful for

My understanding of what matters most
My friendly, warm, people-centered style
My gifts of communication and creativity, which allow me
to advance human aspirations
My passion for helping others become whole

In the storms of life, I can find shelter by

Pulling inward and considering all the hopeful possibilities
Assessing what is most important and finding personal
confirmation for my values system
Being direct with others about my views, letting them know
where I stand

To honor myself and my pathway to God, I can

Gather with kindred spirits for inspiration
and understanding
Champion efforts to create the atmospheres for nurturing
human potential I can so clearly envision
Determine the logical underpinnings of my values and
beliefs in order to confirm what my heart already knows

Chapter 18

ISFP

Introversion, Sensing, Feeling, Perceiving

*Finding spirituality
in the inner world of
personal meaning
and application*

General Description: ISFPs tend to be gentle, compassionate, and considerate. They are often modest and self-effacing in their service to others. They seek cooperative, harmonious, and warm work and home environments. They care about all living things. They aid by providing comfortable atmospheres with color, music, flowers, etc., to please others.

THE GREATEST GIFT FOR ISFPs:
INTROVERTED FEELING WITH SENSING

*Quietly enjoying life, balancing their outward tasks with their inward
needs in an easygoing, flexible, amiable way; doing and saying the
right thing at the right moment.*

THE ISFP ROLE IN COMMUNITY:

*Putting others at ease while providing altruistic acts of charity to those
in need on an individual basis; offering resourceful, behind-the-scenes
assistance for endeavors they support.*

Introverted Feeling is the **dominant function** for ISFPs, the function that develops earliest in life, is most comfortable to use, and is easiest to access. Using the dominant function is the natural avenue for each type to pursue soulwork—this is where the soul resides. In other words, for soulwork to be meaningful, the ISFP's dominant function, introverted Feeling, must be satisfied.

◆

ISFP Spirituality: Atmospheres for Soulwork

For ISFPs, soulwork takes place in the midst of their unpretentious yet full lives. They seldom seek or need huge crowds or daring deeds—ISFPs often find the spiritual right around them in the little things of life as they play out their role of observant bystander. While the initial spiritual pathways for ISFPs may differ, their belief systems help them form their foundational values, which guide the day-to-day events of their lives.

Many ISFPs are encouraged spiritually by what they experience directly. Rather than setting aside structured time for soulwork, ISFPs may tap into their spiritual nature while tending a garden, caring for pets or children, or enjoying their favorite solitary activities. The beauty around them in the world and the ability to nurture other living things reminds them of a Higher Power and helps them listen to their souls.

Tender and vulnerable themselves, ISFPs quickly notice the hurts of others and quietly assist in any practical way they can. Generally, this concern for others is at the root of their spirituality. Many people have been blessed through the efforts of an ISFP without knowing it. Most ISFPs feel closest to God when they can bring a meal, fix a car, baby-sit for someone in an emergency, or visit with an elderly person.

"For me, spirituality is a force that helps me serve others. If the religions of the world didn't at least point us in the direction of goodness, there'd be a lot more suffering and chaos. I can put up with the weaknesses of organized

religion because I wonder if the world would even have survived this long without it!"

VAL, 45, OFFICE MANAGER

ISFPs frequently object to rules and restrictions for spirituality, as they can result in people being hurt or ostracized. Most of all, ISFPs are attracted to places where consideration of others is key. They prefer environments where the unique needs of individuals are recognized and addressed in special ways. By modeling cooperation and inclusion, ISFPs often unconsciously bring people together in a spirit of harmony and joyful teamwork for the task at hand.

"During my childhood, my family participated together in our spiritual community. I enjoyed being with my friends each week, but there were so many requirements—things to memorize, duties to perform, places to be, etc. As I grew older, I took a hard look at all of the rules and regulations that our particular tradition placed upon us. What I saw pushed me further and further away.

"I don't like the concept that a few people decide who is in and who is out. We were taught that all other faiths, even those very close to our tradition, were wrong and to be avoided. Instead of nurturing all people and helping them grow, the authorities' attitude was, 'Just do as we say!' I certainly didn't want to do as they did. Eventually, I left that place to claim for myself what is really important to me as a spiritual person."

CALEB, 47, INDEPENDENT CONTRACTOR

"One of my close friends is, in my mind, an ideal, joyful servant to other people. When I learned that she found inspiration in her spirituality to live out her values and beliefs, I became more interested in my own soulwork. Her particular religious community, where I frequently attend, encourages open discussion of issues for which there are no easy answers. It's large enough that I can choose my activities but stay anonymous when I so desire. There are many avenues for me to quietly act on what I believe. I think God is about helping the walking wounded of the world, not creating more of them through insensitivity and judgmentalism."

BRITTE, 36, SMALL-BUSINESS OWNER

Spiritual Practices Using Introverted Feeling

Whether soulwork is new to ISFPs or they desire to enrich their spiritual practices, pathways that shape and deepen their core values are most rewarding. Some of these activities and methods include:

- Spending time alone in a favorite setting—the woods, the kitchen, with a friend, or where other living things and aspects of nature can be appreciated.
- Attending large-group learning or worship experiences *if* they don't have to share personally or talk with others. ISFPs prefer being lost in a crowd.
  "Though I am very happy in my spiritual community, I find the 'coffee time' awkward and uncomfortable. I feel very self-conscious even though I can sometimes get into a great conversation. More often than not, it is an unsatisfactory experience for me—milling around, wondering how to connect."

  BJORN, 43, HUMAN RESOURCES

- Studying practical subjects that have a spiritual component, such as workshops on marriage, parenting, communication, organizational skills, etc. With their wealth of common sense, many ISFPs like putting their time toward something that can be useful.
  "Our men's group once did a seminar on time management. The materials were full of suggestions that could be implemented immediately. The presenters made us feel as if everyone, not just me, had these problems."

  KIRBY, 32, POLICE OFFICER

- Joining a small, close-knit group (a few *carefully chosen* others) for conversation focused on applying spirituality to their lives.
  "My wife and I belonged to a small study group for seven years. There were just four couples and during those years we supported each other through major, traumatic events. It was a highly significant part of our connection to our spiritual community and was also extremely helpful in our lives."

  DAN, 59, PHYSICAL THERAPIST

- Performing personal acts of kindness for people and helping them learn about spiritual matters in simple and direct ways. ISFPs are often able to observe just what others need and then provide it just at the right time in the right way, often to the surprise of others.

Clouds That Hinder Soulwork

When the gifts of the dominant function of introverted Feeling are violated, or if ISFPs are not affirmed in their strengths, the desire to ascertain their values through soulwork may be weakened or even extinguished. Major factors that can get in the way of ISFP spirituality include:

- Being so busy with all of the immediate needs they see that they can't find time for soulwork.
  "I do value myself, but often I don't have the presence of mind to think of how my 'good deeds' might tax my own physical, spiritual, or emotional resources. Before I know it, I'm exhausted, there's no dinner ready for my own family, and I barely have enough energy to hug my kids as they return from school."
  BONNEE, 28, HOMEMAKER

- Having to do too much socializing or sharing in public settings or in open forums. Many ISFPs dislike being put on the spot to express their spiritual beliefs.
- Finding it difficult to overcome rejection. When ISFPs have been hurt or cast aside by the criticism or actions of others, they may not wish to be included again.
  "I've been disappointed by many people in my life, so I've avoided those situations that can lead to similar rejection. However, in all of this, there is one constant—I have discovered that God doesn't let me down."
  MICHELLE, 54, DENTAL ASSISTANT

- Undervaluing themselves or the contributions they make in the spiritual domain. Because ISFPs like to serve behind the scenes, they and others may discount their own abilities or contributions.

- Struggling to convey the ideals and values they hold so deeply. Others often miss out on nuggets of insight from ISFPs because at times, it can be difficult for them to articulate something of such great importance.

"I can't put into words what God means to me. What comes out sounds either childish or flat—and my relationship with God is anything but that. So I choose not to say anything rather than fall short of the way I feel."

KAY, 63, RETIRED TEACHER

The Second Gift for ISFPs: Extraverted Sensing

ISFPs have extraverted Sensing as their **auxiliary function.** The gifts of extraverted Sensing include experiencing the sacred in what is immediate and real while engaging fully in the active life given to us.

While ISFPs tend to begin their spiritual journey in solitude, their auxiliary function of extraverted Sensing often fosters a need to gather with others, whether in a small group or a large organization. ISFPs are drawn to warm and supportive people who can provide concrete examples of ways in which soulwork has helped them—what they did and what outcomes resulted.

Extraverted Sensing also gives most ISFPs an awareness of the needs of others.

"I have a lot in common with the earthworm—and people who don't consider that a noble comparison forget the role that worms play in aerating soil and making it possible for plants to grow strong and healthy. They aren't visible but they do a lot of good. I don't draw attention to myself as I work alongside others, so they are often surprised by the knowledge I have about them and the unique help I can offer when I suddenly pop into the picture."

JAN, 58, NURSE

ISFPs also use the outer world of Sensing to connect with traditions and role models from the past that are meaningful to them.

"When I go antiquing, I am drawn to the beauty of certain items, but I also think about the history of each piece—where the first owners might have lived, how it might have graced their home, and what their lives might have been like. My grandma's china set began my interest in antiques. Grandma was very spiritual; when I set the table with the same dishes she used, I gain a sense of support. I share her beliefs in God. From her stories I know she gained strength from her spirituality. That same strength is available to me as well."

KATHLEEN, 31, SMALL-BUSINESS OWNER

Thus, the auxiliary function provides balance: While introverted Feeling provides ISFPs with a deeply rooted set of values and beliefs, extraverted Sensing gives them an appreciation of the world around them and an awareness of all the beauty to be found in God's creation. This brings their soulwork from their private world into their relationships with others.

The Third Gift for ISFPs: Intuition

Not as much is documented or agreed upon about how the third, or tertiary, function expresses itself in any of the 16 types.* The **third function** for ISFPs is Intuition. The domain of the Intuitive function includes focusing on the unseen and paying attention to imagination, insights, and information relating to future possibilities.

◈

For all of the 16 types, the third function tends to evolve later in life, typically after the first two functions are clearly developed. How well

---

Whether the third function is extraverted or introverted is not well documented in theory or practice. We therefore suggest that people observe how they use it in both the outer (extraverted) and inner (introverted) worlds at different times to see which is most helpful.

ISFPs can access their third function, Intuition, depends on their degree of comfort with and exposure to imaginative, creative endeavors. Family, school, or recreational pursuits may help ISFPs find opportunities for their Intuition in the midst of a largely Sensing world.

As they seek to enrich their spirituality, many ISFPs use their third function, Intuition, to:

- Discover new insights about their tradition or sacred readings, either through creative thinking exercises, studying myths and symbolism, or by creative activities with others who enjoy using their imaginations; and
- Explore things that cannot easily be explained. In addition to finding answers through what they can tangibly observe or experience, ISFPs may become more willing to consider less rational explanations.

ISFPs in the Storms of Life

The Least Accessible Gift for ISFPs:
Extraverted Thinking

For all of the 16 types, the fourth function is called the **inferior function** because it is the most difficult to use consciously and effectively. The inferior function can be a source of irritation and oversights that can threaten relationships, careers, meaning and purpose, or even competency—but at its best can be a source of rest or richness in the storms of life, in moving toward deeper spirituality, or in exploring issues as we age. For ISFPs, the inferior function is extraverted Thinking.

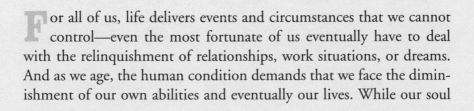

For all of us, life delivers events and circumstances that we cannot control—even the most fortunate of us eventually have to deal with the relinquishment of relationships, work situations, or dreams. And as we age, the human condition demands that we face the diminishment of our own abilities and eventually our lives. While our soul

work may help us prepare for and weather these storms, knowing our psychological type can help us understand how these storms will affect us and where we might intentionally seek refuge.

The dominant introverted Feeling function of ISFPs provides some natural coping skills. Their strong beliefs and their values base help them maintain emotional balance through many of the smaller crises. In addition, with their strong emphasis on serving others, ISFPs may keep themselves busy trying to help whomever else is affected. They tend to know instinctively when to act and when to wait, when to speak and when to keep quiet. They'll cook, repair, visit, write, assist, or nurse to help out and, when they need help, these favors are often returned to them.

The auxiliary function of extraverted Sensing also provides some help. Because their deep convictions and sensitivity sometimes result in ISFPs being personally hurt, many find solace in checking out the facts surrounding the events. They can use their Sensing function to ask themselves questions such as: What was actually said and done? Were the differences of a personal nature or more situation-specific? If ISFPs can step back from the crisis for awhile, sometimes their common sense helps them see new realities that can rectify the event.

Other ISFPs regain their energy by tackling a project or activity that lets their established skills shine. They might focus on a routine project at work or their favorite craft or hobby, or find a way to enjoy nature through walking and other pursuits.

"I am good at golf. Getting out on my favorite course helps me forget whatever upset me. I know which clubs to use, the lay of the ground, how to correct for the wind—things work out for me the way they are supposed to and I feel refreshed."

TAD, 23, STUDENT

When the Storms Overwhelm

However, the storms of life often swell beyond our natural capacity to cope. While life's tragedies strain all of us, no matter how intense our soulwork and regardless of our psychological type, the stormy times for ISFPs can be intensified if the circumstances include any of the following factors:

- When the storms bring conflicts among those close to them. ISFPs may work feverishly to smooth over conflicts and may withdraw if they perceive that there is too much disharmony or if they feel they could be at fault.
  "The rest of my work team calls on me whenever there are disputes. I try to help people see one side or the other and bring down the emotional levels. However, I'd much rather flee when they fight with each other."

  ALLI, 29, PRESCHOOL TEACHER

- When a crisis makes their normally private lives more public. ISFPs may become prematurely resigned to a situation if they believe they have lost face.
  "We knew our daughter suffered from depression and had sought medical help. However, when she attempted suicide we were devastated. We told only a few close, trusted friends and of course the rest of the family. We weren't trying to hide it, we just wanted the space for her and ourselves to recover and heal."

  ANDREA, 60, LEGAL SECRETARY

- When they are pressured to make major decisions with long-range implications. For ISFPs, the process of living is much more important than setting goals. In the midst of a crisis, ISFPs may resist looking at the big picture, taking each day one step at a time.
- When they sense the possibility of loss or failure in a relationship.

In the most despairing moments, all types can be caught by overuse of their strengths, relying too much on their dominant function. The worst time for ISFPs is when they go beyond their own emotional and/or physical limits to be of service to others. Their natural tendency to help can become their undoing because in the process they may deny their own needs in the interest of others. They have overused their dominant Feeling function by trying to make everyone happy. When these dark times come, ISFPs may lose their natural gentle and caring demeanor. In the worst storms, a totally different approach to soulwork may be the only refuge.

"The foundation where I worked was in turmoil. Two department heads had quit just a few days before the main fund-raising event of the year. I pitched in, making arrangements, checking on the guest list, finalizing the floral centerpieces, in short, doing the work of three people. Late one evening as I was helping to set up the banquet tables, I started listening to myself lord over the volunteers, berating them for crooked fork placements and bringing the wrong name tags. 'This isn't me,' I thought. I was so embarrassed that I simply left. If I hadn't, I'm sure I would have continued on and chased away any remaining volunteers!"

LISA, 33, RECREATION MANAGER

"When my father was dying, I honestly tried to be two places at once for weeks on end. I had the nursing skills to make him more comfortable and knew his special tastes in food, reading materials, flowers, friends, and all of the other little things that could brighten his day. However, I also had a family of my own that needed my attention.

"Finally one morning I found myself too exhausted to crawl out of bed. I called a friend to cover a commitment I couldn't let slide that day. Later, she appeared at my door to deliver a lecture about my not doing my father or family any good by running myself into the ground. She was right—I needed to be on the receiving *end of service as well as the giving end, but at the time I felt unappreciated for what I* was *doing."*

KIM, 51, BOOKKEEPER

Clues that ISFPs are being overwhelmed:

- Hasty actions, critical comments, or abnormal directive and abrupt take-charge behavior
- Overly logical or analytical about a situation, perhaps in the process using faulty reasoning

---

How to help ISFPs:	• Provide an appropriate framework and objectivity for the decisions they face

For self-help:	• Pull back from service to others • Work through a situation logically with someone who can offer support and affirmation

The Gifts of the Inferior Function—Rest and Richness

Even though using one's inferior function is stressful, an irony of psychological type is that *a path to serenity and rest is to intentionally use the inferior function*. For the ISFP, the inferior function of Intuition is opposite the dominant function of Sensing. Therefore, its *conscious use* requires shutting down what is most natural and easy—the Sensing function, which may have gotten out of control while trying to cope with the storm.

For ISFPs, pursuing activities that use their inferior function, extraverted Thinking, forces them to set aside their subjectivity and approach the situation from a more objective, logical perspective. Ways to intentionally engage the extraverted Thinking function include:

- Stepping back from the situation, determining through cause/effect statements what happened and what universal truths were violated. Some ISFPs memorize certain passages from sacred or secular readings, giving them a basis for remembering what holds true in any situation. Using this approach often stops the cycle of ISFPs making excuses for the other people involved or feeling depressed or guilty about the situation.
- Organizing or reorganizing something that is important or will save time—a computer database, a color-coded system for storage, or perhaps a better format for some business forms. Using efficiency and sound reasoning at these times can help in sort-

ing out other issues while bringing some momentary order as well.

- Engaging the mind in activities that require logic. Some ISFPs read mysteries, where the clues always add up to the right answer; play games such as chess or duplicate bridge that require analysis and strategy; or work double acrostics to remove themselves mentally from the problems at hand.

In soulwork for each type, richness, depth, and development come through the inferior function. As useful as it is to understand the inferior function for the storms of life, it provides more benefits as we seek to grow.

In the first half of life we define ourselves, both in work and relationships, through our dominant and auxiliary functions. In the second half of life, the gifts of our inferior function can aid us as we seek to become all that we can be. When we don't take advantage of this natural development of our psychological type, we can become stuck.

Midlife also gives clarity to the brevity of our lives. This compels many of us almost unconsciously to seek richness from unfamiliar experiences as well as to complete the psychological tasks we may have bypassed at an earlier age. As we journey toward wholeness and completion, we can open ourselves to new avenues that are outside of our routines by relinquishing the control our dominant function exerts. Adding spiritual practices that incorporate the attributes of our inferior function can give our soulwork new dimension and zest.

The first two functions, Feeling and Sensing, give ISFPs a set of deeply held ideals and an awareness of the delights of this life. However, to continue to grow, ISFPs need the spiritual richness of extraverted Thinking. They may be compelled to search for more intellectual implications for their spirituality.

EXTRAVERTED THINKING SOULWORK

This involves:

- Defining and clarifying truth and universal principles in an impartial manner;

- Bringing intellectual and philosophical insights to spiritual questions;
- Examining the systems and structures of their beliefs or applying logical reasoning to their decisions and values; and
- Allowing doubts to be the catalyst in searching for new understanding, asking critical questions, and analyzing different explanations.

ISFPs become reacquainted with the spiritual as they find meaning in things they previously overlooked. While they may continue many of their favorite methods of soulwork, renewal may come from the spiritual pathways that are naturally the domain of ENTJs and ESTJs:

- *My beliefs and values are now a tool as I try to objectively analyze my spiritual convictions and make choices about my activities. I defined several logical criteria to clarify the best use of my time and narrowed down my charity work to the two most deserving projects. I now understand the personal costs of agreeing too often to serve the needs of others. With this grounding, I feel a new freedom to say "no" to many requests in order to say "yes" to myself.*
- *I finally took a rigorous class on the main teachings of my religion. The lecturer presented logical arguments to prove our major tenets. I now feel more able to explain my beliefs to others. Her logic gave a structure to the things that I've thought about for years.*
- *I never thought of myself as a teacher, but I love passing on my beliefs to children. The process forces me to think in the type of logical steps that will help them understand. In the process, I revisit my own beliefs in a slower, more deliberate manner.*
- *Certain parts of the sacred texts seem true to me in all situations. I've memorized those passages and they've become a part of my way to deal with what is.*
- *After delivering meals as often as I could to the elderly in my small county, I realized that there were many others who really needed this service regularly. I took it upon myself to get our spiritual community to sponsor an official meal-delivery program.*

I am thankful for

My cooperative and considerate nature
My enjoyment of life's precious moments
My capacity to minister to the hurts I see
The ways in which I bring harmony to human endeavors

In the storms of life, I can find shelter by

Accomplishing something that enhances my faith in myself
Being in the world of nature to experience God at work in
this world
Assessing what really happened in tough situations in an
objective way, thereby giving myself a fresh start

To honor myself and my pathway to God, I can

Allow myself time to be spiritual in my own way
Clarify my values so that I can know best how to
serve others
Define and accept a logical basis for what I take on faith in
order to communicate it more easily to others

◈

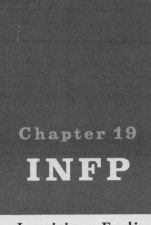

Chapter 19
INFP

Introversion, Intuition, Feeling, Perceiving

Finding spirituality
in the inner world
of the heart
and imagination

General Description: INFPs tend to be inquisitive, gentle, creative, and concerned about the human condition or the common good. They seek to follow their ideals, remind others of what is important in life, and use humor and insight to make their points. INFPs strive to make their inner vision of perfection real in their lives and in the lives of others.

THEIR GREATEST GIFT:
Quiet and insightful as they develop their compelling values; concentrating on issues that matter to people; shifting the focus from what is to what could be better.

THE INFP ROLE IN COMMUNITY:
Working with others to identify ideals and the worthiness of striving to meet them; discerning what has meaning for individuals and communities, then leading through the strength of conviction.

Introverted Feeling is the **dominant function** for INFPs, the function that develops earliest in life, is most comfortable to use, and is easiest to access. Using the dominant function is the natural avenue for each type to pursue soulwork—this is where the soul resides. In other words, for soulwork to be meaningful, the INFP's dominant function, introverted Feeling, must be satisfied.

◈

INFP Spirituality: Atmospheres for Soulwork

INFP spirituality is often intensely personal and well thought through. With introverted Feeling as their dominant function, INFPs usually seek a deep understanding of their values and ideals, tailoring individual soulwork to discern what is important. Although most INFPs regard spirituality as an ongoing journey, they prefer to reach a level of inner certainty in their belief system before welcoming discussions with others. INFPs typically want to share their ideas one-to-one with those who are trusted.

Most INFPs delight in the mysteries of spirituality. They are among the most open of all the 16 psychological types to mysticism—unseen and synchronistic experiences make up the fabric of everyday life. INFPs consider the existence of the spiritual world their referential starting point and are receptive to information from their intuition and other intangible sources. Some of the greatest teachings in many of the world's spiritual traditions on meditation, prayer, and other spiritual disciplines come from INFPs. People generally feel comfortable confiding in them because of their ability to listen, their obvious concern for the nurturing of the spiritual in others, and their openness to the inexplicable.

"Sometimes I ponder why people will share their spiritual insights, issues, or personal concerns with me, even in settings that have no apparent content or discussion of spirituality. Somehow people sense that I think about such things and they risk trusting me with what seems to be intimate knowledge."

CORRINNE, 56, RESEARCH SCIENTIST

For INFPs, personal relationships, either with people or with their Creator, are an important part of their spirituality. Soulwork provides them with a link to others and the important purposes of life. With their concern for living out their ideals, they are often alert for hypocrisy, judgmentalism, and intolerance on the part of organized spiritual communities or "pious individuals."

"I welcome diversity of belief and tradition and feel a tie to anyone who is open to soulwork. No one issue is too big, or for that matter, too small to address. I enjoy the dialogue differences create. I'm sure that God knows there's a diversity in the ways and means of faith. To me, spirituality is definitely not a 'one size fits all' proposition."

PAVEL, 44, PSYCHOLOGIST

The joy of deep understanding, the communion between self and others, and the personal relationship to the Creator are often facets of INFP spirituality.

"I think I was born with a hunger to feed my spiritual self as well as my physical self. I used to read books about Gandhi, St. Joan of Arc, and different religious movements around the world, fascinated by how ordinary people could garner the courage to take such stands. I often checked out Bible encyclopedias, the Koran and its explanations, as well as other sacred texts—all done privately because I felt the need to know for myself about different leaders and spiritual belief systems.

"People are sometimes amazed to hear that I started what became my life's work when still a teenager. I learned early on what I value—helping others find soulwork that is personally meaningful and that honors their search, whatever the source. It's a goal worth pursuing for a lifetime."

MICHAEL, 55, UNITARIAN MINISTER

"So often the impressions I receive from 'out there' are accurate, driving my inherent trust in the unseen world. Perhaps other people could receive the same messages I do, both from the natural world and from the events of life, if they took the time to notice. As I listen to a friend, attempt to express

myself through poetry, or walk through a meadow, I consciously open my mind to what God might be saying to me.

"More often than not, God has plenty to say! I think that's why I've been able to bring to fruition my dream of helping other women through my art. For the past five years, I've followed my 'hunches,' which I believe were really God's advice. The results? A workshop for impoverished women, funded by grants, that virtually no one else thought possible."

SONDRA, 37, ARTIST

Spiritual Paths Using Introverted Feeling

Whether soulwork is new to INFPs or they desire to enrich their spiritual practices, pathways that allow for mysticism, transcendence, and integrity are often the most rewarding. Some of these methods or activities include:

- Engaging in quiet times alone to journal, meditate, and reflect on the values or ideals INFPs wish to live out in their lives.
- Being with a trusted person to discuss matters of the soul and spirit in an intimate way.
  "I have my own inner constellation of interests that often intersect[s] with what is going on in my 'outside' life. I typically share this in little pieces only with my wife when we go for our evening walks. She is a good listener who gently challenges my conclusions and enriches my perceptions. She is truly my soulmate."

ANSEL, 24, TEACHER

- Living out their lives consistently with their values, thus enabling INFPs to move out into the world independent of prevailing opinions with determination and persistence.
- Expressing values or aesthetic sense through artistic, literary, or personal works.
  "In my spare time, I quilt. There are so many possible and creative ways to do quilts that I am never bored or boxed in. And as much as I feel the quiet enjoyment and peace that comes by doing the actual work, I also find a great deal of pleasure in giving the finished quilts

to family members. It is rewarding to see their joy in knowing they have something entirely unique—my quilt for them."

JOHN, 56, QUALITY ASSURANCE MANAGER

- Ministering to those whose needs are unmet, offering compassionate, life-giving, personalized resources. This help may include involvement in human rights, equal access to education, or other social issues. INFPs' passion is often ignited by the hope that they can bring the world toward greater congruence with these values. Sharing with others in times of need often deepens their respect for the quiet acts of courage and altruism they see.

Clouds That Hinder Soulwork

When the gifts of the dominant function of introverted Feeling are violated, or if INFPs are not affirmed in their strengths, the instinctive connection with the spiritual aspects of life may be weakened or even severed. Major factors that can get in the way of INFP spirituality include:

- Being with people who are dogmatic, rigid, or judgmental in their spirituality.
  "I can spot a phony quickly and can be put off by someone who 'knows it all' and hurts people in the process. I stay as far away as possible from those I regard as narrow-minded."

SHELIA, 43, SOCIAL WORKER

- Being misunderstood or having their spiritual experiences discounted. INFPs may have difficulty finding other people who can relate to their understanding of the mystical aspects of life. Others may accuse them of not being grounded in reality.
  "I believe that God often speaks to me, using simple things in nature and small events in my life. I seldom share these insights with other people, though, for I am usually misunderstood."

IRA, 48, CHEF

- Finding out that someone or something has crossed their spiritual values by discrediting or betraying their spiritual community or belief system.

  "I have spent much of my life out in the world, speaking and acting for my beliefs in ways that go decidedly against my way of being. I must be consistent with my internal values to the point of being independent of prevailing opinions. At my best I do this as gently as possible without criticizing or demeaning others. I'm determined and persistent, yet quiet, unless that approach fails to create the changes I clearly see need to be made."

  KIRSTEN, 67, RETIRED COUNSELOR

- Endeavoring to bring the perfection they believe is possible to their spiritual journey. INFPs sometimes get so caught up in their aspirations and desire for wholeness that they willingly search for better spiritual beliefs, ideas, or disciplines, never really settling on any one practice or faith.

  "I think my soulwork habits are similar to my love life. I waited until I was thirty to marry and even then I had misgivings about not having found the perfect *spouse for me. I later discovered that I can* contribute *to the ideal and accept some reality, too!"*

  JEFF, 39, JOURNALIST

The Second Gift for INFPs: Extraverted Intuition
INFPs have extraverted Intuition as their **auxiliary function.** The gifts of extraverted Intuition include seeing future possibilities and many connections in the outer world, and actively pursuing with others ideas that might make things better for people and organizations.

While INFPs tend to begin their spiritual journey in solitude, their auxiliary function of extraverted Intuition often fosters a need for some sort of community setting, whether a small group or a large organization. INFPs tend to hold their spiritual community accountable to its values, remind others of what is best for the common welfare, and provide behind-the-scenes care. They want to help people and organizations reach their fullest potential, using a gentle, encouraging, yet determined style that is well-grounded in their values.

INFPs often influence through their own examples of integrity, loyalty, inspiration, and support. At times, their extraverted Intuition can be so exuberant that they may need to rein it in so that they don't ambush others with their spontaneous ruminating. Extraverted Intuition also allows INFPs to put their ideals into practice in imaginative and creative ways.

"I carry on my spirituality quietly by helping others to discover or understand who they are so they can grow. For these reasons, I've been a volunteer at a homeless shelter, doing what I can to redress injustice even if it's just one person at a time. It truly is a rewarding experience for me and I hope for them as well."

OLIVIA, 27, MUSICIAN

Thus, the auxiliary function brings balance: While introverted Feeling provides a deeply-rooted system of beliefs, extraverted Intuition points INFPs toward those future possibilities that allow their ideals to flower and have an impact on the outer world.

The Third Gift for INFPs: Sensing

Not as much is documented or agreed upon about how the third, or tertiary, function expresses itself in any of the 16 types.* The **third function** for INFPs is Sensing. The domain of the Sensing function includes a firm grasp of reality, attention to details, and an enjoyment of present and everyday circumstances—accepting life as it is.

For all of the 16 types, the third function tends to evolve later in life, typically after the first two functions are clearly developed. How-

---

Whether the third function is extraverted or introverted is not well documented in theory or practice. We therefore suggest that people observe how they use it in both the outer (extraverted) and inner (introverted) worlds at different times to see which is most helpful.

ever, many INFPs are assisted early on in accessing Sensing, their third function, because Sensing predominates in most of the world's cultures and in many early educational curricula and systems. Thus, many INFPs benefit from being able to understand factual and practical matters when they *consciously* try to do so. As they seek to enrich their spirituality, many INFPs use their third function, Sensing, to:

- Add nuance to their spirituality by learning the factual, historical, and practical aspects of a belief system; and
- Pay attention to the impact of soulwork on their current situation, noticing the simple things that bring joy to life—being healthy, experiencing the outdoors, or delighting in day-to-day events.

INFPs in the Storms of Life

The Least Accessible Gift for INFPs:
Extraverted Thinking

For all of the 16 types, the fourth function is called the **inferior function** because it is the most difficult to use consciously and effectively. The inferior function can be a source of irritation and oversights that can threaten relationships, meaning and purpose, careers, or even competency —but at its best can be a source of rest or richness in the storms of life, in moving toward deeper spirituality, or in exploring issues as we age. For INFPs, the inferior function is extraverted Thinking.

For all of us, life delivers events and circumstances that we cannot control—even the most fortunate of us eventually have to deal with the relinquishment of relationships, work situations, or dreams. And as we age, the human condition demands that we face the diminishment of our own abilities and eventually our lives. While our soulwork may help us prepare for and weather these storms, knowing our psychological type can help us understand how these storms will affect us and where we might intentionally seek refuge.

The dominant introverted Feeling function provides some natural coping skills. With their inner focus on what matters most and their way of finding a larger meaning or purpose, INFPs can often see a "silver lining" behind the clouds. Additionally, since INFPs tend to weave spirituality into their everyday lives, they can readily access spiritual resources in times of loss.

The auxiliary function of extraverted Intuition also provides some help. Exploring the larger ramifications and then talking through their situation with others often helps INFPs loosen the grip of an entrenched position on a value or issue they may hold. This helps them become more open and receptive to trying a new process or changing values.

Some INFPs use their extraverted Intuition to gain new insights.

"I had decided that one of several overseas opportunities was the best next step for me, but didn't know how to narrow the field. As I walked the beach in search of an answer, I noticed a dog struggling in the surf. I suddenly knew what to do. A long stint in a foreign country would go against my value for a strong family life. I felt I could be overwhelmed, just as the dog was floundering in the ocean. This led me to choose the overseas option with the shortest possible time away from home."

YASIR, 27, ARCHITECT

When the Storms Overwhelm

However, the storms of life often swell beyond our natural capacity to cope. While life's tragedies strain all of us, no matter how intense our soulwork and regardless of our psychological type, the stormy times for INFPs can be intensified if the circumstances include any of the following factors:

- When the atmosphere or relationship deteriorates into attack, backbiting, or hypocrisy. INFPs may choose to withdraw if the situation is so far out of hand that they believe there's no opportunity for change.
  "Because my beliefs are so personal, when I feel betrayed or discredited, it is often difficult to state my criticisms in ways that are understood. Often, even when I try my best to be objective, others hear me

as supercritical or defensive and then trivialize what I've said. Speaking then is like 'throwing pearls before swine' and I remain quiet to protect what is so valuable to me."

TAMARA, 33, LABORATORY TECHNICIAN

- When INFPs accommodate the wishes of others to retain the relationship or ensure harmony. Their desire for acceptance may encourage them to hang on to a relationship and lead them to being at war with themselves—not accepting the reality of the situation.
- When people seem indifferent to the problems of others, leave them isolated, or treat them poorly.

  "It's quite painful to me when people seem callous or indifferent to the needs and hurts of others, especially when they might be to blame. I know that life is too short to try to change everything, so I've learned the hard way to choose my battles and seek others who treat people well and care about them as much as I do."

ALTHEA, 28, MEDICAL STUDENT

- When their values compel them to lead or speak up, yet the desired outcome is not achieved. Generally INFPs prefer not to take a direct, out-in-front leadership role. However, when their values or people close to them are threatened, beware . . . a strong leader will emerge!

In the most despairing moments, all types can be caught by overuse of their strengths, relying too much on their dominant function. The worst time for INFPs is when they become too intent on their own point of view or conclusions. By overusing their dominant Feeling, they get entrenched in their own beliefs, become unwilling to admit other viewpoints, and move toward isolation from others. In the worst storms, a totally different approach to soulwork may be the only refuge.

"I wanted to serve on the ethics committee of my professional organization because its integrity was so very important to me. Soon I became the spokesperson for the group and traveled and wrote extensively about ethical behaviors and situations. I realized when people started referring to me as

the leader of the 'ethical Police' that I had become too one-sided and harsh—something I so dislike in others!"

NANCY, 59, COUNSELOR

"When they pushed me into early retirement, I was devastated. The rationale offered by the company to which I had devoted twenty-three years seemed weak and insincere. But I didn't object or discuss my fears about the loss of income, status, and more importantly, my work friends and the job I loved. Later, when it was too late, I realized that I should have stood up for myself—a value I espouse to others. I'm just now getting over the blow and my sense of inner turmoil."

DUANE, 59, BIOLOGIST

Clues that INFPs are being overwhelmed:	• Being too objective or closed off to new viewpoints or information • Isolating and/or verbalizing critical and negative remarks about themselves or others
How to help INFPs:	• Encourage them to talk through their emotional state, look to the external world for new ideas and insights, and determine the most logical outcome
For self-help:	• Look beyond the personal impact of the situation, set some new goals and accountabilities for change • Remember that life and people have both a light and a dark side, then adopt more realistic expectations

The Gifts of the Inferior Function—Rest and Richness

Even though using one's inferior function is stressful, an irony of psychological type is that *a path to serenity and rest is to intention-*

ally use the inferior function. For the INFP, the inferior function of Thinking is opposite the dominant function of Feeling. Therefore, its *conscious use* requires shutting down what is most natural and easy— the Thinking function, which may have gotten out of control while trying to cope with the storm.

For INFPs, pursuing activities that use their inferior function, extraverted Thinking, forces them to set aside their subjectivity and approach the situation from a more objective, logical perspective. Ways to intentionally engage the extraverted Thinking function include:

- Seeking the advice of a trusted friend or colleague to work through the pros and cons of different courses of action, discussing rational explanations for the behavior of others, and objectively looking for the cause/effect of the crisis. With that assistance, INFPs can often develop a logical plan of attack—and then can give it one more test by asking, "What does my heart say?"
- Using a ranking system to choose between various alternatives. By listing all the needs or criteria and assigning number values to the options, the correct course of action often becomes clear.
- Engaging the mind in activities that require logic. Some INFPs read mysteries, play games such as chess or duplicate bridge that require analysis and strategy, or work double acrostics to remove themselves mentally from the problems at hand.

In soulwork for each type, richness, depth, and development come through the inferior function. As useful as it is to understand the inferior function for the storms of life, it provides more benefits as we seek to grow.

In the first half of life we define ourselves, both in work and relationships, through our dominant and auxiliary functions. In the second half of life, the gifts of our inferior function can aid us as we seek to become all that we can be. When we don't take advantage of this natural development of our psychological type, we can become stuck.

Midlife also gives clarity to the brevity of our lives. This compels

many of us almost unconsciously to seek richness from unfamiliar experiences as well as to complete the psychological tasks we may have bypassed at an earlier age. As we journey toward wholeness and completion, we can open ourselves to new avenues that are outside of our routines by relinquishing the control our dominant function exerts. Adding spiritual practices that incorporate the attributes of our inferior function can give our soulwork new dimension and zest.

The first two functions, Feeling and Intuition, give INFPs a set of deeply held ideals and a vision of future possibilities. However, to continue to grow, INFPs need the spiritual richness of extraverted Thinking. They may be compelled to search for the intellectual implications of spirituality.

EXTRAVERTED THINKING SOULWORK

This involves:

- Defining and clarifying truth and universal principles in an impartial manner;
- Bringing intellectual and philosophical insights to spiritual questions;
- Examining the systems and structures of their beliefs or applying logical reasoning to their decisions and values; and
- Allowing doubts to be the catalyst in searching for new understanding, asking critical questions, and analyzing different explanations.

INFPs become reacquainted with the spiritual as they find meaning in things they previously overlooked. While they may continue many of their favorite methods of soulwork, renewal may come from the spiritual pathways that are naturally the domain of ESTJs and ENTJs:

- *I used to object to any suggestion that one rule or belief be applied to everyone. Recently, though, I've begun to study some of the laws or precepts that seem to exist in every culture. I want to understand how these maxims came into existence and whether there are other "universal truths" that we should apply uniformly. I'm more willing to take the "tough stand" if that's what's called for, even surprising my rabbi in the process.*

- *It's been a long time since I questioned my spiritual precepts. I used to say that all paths have merit, so I wasn't very motivated to look more deeply. Now, though, I enjoy the process of questioning in order to understand more clearly the spiritual path I have chosen.*

- *I decided that it was time to act on what I believe! I initiated a new outreach group, recruited its members, and even ran all of the organizational meetings. Before, I might have attempted to act alone; now I want to actively convince others to follow my plan!*

- *The dispassionate language of logic used to strike me as unspiritual. Now, however, I find that it allows me to articulate my deeply held beliefs much more clearly and in ways that make it easier for others to understand.*

- *I find I'm enjoying debates with leaders from several spiritual communities. We keep each other on our toes, making sure each person can vigorously defend their positions.*

I am thankful for

My idealism and hope for the world

My intense ideas, which provide me energy to live life deeply and abundantly

My ever-present awareness of the beauty and synchronicity of life's experiences

The way I value the importance of the spiritual journey and the things that give meaning to life

In the storms of life, I can find shelter by

Asking, "What is most important to me?"—and then making a change, sometimes even a radical change

Using a trusted person to help me see things objectively

Dialoguing with myself through journaling, art, or meditating while walking in nature

To honor myself and my pathway to God, I can

Create solitude to tap into my awareness of the spiritual part of my life

Live with personal authenticity and integrity

Add logic and objectivity to my life in order to more clearly understand my heartfelt soulwork

Conclusion

A Closing Thought on Being Wholly Spiritual

Sixteen types, four major paths to spirituality. Does this mean that we each need to chart a distinct spiritual path? Throw out traditions and start anew? Form separate spiritual communities? That spiritual leaders must adapt to each of these paths? Our conclusion is a certain NO.

In spirituality, traveling down just one path can be the route to stagnation, offering little chance of surprise, challenge, or development. For all types, spiritual wholeness develops when we see "how the other half lives"—when we allow for insights and information from spiritual experiences that are different from our initial, more natural paths.

However, for people whose natural paths depart from traditional forms of spirituality—such as those Sensors who prefer finding God spontaneously in the midst of their enjoyment of all that God has given us; Intuitives who break with tradition in favor of innovation and new experiences; Thinkers who are chastened for their customary skepticism; and Feelers who question systems that seem to shut out those who are in most need of help—for everyone's sake, we need to rethink what it means to be spiritual. Otherwise we may lose the opportunity to find avenues that lead toward wholeness. As you finish these pages, take a moment to consider how to best nurture your own soul as well as the spirit in each of us.

Inviting Everyone to Wholeness

What "shoulds" and "oughts" do you or those around you bring to the realm of soulwork? Consider the practices and traditions of your personal spirituality or those of your spiritual community within the framework of Sensing, Intuitive, Thinking, and Feeling soulwork. Sometimes the changes that will allow each type to feel at home are simple, as we heard from the many people we talked to in the course of writing *SoulTypes*.

- One of our friends detests our church's tradition of standing during the worship service to share with strangers. "If only the minister would say, 'Share *with a friend or* a stranger,' I'd feel comfortable."
- Another person we interviewed expressed the need to not be judged for "skipping school" once in a while. "I like my study group, but sometimes on a winter day, my soul would be better fed by setting our lessons aside to go skiing."
- "I wanted the freedom to *not* take a stand," several commented. "Issues aren't always clear, circumstances change. Allow some of my beliefs to be cloudy."
- "If I try to talk about spirituality, my thoughts get muddled. I have to keep it to myself," was another common statement.

For every tradition, practice, or form of spirituality, be open-minded and allow people to react in their own ways to the routines and customs that others view as perfectly normal.

Your Personal Path to Spiritual Richness

However, before you work to increase understanding in those around you, take one more look at your own soulwork. Are you at peace with the requirements you place on yourself? Have you discovered and defined the essentials of your type of spirituality? Are there ways in which your spiritual life could be augmented or deepened?

As an ENFP (Sandra) and INFJ (Jane), our most natural paths to soulwork are through our Intuition and Feeling Functions.

For us, the essence of spirituality is adding insight and understanding to our faith and then sharing it with others. (See p. 309.)

If the two of us fail to nurture these deep spiritual values, our soulwork can quickly go dry. However, our soulwork would be incomplete if we stopped here.

We both need to add *Thinking* to our spirituality. A sprinkling of skepticism and discernment is vital to our teaching, our writing, and our ability to successfully apply our spirituality to what we do and to our decisions.

We need *Sensing* to pull ourselves away from our imaginations and innovations, back to the everyday delights of what God has created, the value of consistency in some pursuits, and the richness and history of spiritual traditions.

Take some time to articulate for yourself the vital practices of your soulwork. Reread the natural paths of your psychological type to find those core purposes or approaches that draw you to spirituality. But then, look at the paths of a type very different from you—your exact opposite (for example, ENFPs would read the ISTJ chapter). What could you gain? What might you be missing?

Often, the key to understanding isn't adapting to everyone else—it is understanding the genuine psychological differences, comprehending the spiritual viewpoint of another, gaining knowledge from a changed perspective, or discovering new forms of soulwork that turn out to be avenues to meaning and growth.

May these passages help you

Rejoice in the special spiritual journey that will best engage
   your soul
Grant new freedom for others to take a different path
Create the patterns of soulwork that can shelter your spirit
   through whatever storms come your way

◈

Suggestions
for Group Study

1. Allow each person to discern their psychological type. You may use the introductory chapters of *SoulTypes* or, with the help of a qualified practitioner, take the MBTI®.

2. Gather in type-alike groups (those who share the same four letters) and study the first page on the chapter for your type. Then, report to the larger group what you would like them to know about the gifts of your type. If some types have only one person, ask them to be a "group" of one.

3. In preparation for the next meeting, read the entire chapter for your type and discuss your type preferences with someone who knows you well. Make note of the ways in which your own personal soulwork matches the chapter description. Also, consider where you are personally on the journey toward wholeness using the stages described on pages 9–11 of Chapter 1. Make note of a step toward a deeper spirituality you hope to take as a result of this study.

1. If the group is small, each person may want to share one thing that stood out for him or her from reading about his or her type and

spirituality. People also can voice questions that arose for them that others in the group might be able to answer or provide some insights.

2. Using the chart on page 29, consider the type dynamics (order of preferences) of the group. How many dominant Sensing, Intuitive, Thinking, and Feeling types are there? Break into discussion groups by dominant functions (the first preference listed in the chart for each type). If the group is large (more than 30), divide further by grouping the introverted Sensing types, extraverted Sensing types, introverted Intuitive types, etc. Using the summary pages on each of the functions (Sensing, page 39; Intuition, page 103; Thinking, page 167; Feeling, page 235) as a guide, discuss:

   a. Your definition of spirituality. What does soulwork look like for your group? When do you feel most spiritual?
   b. With what spiritual practices do you struggle the most? What insights did you gain from *SoulTypes* into the sources of these struggles? What, if any, are the relationships to type?

3. For additional insights, consider major spiritual events in your life. How do these events fit with the path of spiritual growth? You might fill in a chart similar to the one below:

My dominant function is _____	Spiritual milestones that reflect my dominant function:
My auxiliary function is _____	Spiritual milestones that reflect my auxiliary function:
My third function is _____	Ways in which I use my third function in soulwork:
My inferior function is _____	Ways in which my inferior function could enrich or hinder my soulwork:

4. Have each of the four groups (by dominant function) plan an ideal but fictitious retreat/event for soulwork. Each group can decide on location, preferred activities, size of the group, etc. Have each group present their ideas to the entire group. Note the differences and similarities.

5. In preparation for the next meeting, read the summary pages on Sensing and Intuitive spirituality (pages 39 and 103). Then read the chapter for the type that is your opposite (e.g., INFJs read the ESTP chapter) to gain an awareness of the different approaches to spirituality.

SESSION THREE—SENSING AND INTUITIVE SOULWORK

1. Review as a group the summary pages for Sensing and Intuitive soulwork (pages 39 and 103). Discuss:
   a. What surprises are there about what each group considers spiritual?
   b. How might Sensing types and Intuitive types struggle/ flourish within this group study experience? Spiritual setting or community?

2. The first three exercises under "Suggestions for Sensing Soulwork" (page 40) and "Suggestions for Intuitive Soulwork" (page 104) are designed for group discussion.
   a. Instruct each person whose dominant or auxiliary function is Sensing to choose an exercise from among the first three exercises from page 40 and those whose dominant or auxiliary function is Intuition to choose among the first three exercises on page 104 and then try it.
   b. Allow at least 20 minutes for each person to work through his or her chosen exercise. If space allows, spread out—even go outdoors.
   c. As people come back together, have them join with others who chose the same exercise for small-group discussion. Some questions for the groups to consider are:

       i. Was the exercise easy or difficult? Why?

      ii. What about the exercise helped you tap into your type of spirituality?

      iii. What insights did you gain?

    d. Each group can then describe each of the experiences and insights to the entire group.

3. In preparation for the next meeting, read the summary pages for Thinking and Feeling spirituality (pages 167 and 235). For enrichment, Sensing types can try one of the 18 soulwork suggestions for Intuitive types and vice versa.

SESSION FOUR—THINKING AND FEELING SPIRITUALITY

1. The first three exercises under "Suggestions for Thinking Soulwork" (page 168) and "Suggestions for Feeling Soulwork" (page 236) are designed for group discussion.

    a. Instruct each person whose dominant or auxiliary function is Thinking to choose an exercise from among the first three exercises from page 168 and those whose dominant or auxiliary function is Feeling to choose among the first three exercises on page 236, then try it.

    b. Allow at least 20 minutes for each person to work through his or her chosen exercise. If space allows, spread out—even go outdoors.

    c. As people come back together, have them join with others who chose the same exercise as they did for small-group discussion. Some questions to consider are:

      i. Was the exercise easy or difficult? Why?

      ii. What about the exercise helped you tap into your type of spirituality?

      iii. What insights did you gain?

    d. Each group can then describe each of the experiences and insights to the entire group.

2. In preparation for the next meeting, read the Conclusion of *Soul-Types* (page 301). Come up with a phrase that expresses the essence of your spirituality (our example is on page 303). For enrichment, Thinking types can try one of the 18 suggestions for Feeling soulwork and vice versa.

SESSION FIVE—WORKING TOWARD WHOLENESS

1. Discuss your experiences with trying the opposite soulwork suggestions (i.e., Thinking types share what it was like to try an exercise oriented toward Feeling types and vice versa).

2. Form groups by your third functions to discuss the ways in which this function surfaces and the impact it has on your spiritual life.
    a. What are the gifts of this function for your spirituality?
    b. What examples can you share about its existence and use in your spiritual development?
    c. Share any "aha's" with the larger group. Then regroup by your fourth functions and discuss the same questions and one more:
    d. How does your fourth function keep you from being spiritual?

3. Individually, revisit the phrase describing your spirituality (see question 3, session 4). Commit to one spiritual practice to *continue* fervently and one spiritual practice to *start* for exploration and experimentation with your soulwork.

4. Have each person share their commitment to his or her spiritual practices and the phrases that capture the essence of his or her spirituality.

5. Do any evaluation or next-step activity that seems appropriate.

Suggestions
for Further Reading

Corlett, Eleanor S., and Nancy B. Millner. *Navigating Midlife: Using Typology as a Guide*. Palo Alto, CA: Davies-Black Publishing, 1993.

Duncan, Bruce. *Pray Your Way: Your Personality and God*. London, England: Darton, Longman and Todd Ltd., 1993.

Gold, Victor Roland, et al., eds. *The New Testament and Psalms: An Inclusive Version*. New York, Oxford: Oxford University Press, 1995.

Grant, W. Harold, Magdala Thompson, and Thomas E. Clarke. *From Image to Likeness: A Jungian Path in the Gospel Journey*. Ramsey, NJ: Paulist Press, 1983.

Hagberg, Janet. *The Critical Journey*. Dallas, TX: Word Publishing, 1989.

Hall, Calvin S., and Vernon J. Nordby. *A Primer of Jungian Psychology*. New York, NY: The New American Library, Inc., 1973.

Hirsh and Kise, *Looking at Type and Spirituality*. Gainesville, FL: Center for Applications of Psychological Type, 1997.

Johnson, Reginald. *Your Personality and the Spiritual Life*. Wheaton, IL: Victor Books/SP Publications, Inc., 1995.

Michael, Chester P., and Marie C. Norrisey. *Prayer and Temperament: Different Prayer Forms for Different Personality Types*. Charlottesville, VA: The Open Door, Inc., 1991.

Moore, Thomas. *Care of the Soul: A Guide for Cultivating Depth and Sacredness in Everyday Life*. New York, NY: HarperPerennial, 1994.

Moses, Jeffrey. *Oneness: Great Principles Shared by All Religions*. New York, NY: Fawcett Columbine, 1989.

Mulholland, M. Robert, Jr. *Invitation to a Journey: A Road Map for Spiritual Formation*. Downers Grove, IL: InterVarsity Press, 1993.

Myers, Isabel Briggs, and Peter B. Myers. *Gifts Differing*. Palo Alto, CA: Davies-Black Publishing, 1980.

Quenk, Naomi L. *Beside Ourselves: Our Hidden Personality in Everyday Life*. Palo Alto, CA: Davies-Black, 1993.

Richardson, Peter Tufts. *Four Spiritualities: Expressions of Self, Expressions of Spirit*. Palo Alto, CA: Davies-Black, 1996.

Sykes, William. *Visions of Grace: An Anthology of Reflections*. Oxford, England: The Bible Reading Fellowship, 1997.

———. *Visions of Hope: An Anthology of Reflections*. Oxford, England: The Bible Reading Fellowship, 1993.

———. *Visions of Love: An Anthology of Reflections*. Oxford, England: The Bible Reading Fellowship, 1992.

Tagliaferre, Lewis, and Gary L. Harbaugh. *Recovery From Loss: A Personalized Guide to the Grieving Process*. Deerfield Beach, FL: Health Communications, Inc., 1990.

Notes

CHAPTER 1

1. C. F. Andrews, *Mahatma Gandhi's Ideas* (George Allen & Unwin, 1929), 101.
2. Carl Jung, *Modern Man in Search of a Soul* (New York: Harcourt, Brace, Jovanovich, 1933), ch. 5.
3. Thomas Moore, *Care of the Soul* (New York: HarperCollins Publishers, Inc., 1992), 215.
4. Kabir, as quoted in *The Quotable Spirit*, compiled by Peter Lorie and Manuela Dunn Mascetti (New York: Macmillan, 1996), 86.

CHAPTER 3

1. Jung, *Modern Man in Search of a Soul,* ch. 5.

SENSING SPIRITUALITY

1. Robert Browning, *Pippa Passes* (1841), pt. 1.
2. H. C. Beeching, as quoted in *The Oxford Book of Prayer,* George Appleton, editor (Oxford, Oxford University Press, 1995), 61.

CHAPTER 5

1. Ramakrishna, quoted in Solange LeMaitre, *Ramakrishna and the Vitality of Hinduism* (New York: Funk and Wagnalls, 1969), 166.

INTUITIVE SPIRITUALITY

1. Henry Ward Beecher, *Proverbs from Plymouth Pulpit* (Charles Burnet & Co., 1887).
2. Henry David Thoreau, *Journal* (July 14, 1852).

THINKING SPIRITUALITY

1. Kahlil Gibran, *Sand and Foam* (New York: Alfred A. Knopf, 1926).
2. George Appleton, editor, *The Oxford Book of Prayer,* (Oxford: Oxford University Press, 1985), 115.
3. Simone Weil, as quoted in *The Quotable Spirit*, compiled by Peter Lorie and Manuela Dunn Mascetti (New York: Macmillan, 1996), 240.
4. George Fox, as quoted in *Devotional Classics,* edited by Richard Foster and James Bryan Smith (San Francisco: HarperSanFrancisco, 1993), 220.

FEELING SPIRITUALITY

1. Ella Wheeler Wilcox, *The World's Need.*
2. St. Francis, quoted in John Bartlett, *Familiar Quotations*, 16th edition. (Boston: Little Brown, 1992), 123.
3. Holy Bible, New Revised Standard Version (Nashville: Thomas Nelson, 1989).
4. Pattinatar, as quoted in *The Oxford Book of Prayer*, George Appleton, editor (Oxford, Oxford University Press, 1995), 290.

If you would like information on SoulTypes workshop opportunities, please contact us at:

Our email address: SoulTypes@aol.com

Our website: www.LifeKeys.com

Or write to us at:

SoulTypes

P.O. Box 390586

Minneapolis, MN 55439-1417

If you would like to receive a free bookmark printed with soulwork suggestions for your psychological type, please send to the above address:

Your name and address

Your four-letter psychological type

A self-addressed, stamped envelope